Privacy in Britain

Privacy in Britain

Walter F. Pratt

Lewisburg
Bucknell University Press
London: Associated University Presses

Associated University Presses, Inc.
Cranbury, New Jersey 08512

Associated University Presses
Magdalen House
136–148 Tooley Street
London SE1 2TT, England

Library of Congress Cataloging in Publication Data

Pratt, Walter F 1946–
Privacy in Britain.

Bibliography: p.
Includes index.
1. Privacy, Right of—Great Britain. 2. Privacy, Right of—United States. I. Title.
KD1956.P66 342'.41'085 76-50289
ISBN 0-8387-2030-7

PRINTED IN THE UNITED STATES OF AMERICA

to Billy

Contents

Acknowledgments

Many people aided my research, and for their help I am greatly appreciative. Especial thanks go to: Sir E. T. Williams and everyone associated with Rhodes House for making my research both possible and pleasant; Dr. Geoffrey Marshall for supervising the research and writing; Peter Kalis for discussing a draft of the manuscript; Mrs. G. Amlot and the Christopher Kirwans (and even Rex, who had no sense of privacy or propriety) for allowing us the privilege of being part of their family; and, most of all, Dottie.

I also wish to thank Sweet & Maxwell, Ltd., for permission to reprint chapter 1, which appeared in a different form in the summer 1975 issue of *Public Law.*

Privacy in Britain

Introduction

This is the biography of an expression—"right to privacy." It is the story of a vaguely defined concept—*privacy*—and of its steadily expanding use as a defense against ever-more-numerous perceptions of danger. Because these perceptions are as imprecise as the definition of privacy itself, it is difficult to describe the precise contours of the concept being traced. To pretend to do so would be to create an unjustifiably coherent philosophical basis for a popular movement. Nevertheless, even though it is recognized as artificial, a description of the concept can provide a useful preview of what is to come.

For heuristic purposes privacy can be portrayed as falling between two definitional boundaries: the right of an individual to control information about himself and the right to a private sphere. The model is not intended to be rigorously precise, and the boundaries are not always distinct. But, in general, perceiving privacy as the control of information requires imagining the individual as consisting of units of information. Therefore, publishing or otherwise using information without the individual's consent constitutes an invasion of privacy. Arguments of this type gained much of their authority from the traditional concept of *reserve* or *reticence.* Other arguments, those premised on a private-sphere notion, inherited their prestige from values attached to the home. The notion requires envisioning a protective sphere about an individual; entry into the sphere, like entry into a home, requires justification if it is not to be considered an unreasonable invasion of privacy.

Just as the concept of *privacy* has not been rigorously examined, so too the notion of a *right* has not been considered. Much of the discussion has begged the question of the existence of a right. Even so, many of those who have suggested that there should be a legal right to privacy have based their arguments on the importance of such a right in allowing an individual to develop his own personality. These arguments have been predicated upon a concept of autonomy understood as the freedom of an individual to make choices about his own future without unjustified interference. Focusing upon the notion of *choice*, both definitional models believe that an individual is hindered in his selection of alternatives unless he has "time off" or an opportunity to separate himself from contact with other members of society.

This idea of an individual's being separate from society has introduced an additional element of complexity into discussions of privacy. It has meant that arguments for privacy have taken their shape from that to which advocates of privacy are opposed. For example, those who support the spherical analysis would say that a neighbor peering over a fence into another's garden intrudes on that person's privacy—possibly because the owner of the garden cannot choose to sunbathe or to plant his garden in a certain way. In that case the "right to privacy" refers to the right not to be peered at, or more generally, the right to be free from unwanted observation. Others have suggested that a person who attaches a thousand-millimeter lens to his camera and surrepticiously photographs his neighbor's activities also intrudes on privacy. In this instance, one's choices are not immediately affected, though if one were aware of the photography they could be. The right to privacy has thus become the right not to be photographed surrepticiously. A different example has been suggested with regard to computers that store vast quantities of information about people. This argument predicts that the information could be used by the computer operator to control the choices made by an individual. Ultimately, actions would be tailored to fit the prototype in the computer. Another aspect to this argument has proposed that it would be wrong if a person were not aware of the information stored about him because he could not correct it or take other action to counter its potential adverse effect.

Thus, there are really two parts to the discussions of choice. An individual's choices could be affected either if he were aware of the intrusion on his privacy (the peering neighbor or the computer) or if he were not aware of the intrusion (the telephoto lens or the secret computer). In the former case, he might alter his choices because he knows that they are being evaluated by someone else. Proponents of privacy have argued that privacy is necessary to allow experimentation before presenting conclusions to others. In the latter case, because his expectations of privacy have been negated, an individual would be unable to take the necessary defensive measures.

Most of the legislative proposals have not, however, been supported by analysis of either *privacy* or *right*. Instead, the arguments have been made in phrases such as "the right to be let alone." And they have been advanced as remedies for perceived problems rather than to enforce philosophical principles. Although remaining within the definitional boundaries, these proposals have comprised either a general right to privacy or a specific response to a specific problem. Advocates of the general right have argued that the courts are the proper agency to balance the competing claims that would surround a right to privacy. Supporters of specific remedies have rejected the advantages of having the courts attempt a balance and have suggested disadvantages. The most frequently suggested disadvantage has been that a general right to privacy would severely limit the freedom of the press. It has also been argued that a general right would produce uncertainty in the law until the courts developed a body of principles.

Both the ad hoc and the general arguments have developed in response to identifiable events. Because privacy has uniquely been a concept that has taken the shape of that to which it is opposed, the development of claims of a right to privacy can best be traced through those events. But the events that make up the biography often are as ill-defined as the concept itself. This study takes as its benchmark the 1972 Report of the Younger Committee on Privacy. The committee's appointment in 1970 followed several years of intensive legislative activity concerning privacy. On no fewer than thirteen occasions during those years, Parliament debated motions or bills concerned with protecting a right to privacy. The Labour government responded to that spate of activity by appointing a committee under the chairmanship of Sir Kenneth Younger

> to consider whether legislation is needed to give further protection to the individual citizen and to commercial and industrial interests against intrusions into privacy by private organizations, or by companies, and to make recommendations.[1]

From there this story is predominately a search for the origins of the concerns that culminated in that report. The choice to proceed in this way does not imply that privacy "died" in 1972. In that sense this is a most unusual biography, for it follows its subject only to maturation. Although events of succeeding years are not entirely ignored, they are seen as continuations of earlier trends rather than as beginnings of new developments. For example, the allegations surrounding Jeremy Thorpe's resignation as leader of the Liberal party were but variations of the public life—private life conundrum posed in the Profumo affair. Likewise, the reports of Princess Margaret's separation from Lord Snowdon merely recalled numerous allegations of improprieies by the press.

Throughout, the implicit question is how the concerns that led to the Younger Committee reached such a critical point. There is, as well, a comparative element to the query: How was it that the Americans, first through their courts, and later through their legislatures, developed legal sanctions against invasion of privacy, while the British, through either their courts or their legislature, did not?

In part, the answer to the British portion of that query lies in the fact that privacy inheres more in the character of the people and thus requires less protection from the governmental institutions. An American, Ralph Waldo Emerson, recognized that trait during voyages to England in 1833 and 1847. In a book, *English Traits*, published in 1856, he observed: "The motive and end of their [the English] trade and empire is to guard the independence and privacy of their homes."[2]

Almost a century later, Erwin Schrödinger, a German scientist living in Britain, said in a talk on British Broadcasting Company (BBC) Radio:

> Generally speaking I consider the British spirit to be distinguished by a deep reluctance to intrude unnecessarily into a man's privacy, by a great respect towards a single personality, and by a complete understanding that it may be a valuable one in spite of—or even because of—its being an individual phenomenon, deviating strongly or even quaintly from all the others.[3]

Aliens were not the only ones who recognized the trait; for example, George Orwell wrote of a "characteristic which is so much a part of us that we barely notice it, and that is the addiction to hobbies and sparetime occupations, the *privateness* of English life."[4]

Hence, the weakness of the opposition to claims to a right to privacy may be explained by the strength of the tradition of privacy. But the tradition can do little more. It cannot, for example, provide a chronology for the development of privacy as a value. The concept of a *right* to privacy, however, does have an origin in time. It began with an article in the *Harvard Law Review* of December 1890.[5] Paradoxically, the authors of that article relied almost exclusively on English common law decisions to argue that there are ample precedents for judicial protection of a right to privacy. From that argument evolved the many privacy decisions in American courts. And, though British courts have not reached similar conclusions, that same article has provided inspiration and an argumentative method for proponents of privacy legislation in Britain. So it is that this British biography begins with discussion of an article from an American law review.

1

The Warren and Brandeis Argument

i

The *Harvard Law Review* article was written by Samuel Warren and his former law partner, Louis Brandeis, later an associate justice of the Supreme Court of the United States. Precipitated by Warren's irritation about newspaper reports of entertaining done by him and his wife in Boston, the article is important not merely for its seminal character; equally significant is its style of reasoning—both for its own conclusions and for the contrast with British judges. It is through an understanding of that contrast that one may begin to comprehend the reasons for the secondary role played by the judiciary in the development of a concept of privacy in Britain.

The many comparisons between British and American protection of privacy make it particularly important that those divergent judicial reactions to the Warren and Brandeis article be understood. Among other explanations, it is possible to attribute the differences to the separate philosophies of the judicial function and to the written Constitution of the United States. Both are valid explanations; both differences contributed to the success of the Warren and Brandeis argument in the United States and to its failure in English courts. Neither explanation is adequate, however, for both overlook the content of the Warren and Brandeis article. The simplest and most direct explanation is that Warren and Brandeis are wrong: the English cases that they rely upon do not support their conclusion. Moreover, other contemporaneous evidence, not used by Warren and Brandeis, also refutes their supposition that common-law precedents could be interpreted as affording protection for a right to privacy. But before discussing those precedents it will be helpful to summarize the article's argument.

Warren and Brandeis begin their article by describing a conflict between man's increasing need for solitude and the demands of an ever more complex world:

> The intensity and complexity of life, attendant upon advancing civilization, have rendered necessary some retreat from the world, and man, under the refining influence of culture, has become more sensitive to publicity, so that solitude and privacy have become more essential to the individual; but modern enterprise and invention have, through invasions upon his privacy, subjected him to mental pain and distress, far greater than could be inflicted by mere bodily injury.[1]

More succinctly, they maintain that a need exists for protecting the person and "for securing to the individual what Judge Cooley calls the right 'to be let alone.' "[2] There is also a more general harm, for the invasion of an individual's privacy damages others as well. Publication of gossip and trivia tends to lower the standards of the public and to displace the news and opinion that should appear.

The dilemma that Warren and Brandeis pose is whether or not a remedy exists for the first problem that would also solve the second. The ambitious sweep of their affirmative response is evident in the article's second sentence: "Political, social and economic changes entail recognition of new rights, and the common law, in its eternal youth, grows to meet the demands of society."[3] In their view, from its initial purpose of protecting a man's life and property, the common law had grown to protect a man's feelings as well:

> Gradually the scope of these legal rights broadened; and now the right to life has come to mean the right to enjoy life,—the right to be let alone; the right to liberty secures the exercise of extensive civil privileges; and the term "property" has grown to comprise every form of possession—intangible, as well as tangible.[4]

Specifically, they argue that English copyright and intellectual property cases are "but instances and applications of a general right to privacy, which properly understood afford a remedy for the evils under consideration."[5]

At times, however, the authors' rhetoric exceeds their logic, as when they identify the right to life with the right to be let alone. Without explanation, Warren and Brandeis slide from a rarely contested right (to life) to an undefined right (to enjoy life) and finally to "the right to be let alone." Judge Thomas M. Cooley uses this last phrase in his book on torts.[6] But to him this is not the equivalent of the notion of an inviolate personality posited by Warren and Brandeis; it is a right not to be the victim of assault or battery. In his book when he writes of "the right to be let alone" as explicative of "the right to immunity from attacks and injuries,"[7] he is only listing and explaining what he considers to be "rights which every government is expected to recognize." He is not urging the acceptance of a right to prevent publication of the details of entertaining done by Boston socialites.[8]

It is thus important to realize that the expression "the right to be let alone," which has become a trademark of the Warren and Brandeis article, had originally no relation to the concept of privacy, even though Warren and Brandeis use it as synonymous with privacy.[9]

Equally important, the right to be let alone implies a more comprehensive concept than the right to life—the two rights are not in all cases equivalent. Indeed, supporting or protecting the right to life could conflict with the right to be let alone. For example, during an epidemic of disease a government might seek to protect life through compulsory inoculation, a violation of being let alone. Similarly the right to enjoy life could interfere with the right to be let alone: to ensure enjoyment of life a government might be urged to reduce noxious odors and smoke in residential areas. Likewise, regulations to prohibit open burning interfere with the right to be let alone. Although the three concepts may, in instances, be equivalent, they do not have the unqualified synonymity asserted by Warren and Brandeis.

ii

In addition to these synonyms, Warren and Brandeis explain their concept by analogy to other legal principles. According to them, the two common law wellsprings of the right to privacy are the awarding of damages for injury to feelings and the protection of intellectual property. In addition, they distinguish the right from the legal remedies for damage to reputation. Unlike the two former principles, compensation for loss of reputation is not premised upon injured feelings. Instead, reputation is valued for its "material rather than spiritual" worth. "That branch of law simply extends the protection surrounding physical property to certain of the conditions necessary or helpful to worldly prosperity."[10] These distinctions make it clear that though the conduct they seek to proscribe is the unauthorized circulation of information about an individual, the harm they perceive is injury to feelings.

One such nonpropertied action that they report permitted the awarding of damages to parents after the seduction of their daughter. The courts proclaimed that these damages were for the loss of the daughter's services, but to Warren and Brandeis that is only a legal fiction to enable the parents to be compensated for their injured feelings. Once that fiction had been created, "then the feelings of the parent, the dishonour to himself and his family, were accepted as the most important element of damage."[11] In that principle, Warren and Brandeis detect a rudimentary protection for injury to feelings or honor independent of material damage.

Their exposition of the fiction of service is correct, but their deduction that the courts would protect feelings independent of material damage is not. Study of judicial opinions reveals two facts to refute Warren and Brandeis's argument: 1) in seduction cases no damages were awarded unless some service existed; 2) actions for seduction were considered unique and not applicable to other claims for injury to children. The insistence upon material damage, as well as the tone for later decisions, was established in *Robert Marys's Case*.[12] There the judge ruled that a master had no action for the beating of his servant unless he also lost the services of the servant:

> The master has not any damage by the personal beating of his servant, but by reason of a *per quod, viz. per quod servitum*, &c. *amisit* [whereby he lost the service (of his servant)]; so that the original act is not the cause of his action, but the consequent upon it, viz. the loss of his service is the cause of his action; if the master doth not lose the service of his servant, he shall not have an action.[13]

Elaborating on that decision, Chief Justice Holt explained, in 1704, that no action would lie for getting a "maid or daughter" pregnant; if services were lost because of the pregnancy, however, the loss could be considered as aggravation in an action for entering the house without permission.[14] Lord Mansfield followed the precedent and refused to award damages to a woman because at the time of the seduction her daughter had been supporting herself and therefore could not be considered a servant.[15] And in 1809 Lord Ellenborough said that allowing damages for the feelings of parents had "always been considered as an action sui generis," and that the practice of awarding such damages had "become inveterate and cannot now be shaken."[16] In addition, Lord Ellenborough emphasized that the cases were not to be interpreted liberally. He explained that "although by some anomaly, when the loss of service was established, a further compensation was allowed for the injury to the parental feelings, it was necessary to watch that this anomaly should not be carried further, and that the original scope of the action should not be entirely lost sight of."[17]

The Court of Exchequer provided no exceptions to those sentiments that strictly confine the scope of the recovery. Pollock C.B. said that the mother of a girl who had been debauched could not recover damages because there had been no actual loss of services—the girl worked for someone else. In this case, Chief Baron Pollock observed: "The entire services of the girl belonged to her master. However painful it may be that there should be a wrong without a remedy, we must leave the law as we find it. We cannot make that a service which was no service."[18]

The singularity of the seduction action was emphasized by the courts' refusal to award damages for injured parental feelings after an injury to a son. Abbott C.J. once instructed a jury that they could only consider the loss suffered by the father from deprivation of his son's services and that they could not consider injury to the father's feelings.[19]

Even though courts were willing to presume that a daughter provided services to her father, they still required some basis for that presumption—for example, that the daughter was a minor and lived with the family or that she was returning to the family after working for another. Kelly C.B. summarized the requirement: "It has been truly said that the action of seduction is founded on a fiction; but for that fiction there must be some foundation, however slender, in fact."[20]

iii

In their argument Warren and Brandeis recognize the difficulties in attempting to expand such a restricted legal fiction. They therefore rely primarily upon their second source for the right to privacy—the protection of intellectual property. To provide that protection, they explain, "the common law secures to each individual the right of determining, ordinarily, to what extent his thoughts, sentiments, and emotions shall be communicated to others."[21] They derive their conclusion from decisions protecting literary property based upon the principle that the author of a literary or artistic work has an absolute right to determine whether and when his work will be published. Only if the author himself communicates the work to the public is the right lost. The right derives from the common law and is not a creation of stature. In addition, it is distinct from copyright, which becomes operative *after* publication, while the principle protecting an author is operative *until* publication. Warren and Brandeis variously define the principle as an instance of the general right to privacy,[22] of the general right to be let alone,[23] and of inviolate personality.[24] Regardless of the operative name, the courts' purpose according to Warren and Brandeis is to allow an individual to prohibit publication of facts about himself.

Warren and Brandeis attempt to prove their contention by almost exclusive reliance upon the single English case of *Prince Albert* v. *Strange*,[25] which was somewhat of an aberration from other cases because of the involvement of the Royal Family. The case began when Prince Albert sought an injunction to prohibit Strange's announced exhibition of etchings done by Queen Victoria and Prince Albert. To accompany the exhibition, Strange planned to publish a descriptive catalogue that would include a facsimile signature of either Queen Victoria or Prince Albert. Although individual copies made by the palace printer had been given to friends of the Queen and the Prince, neither the entire collection nor individual etchings had been made public. Strange's method of acquiring copies was never determined, but a consensus arose among the parties to the dispute that a helper to the palace printer had been Strange's source.

Before the vice-chancellor, counsel for Strange opposed the injunction by arguing that Strange had committed no impropriety, that the catalogue was the product of his own labor and therefore his property, and that interference with him would be interference with freedom of the press. To Sir John Romilly, the solicitor general who appeared for Prince Albert, the case presented a plain question of law:

> The case does not turn upon the question of copyright, but upon the clear and absolute property which Her Majesty and His Royal Highness had in the etchings. . . . The principle is that the Court

> will restrain any person from making use of the property of another, contrary to the will and disposition of the owner.[26]

A second, and equally plain reason for granting the injunction was that there had been a breech of trust by the printer's helper, from whom Strange had acquired the etchings.

But the solicitor general also thought that there were more indefinite principles involved. He urged the court to accept that there had been "the abstraction of one attribute of property, which was often its most valuable quality, namely, privacy."[27] In explaining that principle, Sir John anticipated the Warren and Brandeis article: "All the cases in which the Court had interfered to protect unpublished letters or manuscripts, or that ideal property which a man acquires in the remarks made by himself, proceed upon that principle of protecting privacy."[28] Warren and Brandeis adopt that contention as the thesis of their argument. They excerpt statements from the opinions of the vice-chancellor, Sir J. L. Knight Bruce, and the chancellor, Lord Cottenham, to demonstrate that the courts were in reality implementing not a narrow doctrine of protecting property but a broader doctrine of privacy, or inviolate personality.

To define the court-protected concept of inviolate personality, Warren and Brandeis append explanatory phrases to their basic argument that the common law secured the right of the individual to determine "to what extent his thoughts, sentiments, and emotions shall be communicated to others." They explain that neither the form nor the value of the expression affects the right. "In every such case the individual is entitled to decide whether that which is his shall be given to the public."[29] This right exists only so long as no publication is made, and, as has been mentioned, the right to privacy differs from copyright, which exists only after publication.

From these explanations they turn to the theoretical bases for the right. On the one hand, the courts had said that property formed the basis for their decisions. But Warren and Brandeis maintain that the "common acceptation" of property is inadequate for the courts' meaning because the value of the protected property accrued not from the profits that might be made, but from "the peace of mind or the relief afforded by the ability to prevent any publication at all."[30] As an example of this concept they refer to *Prince Albert v. Strange*, which prohibited both the reproduction of the etchings and any descriptive catalogue. On the other hand, property might be retained as the central concept. If so, they argue, then it need be realized that "the end accomplished by the gossip-monger is attained by the use of that which is another's, the facts relating to his private life, which he has seen fit to keep private."[31]

"These considerations," they write, "lead to the conclusion that the protection afforded to thoughts, sentiments, and emotions, expressed through the medium of writing or of the arts, so far as it consists in preventing publication, is merely an instance of the enforcement of the more general right of the individual to be left alone."[32] They continue: "The principle which protects personal writings and all other personal productions, not against theft and physical appropriation, but against publication in any form, is in reality not the principle of private property, but that of inviolate personality."[33] And they conclude: "No basis is discerned upon which the right to restrain publication and reproduction of such so-called literary and artistic works can be rested, except the right to privacy, as a part of the more general right to the immunity of the person,—the right to one's personality."[34]

iv

With these thoughts of Warren and Brandeis in mind, it is possible to examine the precedents they cite, and the ones they do not, to determine the validity of their conclusions.

The case most frequently mentioned is *Prince Albert* v. *Strange*. In his introductory comments, Vice-Chancellor Knight Bruce evinced no inclination to accept the privacy principle. He thought it "very probable" that Strange never believed that an exhibition of the etchings would be possible. Strange had printed only fifty copies of the catalogue, he had hired no hall for the display, and no times or prices of admission had been indicated. The vice-chancellor thought that Strange had printed the catalogue merely to be "bought off."[35] A second preliminary observation concerned Strange's title to the etchings; Strange could acquire no better title to them than the printer's helper.

Following his introductory comments, the vice-chancellor turned first to a search for the applicable rule of law. The general principle, as established in *Donaldson* v. *Beckett*,[36] was that an author has the absolute right to the first printing of his manuscript and has an action against anyone who attempts to interfere with that right. This common-law right of an author had been recognized by other courts and had not been confined to instances in which the auhor retained the work in absolute secrecy. As the vice-chancellor said, "The right is not lost by partial and limited communications not made with a view to general publication."[37] Nor could a work never published be translated, abridged, summarized or even reviewed, "for a review professes to treat of the general character of the work reviewed, to analyse or dissect it, and to shew from the contents some reason for the praise or dispraise which it may be the particular critic's task to disseminate."[38] Similarly, the law would not permit a more circumspect use of an unpublished manuscript by a catalogue of works. The rule of law depended neither upon the form of the piracy nor upon the loss or gain; the rule was simple: "The author of manuscripts, whether he is famous or obscure, low or high, has a right to say of them, if innocent, that whether interesting or dull, light or heavy, saleable or unsaleable, they shall not, without his consent, be published."[39]

The vice-chancellor's second aim was to ascertain the foundation of this rule of law. The products of the mind expressed in writing were not protected as literary works, because those who had originated the common law were not "patrons of letters." Instead, they had been concerned with protecting property. Thus it was as a species of property that the common law protected such works: "Upon the principle, therefore, of protecting property, it is that the common law, in cases not aided nor prejudiced by statute, shelters the privacy and seclusion of thoughts and sentiments committed to writing, and desired by the author to remain not generally known."[40] But the principle was not limited to the protection of literary subjects: "Wherever the produce of labour is liable to invasion in an analogous manner, there must, I suppose, be a title to analogous protection or redress."[41] These analogous products of labor included mechanical works or works of art.

With the rule of law thus stated, and the principle supporting it, the vice-chancellor had no difficulty bringing the disputed royal etchings within the rule: "We cannot but see that the etchings executed by the Plaintiff and his Consort for their private use, the product of their labour, and belonging to themselves, they were entitled to retain in a state of privacy, to withhold from publication."[42] Since there was sufficient evidence to prove that the etchings had been obtained without the consent of either Prince Albert or Queen Victoria, the vice-chancellor was certain that there had been interference with their property. "The Defendant appears to me," he observed, "to have been seeking to make use, for his own purpose, of what does not belong to him."[43]

Even without examining the specific quotations selected by Warren and Brandeis from the vice-chancellor's opinion, it should be evident that it would be difficult to interpret the opinion in such a way that thoughts, sentiments, and emotions not committed to paper or made lasting in some form would have been protected by the English courts in 1890. Moreover, a closer analysis of the vice-chancellor's and other opinions will show that the courts were not protecting a concept as indeterminate as privacy.

Warren and Brandeis include two lengthy quotations from Vice-Chancellor Knight Bruce as a footnote to their statement that "neither does the existence of the right [to intellectual and artistic property] depend upon the nature or value of the thought or emotion, nor upon the excellence of the means of expression." The sentences quoted are:

> Assuming the law to be so, what is its foundation in this respect? It is not, I conceive, referable to any consideration peculiarly literary. Those with whom our common law originated had not probably among their many merits that of being patrons of letters; but they knew the duty and necessity of protecting property, and with that general object laid down rules providently expansive,—rules capable of adapting themselves to the various forms and modes of property which peace and cultivation might discover and introduce.
>
> The produce of mental labor, thoughts and sentiments, recorded and preserved by writing, became, as knowledge went onward and spread, and the culture of man's understanding advanced, a kind of property impossible to disregard, and the interference of modern legislation upon the subject, by the stat. 8 Anne, professing by its title to be "For the encouragement of learning," and using the words "taken the liberty," in the preamble, whether it operated in augmentation or diminution of the private rights of authors, having left them to some extent untouched, it was found that the common law, in providing for the protection of property, provided for their security, at least before general publication by the writer's consent.[44]

And, to their statement that "in every such case the individual is entitled to decide whether that which is his shall be given to the public,"[45] they append another quotation:

> The question, however, does not turn upon the form or amount of mischief or advantage, loss or gain. The author of manuscripts, whether he is famous or obscure, low or high, has a right to say of them, if innocent, that whether interesting or dull, light or heavy, saleable or unsaleable, they shall not, without his consent, be published.[46]

The second of these quotations actually preceded the first in the vice-chancellor's opinion, and, rather than ending in a period as Warren and Brandeis indicate, there was a semicolon, and Vice-Chancellor Knight Bruce continued with this statement: "and I think, as I have said, that to use a dishonest knowledge of them [an author's manuscripts] for the purpose of composing and publishing, and so to compose and publish a catalogue of them, amounts to a publication of them within the principle of the rule."[47] In other words, the method of acquisition of the knowledge was important to the vice-chancellor, who was directing his remarks toward the facts of the specific case. The paragraphs that followed those quoted by Warren and Brandeis show that the vice-chancellor sought to protect property, not a claim of inviolate personality, as Warren and Brandeis argue. In those paragraphs he discussed the principle upon which the common law doctrine was based—a principle of protecting property, albeit a particular type of property "not exclusively corporeal." The vice-chancellor observed that other courts had protected manuscripts as exertions of labor against use by someone who had not made similar exertions; they had not protected the manuscripts to protect the feelings of the authors.

To support his analysis the vice-chancellor referred to this statement by Lord Eldon: "It is to prevent the use of that which is the exclusive property of another, that an Injunction is granted."[48] Warren and Brandeis themselves quote from another of Lord Eldon's opinions to support their contention that the principle underlying the decisions was one based on property.[49] Lord Eldon's opinion had been delivered in a case concerning the publication of letters. In it he disavowed the implication that Warren and Brandeis seek to establish (that the cases were actually based on a principle of personality):

> I do not say that I am to interfere because the letters are written in confidence, or because the publication of them may wound the feelings of the Plaintiff; but if mischievous effects of that kind

> can be apprehended in cases in which this Court has been accustomed, on the ground of property, to forbid publication, it would not become me to abandon the jurisdiction which my predecessors have exercised, and refuse to forbid it [publication].[50]

Warren and Brandeis next mention the *Prince Albert* decision in the same note in which they refer to Lord Eldon's opinion. They accept the courts' statements that the right was based upon property but question how the usual concept of property could be used to protect value that was found not in the right to profits from publication "but in the peace of mind or the relief afforded by the ability to prevent any publication at all."[51] The answer that the English courts gave was that the property concept could not be so used; the courts did not protect this "value." In fact, as Warren and Brandeis admit, the courts were not concerned with value[52]—they were protecting no more than the products of labor.[53]

The next quotation from the *Prince Albert* decision follows a passage in which Warren and Brandeis assert that neither the contents of a man's diary nor a list of letters written by a man could be published. Of the publication of a diary entry that a man had not dined with his wife on a particular day, they claim that the matter protected was "not the intellectual act of recording the fact that the husband did not dine with his wife, but that fact itself. It is not the intellectual product, but the domestic occurrence."[54] Actually neither the intellectual act nor the fact itself would have been protected by the courts. Had a case arisen, the key issue would have concerned publication of the contents of a diary without the writer's permission. That case would have readily been decided on grounds of property. The other example that Warren and Brandeis suggest involves publication of a list of letters. Although they admit that copyright would give no protection for the list, they argue that "the famous case" of *Prince Albert* v. *Strange* would provide protection because there the court had prohibited both the reproduction and the description of the etchings.[55] Yet newspapers that reported the *Prince Albert* case included a list of the etchings.[56] Moreover, the decision did not prohibit the publication of a list; it prohibited the publication of a description that, according to the lord chancellor, would have the same effect as publication of a copy—"to make known to the public more or less of the unpublished work and composition of the author, which he is entitled to keep wholly for his private use and pleasure, and to withhold altogether, or so far as he may please, from the knowledge of others."[57] Quite simply, if either example had arisen, the courts would not have diverged from the established principle of protecting property.

The courts had said that they were protecting property but Warren and Brandeis detect "recognitions of a more liberal doctrine."[58] Actually they mention only the *Prince Albert* case to evidence this more liberal doctrine. They select the vice-chancellor's comment that to publish of a man that he had "written to particular persons, or on particular subjects" would be an injurious disclosure of private matters.[59] Although the vice-chancellor had not said that such publication would be actionable on grounds other than property, Warren and Brandeis inquire if that comment were law, then why should not the law also prohibit publication of matters that would embitter a man's life, but not ruin it.

This question created as false an issue as the previous examples of publishing lists of letters. Warren and Brandeis never explain how their theory can be made to coincide with the rule of law as stated by Vice-Chancellor Knight Bruce. No amount of citation from the vice-chancellor's dicta can justify the conclusion that the protection afforded was for a right to be let alone, or a right to inviolate personality, or a right to privacy. Such a broad doctrine was incompatible with the words of the vice-chancellor's opinion. Although *privacy* appears repeatedly in that opinion, the word was no more than ancillary to the breach-of-trust and property doctrines.

Alert to the vulnerability of their argument, Warren and Brandeis are willing to retreat to more traditional phraseology. After all, since the gossipmonger actually used that which belonged to another, even "the fiction of property in a narrow sense" could provide some protection.[60] But their fall-back position is not invulnerable. Their "narrow sense" of property is never defined. If by it they mean some primordial notion that property must be tangible, then their own statement is inconsistent, for mere facts cannot be tangible. Furthermore, at least since 1789 the courts had acknowledged a "broader" sense of property. In *Millar* v. *Taylor*,[61] Aston J. said that though property had originally been defined by occupancy, changed circumstances required new definitions. The new characteristic was simply "a capacity to be distinguished."[62]

In no instance cited by Warren and Brandeis had a court protected facts relating to private life alone—all their citations involve instances of protection granted to a manuscript or to other distinguishable evidence of intellectual effort. The decisive failure of the article is its inability to establish the existence of precedent that would protect inviolate personality, or the right to be let alone, or the right to privacy.

V

In addition to the property doctrine there was another concept that had afforded protection against wrongful publication—breach of an implied contract or breach of trust or confidence. There, too, Warren and Brandeis believe that they have found evidence of a principle that transcends the facts of any one case. After discussing four illustrative cases they explain that principle in these words:

> The principle which protects personal writings and any other productions of the intellect or of the emotions, is the right to privacy, and the law has no new principle to formulate when it extends this protection to the personal appearance, sayings, acts, and to personal relation, domestic or otherwise.[63]

Their note to this statement concerns the adaptability of the law and ends: "The cases referred to above show that the common law has for a century and a half protected privacy in certain cases, and to grant the further protection now suggested would be merely another application of an existing rule."[64] Their reassuring conservatism is but camouflage for an expansive interpretation of English precedents. Once again, however, their interpretation of the law is inaccurate.

The first case they mention, *Abernathy* v. *Hutchinson*,[65] concerns lectures delivered by a Dr. Abernathy that were published without his consent in *Lancet*. Speaking from written notes, Dr. Abernathy delivered the lectures to students who had paid a fee for admission to his course on surgery. The doctor sought an injunction to restrain future publication. Warren and Brandeis write that "Lord Eldon doubted whether there could be property in lectures which had not been reduced to writing, but granted the injunction on the ground of breach of confidence."[66] What Lord Eldon, then the lord chancellor, actually said was that because there had been no decision in a court of law as to whether property existed in sentiments and language, he felt unable, as an equity judge, to grant an injunction on that point.[67] He refused the injunction on that ground, but he allowed a new motion to be brought on grounds of breach of contract or trust. This new request was granted, for the reason quoted by

Warren and Brandeis: those attending the lectures could use them as they wished for their own information, but they could not publish them for profit. In a passage not mentioned by Warren and Brandeis, the lord chancellor said that "the injunction ought to go upon the ground of property."[68] Lord Eldon concluded that since "the lectures must have been procured in an undue manner from those who were under a contract not to publish for profit, there was sufficient to authorise the Court to say, the defendants shall not publish."[69]

The second case cited in this group is Lord Chancellor Cottenham's opinion, on appeal, in *Prince Albert* v. *Strange*.[70] Warren and Brandeis briefly mention that the lord chancellor upheld the vice-chancellor on grounds of property and breach of trust, confidence, or contract. They do not mention that the lord chancellor was more restrained in his treatment of the case than had been the vice-chancellor. Lord Cottenham observed: "The importance which has been attached to this case arises entirely from the exalted station of the Plaintiff, and cannot be referred to any difficulty in the case itself."[71] Later he explained why the case was not difficult: "The property of an author or composer of any work, whether of literature, art, or science, in such work unpublished and kept for his private use or pleasure, cannot be disputed, after the many decisions in which that proposition has been affirmed or assumed."[72] He emphasized the ease with which he thought the case could be decided when he remarked that "it would be a waste of time to refer in detail to the cases upon this subject."[73] According to the lord chancellor, the cases usually presented the question as to whether the author's property right had been waived. He interpreted *Abernathy* as assuming the right of property but having to decide whether oral delivery was a publication. Since he found that the prince had established his exclusive right to the etchings and that Strange had established no right to them, the injunction was allowed to stand.

A concluding point made by the lord chancellor is partially quoted by Warren and Brandeis after their comment about preserving the fiction of property in the narrow sense.[74] The statement in their article says, in part: "Lord Cottenham stated that a man 'is entitled to be protected in the exclusive use and enjoyment of that which is exclusively his.' " (The rest of the sentence referred to a later portion of the opinion.)[75] The full statement in the opinion said:

In that [*Tipping* v. *Clarke*[76]], as in this case, the matter or thing

> of which the party has obtained knowledge, being the exclusive property of the owner, he has a right to the interposition of this Court to prevent any use being made of it, that is to say, he is entitled to be protected in the exclusive use and enjoyment of that which is exclusively his.[77]

Thus, what the lord chancellor was saying was that the individual was entitled to the exclusive use and enjoyment of the property that belonged to him; there was no intended implication that "facts relating to his private life" would be included within this definition.

The notion of privacy, which had such redundant use in the vice-chancellor's opinion, was relegated to "some minor points" in the lord chancellor's opinion: the injunction should remain in force before the issue went to trial because to refuse the injunction would allow Strange to publish the catalogue and thereby make public the etchings and destroy their private character.[78] Privacy was a characteristic of the etchings; it was not the right protected.

The other two cases that Warren and Brandeis mention deserve little attention. One, *Tuck* v. *Priester*,[79] is of no value to Warren and Brandeis because it did not consider the right of an individual to control information about himself. The case involved an alleged infringement of a purchased copyright for a painting.

Warren and Brandeis offer scant original analysis of *Tuck*. Instead, they present almost verbatim the description of *Tuck* in North J.'s opinion in a fourth case, *Pollard* v. *Photographic Co.*[80] Little need be added to their remarks about *Pollard*. They correctly report that the judge found an implied contract between the photographer and his subject not to sell the prints without the subject's consent. There was nothing in the opinion that would imply protection for feelings or privacy.

Warren and Brandeis express concern that "modern devices afford abundant opportunities for the perpetuation of such wrongs [use of photographs without permission] without any participation by the injured party."[81] Because photographs could be taken surreptitiously in 1890, it was possible that no contract could be implied; some protection was felt necessary for that situation. Warren and Brandeis posit that protection could only come from the right to inviolate personality. But before 1890 no court had protected inviolate personality, or a right to be let alone, or a right to privacy, independent of property rights. However compelling Warren and Brandeis's argument may be, they are wrong when they urge that privacy can be protected by extrapolation from court decisions.

vi

Cases other than those already mentioned also show that the courts were protecting property and not a nebulous concept of inviolate personality. Part of Justice Erle's advice to the House of Lords in the case of *Jeffreys* v. *Boosey*[82] is quoted by Warren and Brandeis. In his decision in that case, Lord St. Leonards summarized the common law right of an author in these words: "The common law does give a man who has composed a work a right to that composition, just as he has a right to any other part of his personal property."[83]

In another case Lord Watson reiterated the point when, only three years before Warren and Brandeis published their article, he said:

> The author of a lecture on moral philosophy [the subject of the injunction sought], or of any other original composition, retains a right of property in his work which entitles him to prevent its publication by others until it has, with his consent, been communicated to the public.[84]

Warren and Brandeis also use examples of various decisions relating to personal letters. *Gee* v. *Pritchard*[85] has been discussed, as has the artificial example of the publication of a list of letters that a man had written. Warren and Brandeis observe that the protection given letters was, like that for manuscripts, independent of the value or literary merit of the contents. A final comment upon letters is used as an instance of the courts' groping for a principle to protect adequately the sender of letters; the principle developed was of property in the contents. But Warren and Brandeis think that this is not adequate, particularly for the recipient of an unsolicited letter. They argue that the obligation of this recipient was "simply to observe the legal right of the sender, whatever it may be, and whether it be called his right of property in the contents of the letter, or his right to privacy."[86]

In 1890 the law concerning letters offered no such option for denominating the right—the right of the author was his right to say whether the produce of his intellectual labor was to be published or not. Lord Chancellor Eldon, in *Gee*, believed that there was sufficient property in letters to grant an injunction.[87] MacGillivray's textbook on the law of letters, published in 1907, concludes that all cases in which the plaintiff had successfully sought an injunction were ones in which "the plaintiff had undoubtedly a right of property which had been invaded, or of which invasion was threatened."[88] Later in the book MacGillivray does write of an action for injured feelings, but he explains: "This in itself is clearly no cause of action . . . and injury to feelings, apart from the exceptional case of defamation, never seems to have been held as a ground for supporting an action which could not be supported on other grounds."[89]

These miscellaneous cases dealing with similar principles to those used by Warren and Brandeis are further indications of the incorrect analysis offered by Warren and Brandeis.

vii

Warren and Brandeis do not contend that their right to privacy is absolute; they suggest six limitations:

1. The right to privacy does not prohibit any publication of matter which is of public or general interest.
2. The right to privacy does not prohibit the communication of any matter, though in its nature private, when the publication is made under circumstances which would render it a privileged communication according to the law of slander and libel.
3. The law would probably not grant any redress for the invasion of privacy by oral publication in the absence of special damage.
4. The right to privacy ceases upon the publication of the facts by the individual, or with his consent.
5. The truth of the matter published does not afford a defence.
6. The absence of "malice" in the publisher does not afford a defence.[90]

Among the explanatory comments about the first limitation are these sentences:

> The design of the law must be to protect those persons with whose affairs the community has no legitimate concern, from being dragged into an undesirable and undesired publicity and to protect all persons, whatsoever; [sic] their position or station, from having matters which they may properly prefer to keep private, made public against their will. It is the unwarranted invasion of individual privacy which is reprehended, and to be, so far as possible, prevented. . . .[91]

> The general object in view is to protect the privacy of private life, and to whatever degree and in whatever connection a man's life has ceased to be private, before the publication under consideration has been made, to that extent the protection is to be withdrawn.[92]

The last five of the qualifications are modifications of the defenses available for defamation actions. In effect, they mean that the first limitation is to be the test for any application of the right to privacy. But Warren and Brandeis fail to analyze the scope of "public or general interest." The law protecting an author's manuscript had nothing to do with whether the author was a public figure or whether the community had a legitimate concern with him. Prince Albert and Queen Victoria were public figures with whom the public would legitimately have been concerned (Strange had intended to profit from that concern) but neither the vice-chancellor nor the lord-chancellor predicated his decision upon the public's interest.

To illustrate the problem that they perceive, Warren and Brandeis refer to a case involving a woman who had been performing a role, in a Broadway theater, that required her to appear in tights.[93] Without her permission a photographer had taken her picture. The use of such photographs without consent is something Warren and Brandeis seek to restrain by their right to privacy. Yet their qualification concerning the extent to which a person's life had been made public seems to negate any protection for a woman appearing on a public stage.

Warren and Brandeis want a right that would prevent the publication of a picture of anyone without the consent of that person or of an article about Warren's entertaining guests—a right that would allow an individual to control information about himself, subject to an overriding "public or general interest." Their analogies fail. Damages for injuries sustained by parental feelings when a daughter was seduced were a sui generis action and not one to be extended by the courts. Protection given intellectual and artistic efforts was dependent upon the existence of some tangible manifestation of those efforts; no protection was given for mere ideas nor would it have been given to information about entertaining. In the areas of the law discussed by Warren and Brandeis there was no precedent for a right to privacy.

2

Judicial Precedent in Britain

i

The portrait of the common law sketched by Warren and Brandeis is not merely inaccurate. It is also incomplete. In selectively focusing on decisions that protected the products of intellectual efforts, they ignore other potentially relevant cases. But the relevance was only potential. The courts never grounded a decision on a concept of personality or privacy. To provide some coherence to a discussion of this diverse collection of additional cases, four groups of questions can be superimposed over a body of law that did not overtly acknowledge a right of privacy:

1. Confidential information: What makes certain information confidential and in what special ways does the law regard this information?

2. Privilege: Who is authorized by the law to refuse to tell a court information about an individual? Do those who have this privilege have any other common characteristic?

3. Damages: Under what circumstances will the law award damages for the dissemination of information about a person?

4. Home: Does the law offer any special protection for the relationship centered in the home? What limitations does the law place upon entry into or extraction of information from the home? What limitations does the law impose upon itself in its relation to life in the home?

As with the cases mentioned by Warren and Brandeis, it is not sufficient to show that these other precedents protected privacy indirectly. To provide a foundation upon which a right to privacy may be built it is necessary to find a group of precedents that afford protection for privacy independent of other factors or relationships.

One aspect of a right to control information is mentioned in the Warren and Brandeis article—the courts would deduce that a special duty existed when an employee had access to the confidential information of a business. Two cases are listed: *Yovatt* v. *Winyard*[1] and *Morison* v. *Moat*.[2] Both *Yovatt* and *Morison* had been decided on grounds of a breach of contract or an abuse of a confidence. But Warren and Brandeis think that there must be recognition of a more general right to privacy because the courts must protect confidential information regardless of the relationship and not only when the person using the information is an employee. Closer attention to the holdings in each case will show that Warren and Brandeis's generalization is unwarranted.

Morison v. *Moat* arose out of a dispute between the sons of the original partners to an agreement to manufacture medicine. The elder Morison had been described in the agreement as inventor and sole proprietor of the medicine; the elder Moat was to promote the manufacture and sale of the medicine and was not to communicate the recipe for the medicine to anyone. Morison was to tell the recipe only to any agreed-upon new partner. Morison's two sons (the plaintiffs in the case) were introduced as partners; when the elder Morison died they were legatees of the recipe. At the time that the junior Moat was appointed to transact business for his ailing father, the younger Morison agreed that he should be a "sleeping partner" who would not interfere with business. Later, after the original partnership was dissolved and the assets divided, the younger Moat began manufacturing the medicine based on the recipe he had been given by his father. The Morison brothers successfully sought an injunction to restrain him. The vice-chancellor, Sir George James Turner, did not interpret the issues broadly. Instead, he confined his opinion to considering whether the court should grant an injunction "upon the ground of breach of faith or of contract."[3] Furthermore, there is a statement in his opinion that directly contradicts the expansiveness of the Warren and Brandeis argument:

> What we have to deal with here is, not the right of the Plaintiffs against the world, but their right against the Defendant. It may

> well be that the Plaintiffs have no title against the world in general, and may yet have a good title against this Defendant.[4]

The *Yovatt* case also concerned an agreement about medicines. Yovatt had agreed to instruct Winyard in veterinary medicine but had not agreed to teach him the composition of medicines. Yovatt was granted an injunction to prohibit Winyard's using the medicines. The report of Lord Chancellor Eldon's opinion was brief and gave only breach of trust and confidence as a ground for the injunction.

Two other cases further illustrate the method by which the courts protected confidential information. *Tipping* v. *Clarke*[5] involved a bank clerk who, after arguing with his employer, had threatened to reveal the employer's accounts. Commenting upon the obligation of the clerk, Vice-Chancellor Sir James Wigram said that "it is clear that every clerk employed in a merchant's counting-house is under an implied contract that he will not make public that which he learns in the execution of his duty as a clerk."[6]

A second case illustrates that the protection afforded these confidences was not unlimited. As Vice-Chancellor Wood said in *Gartside* v. *Outram*,[7] "there is no confidence as to the disclosure of iniquity." The vice-chancellor believed that there was property in the secrets of business but not in fraud. "The real ground of the jurisdiction," he said later, "as it is properly put, is founded first upon property, because the Court attempts not to interfere with morals, except in administering civil rights connected with rights of property."[8]

The principles protecting confidential information, so long as it was lawful, or "innocent," to use Lord Eldon's phrase, were applied to relationships other than those of employer-employee. Among these other relationships were those of agent and principal, banker and client, husband and wife, doctor and patient, and clergy and church members. At times the protection given to these relationships was determined by the extent to which they could be identified with the relationship between an attorney and his client; at other times the protection was extended because of characteristics peculiar to the relationship.

As early as 1577 the special relationship between an attorney, or solicitor, and his client was recognized. The report of *Berd* v. *Lovelace*[9] said:

> Thomas Hawtry, gentleman, was served with a subpoena to testify

> his knowledge touching the cause in variance; and made oath that he hath been, and yet is a solicitor in this suit, and hath received several fees of the defendent; which being informed to the Master of the Rolls, it is ordered that the said Thomas Hawtry shall not be compelled to be deposed, touching the same, and that he shall be in no danger of any contempt, touching the not executing of the said process.

The rule was qualified in 1712 by the Court of King's Bench, which held that an attorney could be compelled to testify about a *fact* that he might come to know other than through his client.[10]

During the eighteenth century, courts followed these two rules closely and without significant modification. They emphasized that the privilege was that of the client and not of the solicitor,[11] and they repeated that the privilege existed only for knowledge gained through the solicitor-client relationship.[12]

Lord Chancellor Brougham provided an exhaustive discussion of this part of the law in his opinion in *Greenough* v. *Gaskell.*[13] After considering all of the precedents, he divided the exceptions to the privilege into four groups: cases in which the communication was made before the attorney was employed or after the employment ended; cases in which the attorney was consulted only as a friend and then refused to act; cases in which there was no actual communication, rather where the attorney learned through his own sight; and "where the matter communicated was not in its nature private, and could in no sense be termed the subject of a confidential disclosure."[14] With those exceptions the rule was based upon the importance of the legal profession:

> But it is out of regard to the interests of justice, which cannot be upholded, and to the administration of justice, which cannot go on, without the aid of men skilled in jurisprudence, in the practice of the Courts, and in those matters affecting rights and obligations which form the subject of all judicial proceedings. If the privilege did not exist at all, every one would be thrown upon his own legal resources; deprived of all professional assistance, a man would not venture to consult any skillful person, or would only dare to tell his counsellor half his case.[15]

Lord Brougham's discussion of the law concerning privilege was the archetype for the nineteenth-century courts. In 1859 Vice-Chancellor

Sir R. T. Kindersley gave a similar reason for the privilege, but his operative phrase was that it was required by "the exigencies of mankind."[16]

These same principles were followed through the decade before the Warren and Brandeis article. Jessel M.R. said the privilege was confined to solicitors, and Brett L J., in the same case, explained that the privilege was limited "entirely to communications which take place for the purpose of obtaining legal advice from professional persons."[17] Like the protection given letters and confidential information, the client's privilege did not exist if the communications were used to facilitate fraud.[18] Only truly confidential communications were privileged; the names of clients, for example, were not.[19]

The privilege granted to a client through his solicitor existed not because the client's personality might be harmed and not because the client had a right to control the dissemination of information about himself. The privilege existed because a solicitor could give the best possible assistance only if he knew all the facts, and a means of ensuring that the solicitor was told all the facts was to guarantee that he would not later be obliged to disclose those facts.

Similarly, procedural considerations were the origin for another privilege, or more appropriately a right—the right not to be compelled to give evidence against oneself. But unlike the lawyer-client privilege, the rationale for this right was seldom explained. Instead, most courts were content to rely upon some form of the Latin dictum *nemo tenetur prodere seipsum* ("no one shall be compelled to accuse [or condemn] himself").[20]

For three centuries judges restated the rule without justifying it. In the seventeenth-century case of *R.* v. *Friend*,[21] Friend, on trial for high treason, did not want to reveal whether he was a Roman Catholic. Lord Chief Justice Holt supported Friend when he said: "No man is bound to answer any question that tends to make him accuse himself, or subject him to any penalties."[22] And Lord Chief Justice Treby, concurring, said "no man is bound to answer any questions that will subject him to a penalty or to infamy."[23] In 1751 in the lord chancellor's court, a challenge to an estate turned upon discovery of the religion of the testator. Lord Chancellor Hardwicke ruled that the question need not be answered because the rule of law was "that a man shall not be obliged to discover what *may* subject him to a penalty, and not what *must* only."[24] Over a century later, Justice James Fitzjames Stephen provided yet another restatement of the right:

> The extent of the privilege is I think this: the man may say, "If you are going to bring a criminal charge, or if I have reason to think a criminal charge is going to be brought against me, I will hold my tongue. Prove what you can, but I am protected from furnishing evidence against myself out of my own mouth."[25]

The only modification of this right was the requirement that the court be convinced that there was real danger of the answer subjecting the person to punishment and that the person claiming the right was not trifling with the court.[26]

This right not to incriminate oneself was procedural and limited to certain types of information; it was not founded upon any concept of controlling all information about an individual. Originating in concepts of the accusatorial system of trial, the right was not an example of recognition of a right to privacy.[27] It seemed, instead, to be an instance of a notion of propriety. Vice-Chancellor Knight Bruce voiced such a concept when he explained an important principle of the judicial function:

> The discovery and vindication and establishment of truth are main purposes certainly of the existence of Courts of Justice; still, for the obtaining of these objects, which, however valuable and important, cannot be usefully pursued without moderation, cannot be either usefully or creditably pursued unfairly or gained by unfair means, not every channel is or ought to be open to them.[28]

A different relationship that presented difficulties to the courts was that of husband and wife. Originally, a party to a suit could not testify (another source for the right not to incriminate oneself). Thus, because a husband and wife were viewed as having identical interests, neither could testify in a case in which the other was a party. Judges expressed this limitation in different ways. Lord Hardwicke C.J. said: "The reason why the law will not suffer a wife to be a witness for or against her husband is, to preserve the peace of families; and therefore I shall never encourage such a consent [the husband in the case had been willing for his wife to testify]."[29] Ashhurst J. said in 1788 that "the ground of her incompetence arises from a principle of public policy, which does not permit husband and wife to give evidence that may even tend to criminate each other."[30]

The lord chief justice of the Common Pleas Court, Lord Alvanley, ruled in 1802 that after a divorce the former wife could not relate the events that occurred during the marriage. The phrases that Lord Alvanley used were reminiscent of judicial opinions of breaches of trust or confidence:

> Miserable indeed would the condition of a husband be, if, when a woman is divorced from him, perhaps for her own misconduct, all the occurrences of his life, entrusted to her while the most perfect and unbounded confidence existed between them, should be divulged in a court of justice. . . . it never shall be endured that the confidence which the law has created while the parties remained in the most intimate of all relations, shall be broken whenever by the misconduct of one party (for misconduct alone can have that effect), the relation has been dissolved.[31]

After a statute made a party to a suit competent as a witness in the case, the courts had to decide the status of a spouse under the new law.[32] Although Lord Campbell C.J. thought that the law would be improved if a spouse's testimony were admissible, subject to a restriction not "to divulge confidential communications or to criminate each other," he believed it to be his duty to state the law and not to apply his own opinion. Therefore he felt obliged to conclude that the spouse was still not a competent witness.[33] Wrightman J. concurred in the interpretation of the statute and added:

> The objection to admitting the wife of a party is not merely on the ground of her identity in interest with her husband, but depends upon a broader view of the relation of husband and wife, and on the interest which the public have in the preservation of domestic peace and confidence between married persons.[34]

Crompton J. followed still a third path of reasoning to reach the same result: because the statute did not say that the wife's testimony was to be admissible, it must remain inadmissible.

There was in all three areas of law a paucity of evidence to support a general right to privacy. The right not to incriminate oneself exemplified the law's treatment of an individual in his relationship with the accusatorial process: those who charged an individual could not rely upon him to provide the evidence of guilt. The courts viewed the marriage relationship as so uniquely intimate that its confidences should not be broken—a view that evolved in part from a belief that spouses had an identity of interests. Communications between a solicitor and his client were protected because the courts had a participatory interest in ensuring the furtherance of efforts to do justice.

Once outside those central areas, the courts granted protection less willingly. Commercially, other than the employer-employee relationship, the banker-client relationship was the most frequent subject of litigation. In the case of *Loyd* v. *Freshfield*[35] an allegation was made that Loyd had been negligent in loaning money to one of two partners. The clerk of the bankers was called to tell the balance in the partners' account on a particular day. Abbott C.J. ruled that the balance of the account was not a confidential communication and that the clerk must answer the question.[36]

Another case, thirty-six years later, concerned the disclosure by the Bank of London of a customer's account to another of their customers, who was also a creditor of the initial customer. The customer whose account was disclosed sued the bank. Erle C.J. said that whether the bank had a duty not to disclose the customer's account was a question for the jury.[37] The jury then decided that it was the "duty of a banker in no way to disclose the state of his customer's account." And Chief Justice Erle suggested that, though the bank could say that there were "no sufficient assets" in the account, it could not report that the account lacked a specific amount to meet a bill.[38]

The Court of Exchequer refused in 1868 to say whether a banker had a duty to his client not to reveal details of the account to anyone. The case on appeal to the court concerned a bank's action in reporting a client's balance to a moneylender with the intent of obtaining assistance for the client. The jury returned a verdict for the bank.[39] Thus, prior to 1890 the courts had not defined a definite duty not to disclose a client's account. Whatever duty existed did not find support in a notion of inviolate personality.

The more personal relationships between an individual and his religious adviser or between an individual and his medical adviser would ostensibly be deserving of more protection than those between a banker and his client. The courts, however, frequently stated that no privilege existed for these communications. In 1791 Lord Kenyon C.J. commented that the relation of priest to individual was unknown to the law.[40] Likewise, Lord Langdale M.R. observed that no privilege extended to clergymen, who, along with other "persons in most closely confidential relation," were "bound to disclose communications made to them."[41]

In 1860 a priest was jailed for contempt of court after he refused to identify the person from whom he had received a watch. The watch had been stolen; the priest returned it to the police and reported that he had received it during a confession. Although Hill J. explained that he was not asking about the confession but rather about the name of the man who gave the watch, the priest refused to answer and was jailed.[42] Other than this instance of contempt of court, dicta must be relied upon to trace the denial of privilege to religious advisers. Jessel M.R., in an inclusive opinion, said: "Communications made to a priest in the confessional on matters perhaps considered by the penitent to be more important even than his life or his fortune, are not protected."[43]

Although less reliance must be placed upon dicta alone, the instances of refusing privilege to doctors are as conclusive as those concerning priests. In the trial of the duchess of Kingston for bigamy, Lord Mansfield assumed that the lords thought that a surgeon had no privilege to refuse to answer a material question in court. "If a surgeon was voluntarily to reveal these secrets," Lord Mansfield was reported as saying, "to be sure he would be guilty of a breech of honour, and of great indiscretion; but, to give that information in a court of justice, which by the law of the land he is bound to do, will never be imputed to him as any indiscretion whatever."[44] Another surgeon, who refused to testify about a confession made to him by a woman accused of murdering a child, was told by Park J.: "That is no sufficient reason to prevent disclosure for the purposes of justice."[45]

Before 1851 all cases concerned the privilege of a doctor to refuse to give evidence in court; there was no report of an action against a doctor for revealing information about a patient. In that year the Court of Sessions in Scotland decided that a medical man could not make public the information learned in a consultation without creating a basis for an action against him. The case was reported as *A.B.* v. *C.D.*[46] A.B.'s child had been born only six months after A.B.'s marriage; before baptism the kirk session required medical evidence of the child's legitimacy. After examining the child, the doctor, C.D., wrote in his report that the child had been conceived before the marriage; this report was left at the home of the minister, who later entered it in the minutes of the kirk session. A.B. brought an action for C.D.'s "gross violation of professional confidence." As Lord Fullerton understood the case, the issue was "not whether the communications to a medical adviser are privileged—that cannot be maintained; but whether the relation between such an adviser and the person who consults him, is or is not one which may imply an obligation to secrecy, forming a proper ground of action if it be violated."[47] Lord Fullerton thought that the doctor's action was a ground for an action. The English legal publication *Justice of the Peace* wrote of Lord Fullerton's opinion: "This seems so consonant to common sense and the general benefit of mankind that we cannot but think any English court, if occasion offered [and it had not], would take the same line."[48]

Although generally no privilege existed for communications with medical men, an exception existed if it could be proved that the communications had been made to assist in litigation or with the intention of informing a solicitor. The reported cases on this exception, however, did not protect the person medically examined (from whom information was taken) but instead protected a report made for a railroad company from discovery by the examined person.[49] Even these exceptions did not provide a hint of protection for any semblance of a right to control information about oneself.

A similar exception was made for communications between one person and another acting as his agent for the purpose of obtaining information for litigation. As Sir W. Page Wood V.-Ch. worded the rule, the test was whether the agent, at a distant place, "was discharging a duty which properly devolved upon the solicitor, and which would have been performed by the solicitor" if circumstances had permitted his doing so.[50] This privilege did not extend to an agent who had been sent to negotiate with the other party.[51]

Prior to 1890, with few exceptions, the instances of information-control all arose in the context of a trial in which the basic interests of the court in furthering justice or in finding the truth rather than any issue of individual personality predominated. There was no indication that the rights and privileges recognized by the courts were to be exercised against the world, or in the absence of a special relationship. As Warren and Brandeis correctly recognize, to provide protection for a right to privacy the right must be exercisable against anyone and not merely against a specific individual who existed only in certain determined fact situations.[52] Yet the decisions were based on the facts of the particular case, and the rights were exercised in that context. The closest anyone came to a common principle was Vice-Chancellor Knight Bruce's comment that truth should be pursued with moderation.[53]

In addition, these cases, which were potentially related to information-control, provided little support for a right to privacy because they involved procedural questions and not actions for damages. There were, to be sure, scattered dicta that implied that an action might be successful for a bank's disclosure of the balance in an account or a doctor's voluntary disclosure of certain facts. But to found a right to privacy upon such dicta alone would produce an extremely ephemereal right.

ii

The tenuous nature of any claim for damages based upon invasion of privacy can be further exemplified by the principles upon which the courts awarded damages. Warren and Brandeis advocate the right to privacy to provide compensation for injury to feelings caused by the publication of personal facts that an individual wanted to keep private. They have no doubt that such publication causes "mental pain and distress, far greater than could be inflicted by mere bodily injury."[54] But the courts were not so persuaded. They had refused to grant an injunction to prevent damage to feelings, separate from any property considerations. Moreover, when they did award damages, their insistence that the injury be significant belied any inclination to adopt the privacy concept.

Three years after the *Prince Albert* decision Vice-Chancellor Knight Bruce offered guidance for other judges. To determine whether damages should be awarded for nuisance, a judge should ask himself this question:

> Ought this inconvenience to be considered in fact as more than fanciful, more than one of mere delicacy or fastidiousness, as an inconvenience materially interfering with the ordinary comfort physically of human existence, not merely according to elegant or dainty modes and habits of living, but according to plain and sober and simple notions among English people?[55]

The vice-chancellor's statement was part of his opinion granting an injunction to restrain the burning of bricks in a manner offensive to a neighbor.

St. Helen's Smelting Co. v. *Tipping*[56] was a similar case. Tipping sought to recover for damage done to his trees and crops by noxious vapors and gases from the smelting process. A jury decided in his favor. In the House of Lords, the lord chancellor, Lord Westbury, said that it was necessary to distinguish between a nuisance that produced a material injury and one that produced personal discomfort: "With regard to the latter, namely, the personal inconvenience and interference with one's enjoyment, one's quiet, one's personal freedom, anything that discomposes or injuriously affects the senses or the nerves, whether that may or may not be denominated a nuisance, must undoubtedly depend greatly on the circumstances of the place where the thing complained of actually occurs."[57] Lord Wensleydale and Lord Cranworth agreed with the lord chancellor that the jury's verdict should be upheld. Lord Wensleydale added that because the court must look at everything from a reasonable point of view, "the law does not regard trifling and small inconveniences, but only regards sensible inconveniences, injuries which sensibly diminish the comfort, enjoyment or value of the property which is affected."[58]

In *Tod-Heatly* v. *Benham*[59] the Court of Appeal applied Vice-Chancellor Knight Bruce's guidance to a covenant in a lease by which the lessee agreed not to do anything "which shall or may be or grow to the annoyance, nuisance, grievance, or damage of the lessor . . . or the inhabitants of the neighbouring or adjoining houses." Neighbors complained that opening a hospital to treat poor outpatients violated the covenant by introducing the possibility of infection into the neighborhood. The lessee, a doctor, appealed from the judge's decision against him. Cotton L.J. thought that judges "must not take that to be an annoyance or grievance which would only be so to some sensitive persons." Judges, he believed, should rely upon the evidence of the case and not upon their own sentiments to determine what "would be an annoyance or grievance to reasonable, sensible people; and, in my opinion, an act which is an interference with the pleasurable enjoyment of a house is an annoyance or grievance, and within the definition given by V.-C. Knight-Bruce in *Walter* v. *Selfe*."[60] Bowen L.J. concurred, and included in his opinion this statement:

> If you find there is anything which disturbs his [the ordinary, sensible, English inhabitant of a house] reasonable peace of mind, that seems to me to be an annoyance, although it may not appear to amount to physical detriment to comfort. You must take sensible people, you must not take fanciful people on the one side or skilled people on the other.[61]

The Court of Appeal upheld the ruling of the lower court.

In each instance the court awarded damages only insofar as property was affected. As with intellectual effort, a nexus with property was a necessary condition for the awarding of damages. Entirely missing from the opinions was any hint of a self-sufficient right to privacy. A similar essential condition existed in defamation cases, in which the courts required a loss of commercial value. Once again there was no allowance for recovery for injury to feelings.

At first glance, defamation cases appear to be a part of the law that did relate to feelings. Warren and Brandeis, however, distinguish defamation law from the right to privacy that they advocate: damages for defamatory statements were awarded because the person's image as held by others was lowered, while privacy concerned an individual's internal feelings and estimation of himself; defamation tended to be based upon injury to commercial values, while privacy was concerned with feelings alone.[62] Nevertheless, the judicial reservations about awarding damages solely for the injury done to feelings by defamatory statements are additional evidence of the lack of support for a right to privacy.

The report of a decision by Lord Chancellor Egerton and two chief justices in 1607 said that action would lie for a libelous letter published to others, "for it is an offence to the King, and is a great motive to revenge, and tends to the breaking of the peace and great mischief."[63] Similarly, over two hundred years later, Best J. said that the writer of a libelous letter was prosecuted because the letter tended to provoke a breach of the peace.[64] Further, because the letter had appeared in a newspaper, he added: "The liberty of the press cannot be carried to this extent without violating another equally sacred right; namely the right of character. . . . Where vituperation begins, the liberty of the press ends."[65]

There was another relevant principle: a public man could be commented upon with greater latitude than could a private man. As Parke B. (later Lord Wensleydale) said: "There is a difference between publications relating to public and private individuals. Every subject has a right to comment on those acts of public men which concern him as a subject of the realm, if he do not make his commentary a cloak for malice and slander."[66] That case involved a former mayor who was easily categorized as a public figure. But a parish vicar who presided at a charitable society was not so readily classified. Even so, the Exchequer Court ruled that the vicar's sermons were public—they were, after all, "public sermons"—but the charity was private and subject to comment only under more stringent controls. But as Alderson B. acknowledged, it was not easy to distinguish that which was public from that which was private:

> It seems there is a distinction, although I must say I really can hardly tell what the limits of it are, between the comments on a man's public conduct and upon his private conduct. I can understand that you have a right to comment on the public acts of a minister, upon the public acts of a general, upon the public judgments of a judge, upon the public skill of an actor,—I can understand that; but, I do not know where the limit can be drawn distinctly, between where the comment is to cease, as being applied solely to a man's public conduct, and where it is to begin, as applicable to his private character; because, although it is quite competent for a person to speak of a judgment of a judge, as being an extremely erroneous and foolish one, . . . and although it is perfectly competent for persons to say of an actor that he is a remarkably bad actor, and ought not to be permitted to perform such and such parts, because he performs them so ill, yet you ought not to be allowed to say of an actor that he has disgraced himself in private life; nor to say of a judge, or of a minister, that he has committed a felony, or anything of that description, which is in no way connected with his public conduct or public judgment; and therefore there must be some limits, although I do not distinctly see exactly where those limits are to be drawn.[67]

The sense of the distinction between a public man and a private man was echoed by Lord Chief Justice Cockburn when he told a jury that "those who filled a public position must not be too thin-skinned in reference to comments made upon them," and he added that "the criticism of the press was the best security for the proper discharge of public duties."[68] In different words, Willes J. expressed the same principle when he said:

> The principle upon which these cases are founded is a universal one, that the public convenience is to be preferred to private interests, and that communications which the interests of society require to be unfettered may freely be made by persons acting honestly without actual malice, not withstanding that they involve relevant comments condemnatory of individuals.[69]

Any definition of fair comment was not easy to phrase. Lord Esher M.R. said it must be left to the jury to determine what is fair.[70] He also recognized the difficulties: "It is very easy to say what would be clearly beyond that limit [of fair comment]; if, for instance, the writer attacked the private character of the author. But it is much more difficult to say what is within the limit."[71]

Indeterminate though it might be, a boundary between public and private life was acknowledged by the courts. Yet acknowledgment did not encompass awarding damages for publishing information about the private sphere if the only claim was injured feelings. Three nineteenth-century cases of alleged slander illustrate the unwillingness of the judges to award compensation for injury to feelings alone. The case of *Allsop* v. *Allsop*[72] was brought by William and Hannah Allsop against Thomas Allsop for his claim to have had sexual relations with Hannah while she was married to William. According to the plaintiffs, the result of the statement was that Mrs. Allsop lost the society of her neighbors and then became ill; her husband was put to the expense of curing her. The court had to determine whether the illness was sufficient special damage to constitute a cause of action. In explaining the decision not to award compensation, Pollock C.B. referred the fact that "the Courts here have always taken care that parties shall not be responsible for fanciful or remote damages, or in fact any that do not fairly and naturally result from the wrongful act itself." He continued: "This particular damage depends on the temperament of the party affected, and it may be laid down that illness arising from the excitement which the slanderous language may produce is not that sort of damage which forms a ground of action."[73]

In the second case, *Lynch* v. *Knight*,[74] the question was whether damages could be awarded to Mrs. Knight for loss of her husband's consortium, which she claimed resulted from statements by Lynch. The House of Lords reversed the lower court's decision in favor of Mrs. Knight because they felt that her husband's conduct was not the natural and reasonable consequence of the words. Lord Wensleydale specifically mentioned the question of injury to feelings:

> Mental pain or anxiety the law cannot value, and does not pretend to redress, when the unlawful act complained of causes that alone; though where a material damage occurs, and is connected with it, it is impossible a jury, in estimating it, should altogether overlook the feelings of the party interested.[75]

Different offending statements were reported in a third case, *Weldon* v. *De Bathe*.[76] There someone had told a husband that his wife was not properly managing their house. The wife claimed that she had suffered grief. In upholding the lower court's decision against the wife, Brett M.R. reasoned that "mere injury to the feelings of the plaintiff is not any such special damage [which was required by the law to support an action], and cannot make words not otherwise actionable the subject of an action."[77]

Insofar as the civil law was concerned, the courts had not evinced any significant tendency to protect privacy as an independent concept. What protection there was depended upon the existence of a special relationship, such as that of solicitor-client, or upon injury done to property or reputation. The judges were wary of awarding damages for injury done to feelings—an injury they could not even pretend to quantify.

iii

The one area in which the concept of privacy had a function, albeit an ambiguous one, was the criminal law. In one sense, *privacy* described that which was left unregulated by the criminal law. In another sense, *privacy* was used to justify the exclusion of the criminal law from a particular area. Sir James Fitzjames Stephen uses both senses in his book *Liberty, Equality, Fraternity*.[78] He writes that because the criminal law was "the most powerful and by far the roughest engine which society can use for any purpose," careful consideration must precede its use. To indict a man for a minor act such as ingratitude or perfidy "it would be necessary to go into an infinite number of delicate and subtle inquiries which would tear off all privacy from the lives of a large number of persons."[79] In other paragraphs he is much clearer about his belief in the harm done by attempting to regulate conduct within a private sphere:

> Legislation and public opinion ought in all cases whatever scrupulously to respect privacy. To define the province of privacy distinctly is impossible, but it can be described in general terms. . . .
>
> . . . there is a sphere, none the less real because it is impossible to define its limits within which law and public opinion are intruders likely to do more harm than good. To try to regulate the internal affairs of a family, the relations of love or friendship, or many other things of the same sort, by law or by the coercion of public opinion, is like trying to pull an eyelash out of a man's eye with a pair of tongs. They may put out the eye, but they will never get hold of the eyelash.[80]

Although never so distinctly stated, the courts throughout the late nineteenth century were guided by a similar principle insofar as it related to the family and home life. But when questions of morality and decency arose, the courts tended to enforce Vaughan J.'s dictum that "the law is never better employed than in enforcing the observance of moral duties."[81] This tendency of the courts had been expressed before by Lord Mansfield, who said that the King's Bench Court "is the custos morum of the people, and has the superintendency of offences contra bonos mores: and upon this ground both Sir Charles Sedley and Curl, who had been guilty of offences against good manners, were prosecuted here."[82]

The position of the courts concerning acts committed in private was ambivalent; though special protection was given the home, the courts did not accept the application of the home's privacy attribute in other settings. In 1844 two men were indicted for indecent exposure; their counsel argued that they had been seen casually and that they had, in fact, sought privacy for their act.[83] In spite of counsel's argument, the recorder gave this instruction to the jury: "It cannot be necessary to prove that the parties intended that the public should detect them; they would always seek as much privacy as they could conveniently obtain; but was this such a situation that there was no reasonable probability of their being so discovered?"[84]

R. v. *Watson* involved a man charged with indecent exposure to a twelve-year-old girl in Paddington Churchyard.[85] Lord Denman C.J. said: "The general rule is, that a nuisance must be public; that is, to the injury or offence of several. There is no precedent of such an indictment as the present, and we are not inclined to make one."[86] In 1848, on a point reserved by the lower court, Pollock C.B. and the other judges agreed that a man's act of exposing himself in a public house was not indictable if there was only one other person present—in this case it was the wife of the owner of the public house.[87]

A final topic deserves brief mention in the discussion of the criminal law's relation to privacy claims: eavesdropping. Since the Justice of the Peace Act 1361, a peeping Tom could be bound over to keep the peace.[88] Blackstone's *Commentaries* contains a relevant paragraph:

> *Eavesdropper*, or such as listen under walls or windows, or the eaves of a house, to hearken after discourse, and there-upon to frame slanderous and mischievous tales, are a common nuisance,

and presentable at the court-leet: or indictable at the sessions, and punishable by fine and finding sureties for their good behaviour.[89]

iv

This recurrence of the concomitance of privacy-related concepts with protection for the home makes it appropriate to continue this survey of court decisions with an examination of the direct relationship between the law and the home. The point at which to begin is obvious: Coke's own report of *Semayne's Case*,[90] which included the statement that "the house of every one is his castle." But it is pertinent to consider the remainder of that sentence and another: "The house of every one is his castle, and if thieves come to a man's house to rob or murder, and the owner or his servants kill any one of the thieves in defence of himself and his house, it is no felony and he shall lose nothing."[91] Later in the report there was a qualification:

> The house of any one is only a privilege for himself, and does not extend to protect any person who flies to his house, or the goods of any other which are brought there, to prevent a lawful execution and to escape the process of the law: in such cases after request and denial, the sheriff may break the house.[92]

A second dictum, not so well known, but illustrative of the sympathies of the judges, was Lord Justice Bowen's expressed reluctance to interfere with family life:

> I for one should deeply regret the day, if it ever came, when Courts of Law or Equity thought themselves justified in interfering more than is strictly necessary with the private affairs of the people of this country. Both as regards the conduct of private affairs, and domestic life, the rule is that Courts of Law should not intervene except upon occasion. It is far better that people should be left free.[93]

This opinion of the court that the home deserved protection echoed two eighteenth-century cases that had considered general search warrants: *Entick* v. *Carrington*[94] and *Wilkes* v. *Wood*.[95] Lord Chief Justice Camden's opinion in *Entick* typified the thoughts of the courts.

> Our law holds the property of every man so sacred that no man can set his foot upon his neighbour's close without his leave. If he does, he is a trespasser, though he does no damage at all; if he will tread upon his neighbour's ground, he must justify it by law.[96]

Later judges, not so willing to accept the sweeping breadth of Lord Camden's opinion, balanced the value of property and the rights of the home with the need to discover the facts about crime. A suit for damages from two police officers for their search of a home reached the House of Lords in 1867.[97] The police officers had a search warrant describing certain items, but they also searched private papers and found evidence of participation in the sending of threatening letters. In language very different from Lord Camden, Lord Chancellor Chelmsford said:

> But supposing that in a search which might have been improper originally, there were matters discovered which shewed the complicity of the pursuer in a crime, then I think the officers, I can hardly say would have been justified, but would have been excused by the result of their search.[98]

A potpourri of other cases will illustrate the strength of the dicta and the weakness of the rules of law expressed by the courts concerning homes and privacy.

In *Knowles* v. *Richardson*[99] the court refused to grant an action for a wall that obstructed a view. The court reasoned that a view was a matter of delight and not a matter for damages. But, Twinden J. was reported as asking a rhetorical question: "Why may I not build up a wall that another may not look into my yard?" The brief report provided no clue for the enigmatic inclusion of that question.

Another case began when a gentleman, Merest, and his friend were shooting on his land. Harvey, who was drunk, rode past and asked to join the hunt. Ignoring the refusal of his request, Harvey shot several times and swore loudly. The jury awarded Merest damages of five hundred pounds.[100] Although the ground for appeal was the question of excessive exemplary damages, Gibbs C.J. gave his opinion of Harvey's conduct:

> I wish to know, in a case where a man disregards every principle which actuates the conduct of a gentleman, what is to restrain him except large damages? To be sure, one can hardly conceive

> worse conduct than this. . . . Suppose a gentleman has a paved walk in his paddock, before his windows, and that a man intrudes and walks up and down before the window of his house, and looks in while the owner is at dinner, is the trespasser to be permitted to say, "here is a halfpenny for you, which is the full extent of all the mischief I have done?" Would that be compensation? I cannot say that it would be.[101]

An invasion of privacy was part of the pleadings in *Walker* v. *Brewster.*[102] Walker complained that a result of the fetes sponsored by his neighbor, Brewster, was the gathering of large numbers of people in the area. Some of those people sat on the walls of Walker's grounds and looked into his yard, thus, the complaint said, destroying his privacy. The vice-chancellor, Sir W. Page Wood, did not mention privacy in his opinion but granted the injunction because a nuisance had been created by the large number of people; the vice-chancellor felt that he could not allow a man to make a profit to the irritation of his neighbors.[103]

V

A final group of cases, those concerning ancient lights, also contained remarks about privacy. It was in this aspect of the law of easements that the nineteenth-century courts most often dealt with privacy arguments. Generally, the law held that if a window remained in place for twenty years, the owner of the window then gained a right to prevent any lessening of light or air entering through the window. Often a dispute arose between the possessor of a right to ancient lights and someone who claimed that the window disturbed his privacy. One of the earliest cases was *Cotterell* v. *Griffiths.*[104] Cotterell's windows originally had blinds; when the blinds were removed, Griffiths erected a paling that darkened the windows. Cotterell claimed a loss of his ancient lights; Griffiths responded with a claim of loss of privacy. Lord Kenyon C.J. decided for Cotterell because the paling admitted less light than had the original blinds. He said nothing of privacy.

Chandler v. *Thompson*[105] was a similar case. Chandler enlarged old windows; Thompson erected a new building that obstructed the view but still allowed more light than through the old, smaller windows. The report of the case included the argument by the attorney for the defendant that privacy should be protected. LeBlanc J. acknowledged that he knew of actions for privacy but that he had never known one to succeed. Furthermore, he "had heard it laid down by Lord C.J. Eyre that such an action did not lie, and that the only remedy was to build on the adjoining land opposite to the offensive window."[106]

The basic facts of *Turner* v. *Spooner*[107] were the same as the two earlier cases. Vice-Chancellor Kindersley said of an action for invasion of privacy:

> With regard to the question of privacy, no doubt the owner of a house would prefer that a neighbor should not have the right of looking into his windows or yard, but neither this Court nor a court of law will interfere on the mere ground of invasion of privacy; and a party has a right even to open new windows, although he is thereby enabled to overlook his neighbor's premises, and so interfering, perhaps, with his comfort.[108]

This statement should be compared with one by Turner L.J.:

> That the windows of the house may be overlooked, and its comparative privacy destroyed, and its value thus diminished by the proposed erection [of a photographic studio at the rear of a neighbor's house] (circumstances to which some of the Plaintiffs' witnesses refer), are matters with which, as I apprehend, we have nothing to do. I think, therefore, that the Plaintiffs' case for the injunction wholly fails.[109]

Possibly the strongest rejection of privacy as a ground for action came from the three courts that were asked to decide the case of *Jones* v. *Tapling*.[110] The case was difficult because after Jones had altered the positions of windows in an old warehouse, Tapling constructed a new warehouse that blocked the light to the new windows and the old ones as well (it was impossible to construct and block only the new windows). Jones then restored the old windows and asked the court to order Tapling to remove his warehouse. The only mention of privacy in the equally divided Court of Common Pleas was Keating J.'s comment that he was "not aware of any other system of law, by which the remedy of the owner of land for an invasion of its privacy by his neighbour opening new windows upon it is confined to their obstruction."[111]

Two judges of the Exchequer Chamber were more definite in

their rejection of a cause of action based on invasion of privacy. Bramwell B. said that "it is to be remembered that privacy is not a right. Intrusion on it is no wrong or cause of action."[112] And Blackburn J., though acknowledging that the intrusion on privacy from a large window is greater than from small windows, said:

> But the law does not protect the right to privacy as it does that to light and air. It may be that the reason for this distinction given in the old cases, viz., that light and air are things of necessity, while prospect and privacy are but things of delight, is more quaint than satisfactory; but it is not, I believe, proposed by any one to disturb that distinction now. If it were proposed, I think more substantial reasons for supporting it might be assigned.[113]

From this he concluded that Tapling had no protection for his interference with the legal rights of Jones.

Tapling was no more successful in the House of Lords, where Lord Westbury, the lord chancellor, commented upon the phrase "invasion of privacy by opening windows" by saying: "That is not treated by the law as a wrong for which any remedy is given."[114]

This rejection of an action for an independent right to privacy made certain that the English courts would not evolve a right as suggested by Warren and Brandeis. Without doubt, nothing so vague as an injury to "inviolate personality" would have been approved as a basis for damages; the English courts insisted that damages be awarded only for injuries to measurable concepts such as property or reputation. And they required that these damages be for other than mere injury to feelings. Privilege would be granted only for information that was communicated between solicitor and client; there was no general protection given to the control of information. Only in an area not considered by Warren and Brandeis did privacy play a role in English law—criminal law. When the argument concerned the limits to the powers of government, privacy became a factor. But even in this area the claim was to limit the sphere of the criminal law and not to an independent right of privacy.

Claims of a right to privacy did not develop in England until after the First World War. Once the claims were made, the courts were unable to adapt the law because the precedents were restrictive. This inability meant that attempts to protect privacy concentrated upon the legislature. But before the claims were made in terms of a "right to privacy," there were legislative precedents in areas similar to those that occurred later.

3

Legislative Precedents before the First World War

i

Like the early judicial precedents, early legislative discussions of privacy-related subjects are notable for the absence of a developed concept of a right to privacy. Even though the language of the early legislative debates is much the same as those about privacy between 1967 and 1969, the focus of the concerns differs greatly. Yet with their familiar vocabularies, these predecessors of recent claims of a right to privacy attest the changes as well as the similarities throughout the past three centuries. The early Parliamentary discussions can be conveniently grouped under four headings: newspapers, libel, interception of communications, and the census.

For over three hundred years, attempts to define and to defend freedom of the press have been shaped by contemporaneous issues. Among the earliest regulations of the press was an ordinance of 1643 that permitted the printing of only those publications registered at the Company of Stationers.[1] In the following year Milton published his speech "for the liberty of unlicenc'd printing." Succeeding generations have witnessed recurrent attacks on the press. When the *Observer* began to prosper as a Sunday newspaper in the late eighteenth century, Lord Belgrave proposed a bill to suppress all Sunday newspapers. He theorized that the French Revolution could be attributed to the increased disregard for the laws of God and the neglect and scorn of the day dedicated to His service. Opposing the bill was Richard Sheridan, who said that it would strip the adventuresome of their property and deprive some people of an opportunity to inform themselves on the only day that they did not work.[2]

Lord Belgrave's bill failed; Lord Castlereagh's Newspaper Stamp Duties Bill of 1819 did not.[3] One of the "Six Acts" passed in a special autumn session, it imposed a duty of four pence per number. The bill was opposed by those who said it amounted to an unwarranted interference with the freedom of the press. Supporters, such as George Bankes, said that the opponents were talking about the press of earlier times and not about the contemporary political tracts that could not have been foreseen before the French Revolution. He asked whether it was "not desirable to repress the circulation of those doctrines which threatened to destroy the public morals, and to endanger the public security?"[4] Dr. Joseph Phillimore, regius professor of civil law at Oxford, also supported the bill. His argument was a mixture of the older objections to the politics of the press and the newer denunciation of the press's improprieties:

> If men under the pretense of the liberty of the press, published blasphemies, or libelled their neighbours—if under the pretence of discussing grievances, or promoting petitions, they excited seditious tumults, they must be restrained within proper bounds. Civil liberty would cease to exist without such restraints; in civilised life such restraints must be established as times and circumstances required. In fact, restraints were necessary to the protection of liberty in its most desirable state.[5]

It was not long, however, before the swing of the pendulum reversed and the removal of the stamp duties was advocated.[6] But once collection of the stamp duties had begun, the needs of the Exchequer provided a strong argument in favor of retention. Not until 1855 did a chancellor of the Exchequer admit that the nation's financial situation was strong enough to withstand the predicted loss of revenue.[7] By then the chancellor, Sir George Lewis, was compelled to refute the contention that reducing the stamp duties would only encourage licentious newspapers: "It may, I believe be said with perfect truth, that no immoral or licentious publication has a long life, or obtains an extensive circulation."[8] Sir Edward Bulwer Lytton supported the bill and argued that the press only reflected the tastes of the public.[9] But Henry Drummond disagreed; he thought that the press of 1855 was one of the country's "greatest curses." Furthermore, he believed that the appeal to freedom of the press "was all cant and nonsense; the press was a mercantile speculation; and nothing else." As a commercial venture, the newspapers had to appeal to the taste of the public, which, according to Drummond, was "for gossip—political gossip—and political gossip of one sort or another they must have, cost what it might."[10]

The publication of gossip, political or otherwise, was becoming the primary cause of criticism of the press. By the 1870s political heterodoxy was no longer the dominant refrain of the critics. Proposals were made that the proprietor or printer of a newspaper be positively identified to ensure his availability for a libel action. Among the advocates was Sir Charles Russell, who believed that a class of newspapers "had been started for the purpose of ransacking the private lives of individuals and invading the sacred privileges of homes to pander to the prurient feelings of a certain portion of the public; but in these cases the registered printers and publishers were men of straw, against whom it was useless to proceed."[11]

The libelous tendencies of nonpolitical reports were not, however, the most common cause for condemnation of the press. A more frequent complaint concerned the publication of evidence from divorce courts. That complaint arose as early as 1859, when Parliament passed the Divorce Court Bill but rejected a clause that would have allowed hearings in closed court.[12] In that debate one side argued that publication was a deterrent and an aid to the administration of justice. For example, a Radical M.P., Acton Smee Ayrton, opposed the clause because he thought that publicity would effectively deter a husband who might otherwise mistreat his wife. Ayrton believed that the husband's "conviction that his cruelty, though perpetrated in domestic privacy, might be dragged to light, and made to bring upon him the scorn and reprobation of all right-minded" men would lessen marital misconduct, while secrecy would "tend to encourage domestic vice and domestic immorality."[13]

During the next thirty years, the *Pall Mall Gazette* and other newspapers became the subjects of increasingly critical questions in the House of Commons. But, unlike the Warren and Brandeis article, the evil portrayed was damage to public morals and not intrusion upon the privacy of the parties to a divorce.[14] Those complaints were among the questions considered by the Royal Commission on Divorce and Matrimonial Causes appointed in 1909. After hearing evidence and sponsoring research, the committee accepted "that the evils of excessive publication are real and serious."[15] But it did not consider the divorce proceedings to be a private matter about which the public had no legitimate interest.

Instead, the "English view is that divorce is a grave matter, which concerns the public as well as the parties, and in English courts the characters and the future prospects of the litigants are seriously at stake. This establishes a presumption, which we feel it impossible to ignore, in favour of publicity for divorce, as for other legal proceedings."[16] Because there had been abuses and because the law was uncertain, the committee recommended that judges be given statutory power to close the divorce court entirely, or to order that certain evidence not be published. It also recommended that no evidence be published until the trial was completed and that the publication of pictorial representations of those involved also be prohibited.[17]

Parliament did not accept either recommendation. Moreover, in 1913 the House of Lords rejected the contention that the judges had a residual power to close their courts.[18] Lord Chancellor Viscount Haldane was certain that the Matrimonial Causes Act of 1857 had not given any such discretion to the judges, and that "unless it be strictly necessary for the attainment of justice, there can be no power in the Court to hear in camera either a matrimonial cause or any other where there is a contest between parties."[19] At the end of his remarks he emphasized that "a mere desire to consider feelings of delicacy or to exclude from publicity details which it would not be desirable to publish is not, I repeat, enough as the law now stands."[20]

The press that provoked these reactions was not the same press that had been regulated in the seventeenth century. Equipped with a new tool, the camera, and the ability to print photographs, newspapermen went about their profession with a new sense of mission. For the subjects of the photographs and reports, and other people as well, that mission was intrusive. An article in the *Spectator* of June 1888 provided an apt description of the developing tension between the press and notions of privacy:

> It is not simply that the modern journalist is not ashamed of letting out private secrets; he is apparently conscious of a new claim on the gratitude of men for having done so,—nay, not only on the gratitude of men at large, but on the gratitude especially of the particular man or woman whose secret he has revealed.[21]

ii

Closely related to the debates about newspapers were Parliamentary attempts to modify the law of libel. Of especial relevance to the development of privacy arguments were John Campbell's proposals that truth should not be a defense in a civil action for libel unless the matter was published for the public good. In 1834, as solicitor general, he suggested that a select committee should examine the problems posed by the defense of truth as part of a more general review of the law of libel. As an illustration of the damage that could be done by revealing the truth, he told the story of a young woman who was seduced "by a man of title." She escaped from him and later earned the respect of the community to which she moved. When the seducer located her and she refused to return to him he made known the story of her early life. As a result, she lost her employment. The solicitor general thought it wrong that she should suffer without a remedy (an action for libel would be successfully met with a defense of the truth).[22]

Three years later, as attorney general, he referred to the same story as a "well known anecdote." He still considered that truth ought not to be complete justification, and he believed that "the person who could be guilty of inflicting so enormous an injury on a female, thus circumstanced, was deserving of the most severe punishment."[23] Five years later, as Lord Campbell, he moved for the appointment of a select committee of the House of Lords to study the law of defamation. He suggested that any defense of truth should go to the jury, who would say "whether the publication was for the good of the community."[24] He argued that there were many cases in which society had no interest in being informed of an individual's private history "and when the malicious disclosure of what is true is wrongful, and ought to be punished."[25] The committee was appointed under his chairmanship and eventually included his recommendations in its report.[26] The House of Commons, however, rejected the clause of the bill that would have effected the proposal.[27] The clause was omitted from later bills introduced to amend the law of libel.

Lord Campbell's proposals were not unlike Warren and Brandeis's suggested right in that damages could be awarded for injuries sustained after publication of true statements. Nevertheless they were not the same: Lord Campbell was dealing with injury to reputation; Warren and Brandeis with injury to feelings.

iii

A third area that resembled later privacy arguments involved the interception of communications—either letters or telegrams. In 1735 members of Parliament complained that their letters were being opened. After a committee investigated the allegations, the House of Commons resolved that it was a breach of Parliamentary privilege to open letters to or from members without a written warrant from the principal secretary of state "for every such opening or looking into."[28]

There was a more censorious reaction to the successive petitions presented by a Radical M.P., Thomas Duncombe, on behalf of several foreigners resident in England. Duncombe complained not that their letters had been intercepted or their privacy violated, but that the information so learned had been communicated to a foreign government and that the letters had been resealed so no one could detect that they had been opened.[29] The home secretary, Sir James Graham, refused to comment upon the opening of the letters of one of the foreigners, the Italian republican revolutionary, Joseph Mazzini. Secret committees, however, were appointed to investigate the allegations and the powers of the home secretary.

In a short report the secret committee of the House of Lords said that they had not defined the grounds for the exercise of the power. They thought that it was sufficient "that the exercise of this power can be traced from the earliest institutions in this country for the conveyance of letters."[30] According to them, "The Secretaries of State were in time of war and danger to the State to be made acquainted, if they required it, with letters and communications to foreign parts."[31] The committee accepted the home secretary's explanation that Mazzini's letters had been opened to protect the tranquility of Europe. Although the Commons committee also concluded that the power had long been exercised,[32] neither committee was convinced of the necessity to open letters.

Duncombe was particularly dissatisfied with the report, which he termed "unsatisfactory and evasive."[33] His remarks revealed that his objection was to the secrecy of the practice and not to the violation of the privacy of letters: "If you seize papers under a certain warrant, every individual suspected knows what you are about; but to reseal letters, to commit forgery [of seals], and to send those letters on, I say it is a disgraceful and iniquitous system, and unworthy of any Minister whatever."[34]

Both Sir Robert Peel and Sir James Graham defended the practice on grounds of necessity, especially when dealing with foreign powers. Macaulay disagreed; he admitted that there were convenient ways to discover crime: torture and espionage, for example. But the English had not chosen to adopt those methods. "So I say in the case before us," he continued, "the experience of many years shows us that the benefits arising from the strict observation of the security and secrecy of private life, without the exercise of arbitrary power, much more than counterbalance all the advantages to be derived from a contrary system."[35]

During the First World War, private correspondence was opened and censored.[36] And, as Sir William Harcourt had done in 1881, the government refused to reveal the number of warrants issued.[37] Even though questions were asked about the opening of letters, no serious dispute arose—not even when, during a debate in the House of Commons, Bonar Law read an excerpt from an intercepted letter.[38] In the House of Lords the questions were phrased in almost friendly tones; Viscount Bryce, for example, wanted to ensure that the people who exercised the censorship were "persons of judgment, of experience, and of good feeling."[39]

The only dissonant note occurred when Arthur Ponsonby used an adjournment debate to protest against the practice of resealing letters to conceal that they had been opened:

> I am raising the question of the practice of opening private letters and sticking them down again, so that the writer and the receiver of the letter are unaware that they are being spied upon. It is a most objectionable practice, and that it should be widespread and outside the control of this House is a matter of very grave importance to us.[40]

He complained that the letters of pacifists and Labour leaders were being opened and that the government was also "eavesdropping" by tapping telephones.[41] Ramsay Macdonald alleged that there had been interference with the correspondence of the Independent Labour party. His objections were more general than Ponsonby's:

> Family affairs of the most private and sacred characters are dealt with in letters; letters passing between fathers and sons are opened, read, and probably giggled over by some employé of the Government. . . . People write innocently, knowing to whom they were writing, use loose expressions, allow the pen to run loosely, and say things they would never dream of saying if a third party were present.[42]

The issues in these debates involved what Macdonald termed "fair play." The government was not criticized because it had intruded upon someone's privacy but because it had not followed the unwritten rules of the game—the state was not supposed to use its power secretly against an individual. Most of the objectors would have been satisfied if the letters had been stamped "opened by authority."

iv

Like the interception of communications, the last group of these early legislative measures also involved the collection of information by the government. In this group, however, the collection was made openly through the census. Of the twelve censuses taken before the First World War, two (1861 and 1911) and the first census bill deserve special attention, along with the establishment of the registrar general's office. The first census bill, Thomas Potter's "Bill for Registering the Number of the People," was introduced in 1753.[43] Its preamble explained that it was

> for taking and registering an annual Account of the total number of people, and of the total number of marriages, births, and deaths; and also of the total number of poor receiving alms from every parish and extra-parochial place in Great Britain.[44]

Although passed by the House of Commons, the bill was rejected in the House of Lords. No report was made of the lord's debate, but the objections of William Thornton in the House of Commons were reported at length. He said that the measure was "totally subversive of the last remains of English liberty" and "calculated to divest us of the last remains of our birthright."[45] In his opinion an annual register could only benefit enemies both at home and abroad by alerting them to the nation's wealth or military strength. And he objected to the likely result of the registration:

> To what end then should our number be known, except we are to be pressed into the fleet and the army, or transplanted like felons to the plantations abroad? And what purpose will it answer to know where the kingdom is crowded, and where it is thin, except we are to be driven from place to place as graziers do their cattle? If this be intended, let them brand us at once; but while they treat us like oxen and sheep, let them not insult us with the name of men.[46]

Another opponent of the census provisions, Matthew Ridley, said that he was not superstitious but that he had received letters from the town he represented telling him that the people were filled with "imaginary terrors." He foresaw riotous behavior and predicted that if "epidemical distemper" or public misfortune were by chance to follow the registration, the resulting uproar might threaten "the existence of our present government."[47]

By 1800 concern about shortages of food and increases in population made Parliament anxious to discover the true facts. There was no objection, therefore, when Charles Abbott introduced a bill to require the clergy and parish officers to answer questions about the population.[48] The next three censuses were also based upon returns by the parish officials. Not until the census of 1841 did the registrar general's office supervise the enumeration.

That office was created after the passage of acts to require the registration of births, deaths, and marriages, and to provide a central registry of all deeds. Select committees had investigated both proposals and had rejected arguments similar to privacy claims. The committee to investigate the register of deeds considered that the most prominent objection was to "the exposure of men's affairs."[49] But it was felt that no significant problem would arise and that the advantage to the community would outweigh any slight embarrassment to an individual. The other select committee also foresaw no major difficulties: some "lower classes" initially might not give information about births, deaths, or marriages, but they would soon learn the benefits.[50]

Each succeeding census brought additional questions. The census of 1841 was the first to send a form to each household; that of 1851 was the first to ask a question about average attendance at religious services.[51] In neither instance was there serious objection at the time of the census. The publication of the results of the religious inquiry, however, sparked a dispute between the established Church and the Dissenters about the accuracy of the numbers. That dispute over the use of information reflected a subconscious national concern as well as a religious diversity. Both the concern and the diversity were evident in later censuses, and the anxiety about the use of information cast its shadow far into the future.

The religious diversity dispute was rekindled in 1861 when the government's Census Bill included a penalty for refusal to answer a question about religious profession. During the committee stage in the House of Commons, Dr. Edward Baines moved to strike that clause. He explained that Dissenters and Churchmen alike objected "because—with what seemed to be an instinctive feeling in the minds of Englishmen—they deemed it a duty to resist an authoritative demand on the part of the Government upon a point which they regarded as beyond the legitimate scope of civil interference. The civil governor had a right to inquire into the particulars of the civil condition of the people, such as age, sex, occupation, birthplace, &c, but he had no right to intrude into the domain of conscience."[52] The home secretary, Sir George Lewis, defenced the principle of the religious question but said that the government would not insist on the section in light of the intensity of the opposition and its awareness that, if included, the objections would reduce the validity of other parts.[53]

The censuses of 1871–1901 were taken without disruption; there were unsuccessful attempts to amend each bill to include a religious question. Increasingly, the objection came not from those who opposed certain questions but from those who wanted to ask more questions and at more frequent intervals. One new issue did appear after the passage of the Education Act 1870—the desire of the school boards for information about the number and ages of children. The president of the local government board, C. T. Ritchie, thought that census information should not be given to school boards: "The greatest mistake would be made," he predicted, "if people were led to suppose that the information asked for would be used for the purpose of setting the law against them, either with regard to the attendance of children at school or any other subject."[54]

Unlike all previous censuses, that for 1911 was met with organized opposition: suffragettes said that they would not comply with the census law. The Women's Freedom League adopted a manifesto: "No Votes for Women!—No Census!"[55] The opposition was not to the census. Instead the census was merely an occasion to express other grievances. A series of entertainments was planned for census night by the Women's Social and Political Union to keep women away from their homes at midnight.[56] In spite of the publicity, the number of women who refused to comply with the law was small; even those few who took part in the entertainment were counted by the police.[57]

Before the end of the First World War, then, there was not a developed claim of a right to privacy, and no one in the United Kingdom had suggested the need for such a right. Newspapers were criticized primarily for their political content. Toward the end of the nineteenth century, however, complaints began to emerge about their treatment of people's private lives. The "yellow journalism" that had provoked Warren and Brandeis had not yet reached Britain. In related discussions, truth as a defense in a defamation action was of concern because reputation, not feelings, was injured. Similarly, privacy was not a factor among issues that surrounded the interception of correspondence and the census.

4

Early Complaints about Privacy

i

The end of the First World War had little immediate effect on the development of claims of a right to privacy. In the following two decades, however, concerns about privacy were expressed with increasing frequency. This period also witnessed the first proposals for legislative protection for privacy. Although the concerns were expressed more often, the causes of the concerns remained much the same. Newspapers came to dominate the privacy arguments of these years, but two of the other areas of early legislative concern—the census and libel—continued to be important topics of discussion.

The census scheduled for 1921 provided the first postwar occasion for observing the public's reaction to requests for information. The 1920 Census Bill was introduced in the House of Lords by Viscount Astor, Parliamentary secretary to the minister of health. Describing it as a "perpetual Census Bill," he explained that it provided powers to take a census at regular intervals and eliminated the need for a separate act for each census.[1] In spite of this innovation, the bill passed through the House of Lords without debate. In the House of Commons, however, there were objections to Clause 8, which authorized questions on "any other matters with respect to which it is desirable to obtain statistical information with a view to ascertaining the social or civil condition of the population."[2] Among the objections to this clause were comments by Lieutenant Commander Joseph Kenworthy, who thought it dangerously vague:

> Are they going to take our finger prints? . . . What is the limit of what they may ask? . . . Where is this going to end? I admit

> I have given an extreme case of finger prints. In view of the way we are now docketed and indexed, and so on, and with the whole system of internal espionage, spying on the private life of the people, which is a custom that has sprung up in the War, are they going to use the cloak of the Census still further to pry into the private lives of the people?[3]

The objections were so strong that the minister of health proposed an amendment to require that any questions asked under the clause must first be approved by Parliament. Industrial unrest necessitated the postponement of the census from April to June, but otherwise it was taken without incident.

Only one other census, in 1931, was taken before the Second World War. In the House of Lords, the order for that census was approved without discussion.[4] Questions in the House of Commons primarily concerned the cost of the census and the use of unemployed persons as enumerators.[5] Lacking both opposition to the census itself and cause for symbolic protest, the public's response was equally nonchalant. There were approximately twenty reported refusals to complete the census form.[6] Even then, only eight prosecutions were initiated. By comparison, after the 1921 census there had been only one prosecution.[7]

But the suspicion of the census—Dr. Edward Baines had termed it "an instinctive feeling in the minds of Englishmen"—had not disappeared. The government did not exercise its power to conduct a quinquennial census in 1936. But as the danger of war increased, the declining rate of population loomed as more important. So in October 1937 Sir Kingsley Wood, minister of health, introduced the Population (Statistics) Bill "to make further provision for obtaining statistical information with respect to the population of Great Britain; and for purposes connected therewith."[8]

The minister claimed that the bill was urgently needed and asked the House to approve the collection of information about the population trends. Unlike the two previous census bills, there were objections to this measure. A Labour member, F. W. Pethick-Lawrence, moved an amendment to reject the bill "which instructs the registrars to elicit confidential and intimate information not urgently required for statistical purposes."[9] A similar amendment had been put down by an Opposition Liberal, Kingsley Griffith; both men thought that the proposed questions were irrelevant.[10] Commander Sir Archibald Southby, a Conservative, considered the interest in population admirable, but he believed "that the preservation of a reasonable amount of family and personal privacy" was equally important.[11] A future Labour home secretary, J. Chuter Ede, thought that "people should still be able to keep some secrets in their own breasts, even from the registrar." He was convinced that the public would cooperate only if they did not feel that the questions were "going unnecessarily into private details."[12] All these objections were stilled when Sir Kingsley Wood proposed amendments to specify the questions that were to be asked, to remove the penalty for not answering questions when one had no knowledge of the answers, and to make the information secret and privileged. The bill was also limited to a ten-year term.[13] With those amendments it passed without further difficulty.

ii

The sketchy and spasmodic uses of the concept of privacy in the debate on the Population (Statistics) Bill were in contrast to the repeated uses of the concept in the concurrently developing complaints about journalists' conduct. With the end of the First World War, newspapers resumed their promotional stunts and reports of personalities. Along with that resumption came renewed criticisms that retained many of their prewar elements. In part, however, the greatest adverse reactions were provoked by changes in the newspapers. Newspapers were no longer organs of political viewpoints; they were now bought and sold as investments. Before the financial crisis of 1929 ended the process, nearly half of all British newspapers had become part of one of four major groups (owned by Lord Beaverbrook, the Berry Brothers, the Harmsworths, and Westminster Press).[14] As Kennedy Jones wrote in 1920: "It is truer at the present time than at any other period in the history of the daily paper that the policy and general conduct of the daily Press turns on commercial success."[15]

This emphasis on commercial success produced a new style of journalism that concentrated upon presentation of news; to encourage the public to purchase newspapers their interest had first to be attracted. Two of these styles were described in the *Report on the British Press* published in 1938 by Political and Economic Planning (PEP). The older was the "Northcliffe technique," which "assumed that most news is intrinsically dull and must be sugared by the addition of some external and irrelevant detail, such as 'the girl,' or a famous exploit of the individual in question."[16] Beginning about 1930, another style was developed by the *Daily Express* under the editorship of Arthur Christiansen. The PEP report said that this technique "makes a religion of newsgetting, and assumes that the human interest must be extracted from the news itself without introducing any irrelevant details."[17] A third style was attributed to the *Daily Mirror* and its editorial director at that time, Harry Guy Bartholomew. According to Francis Williams (later Lord Francis-Williams), Bartholomew had an "instinct for journalistic vulgarity"; under him the newspaper was transformed into the "strident caricature of American yellow journalism at its brashest. Stunts, sensations, sex, strip cartoons, radical crusades took pride of place in its daily menu even if it meant leaving out the news everyone else considered important."[18]

Newspapers changed styles to attract readers. Each new campaign in the circulation was marked by new contests, gimmicks, and other strategies. For some newspapers there were more readers; for all newspapers there were more critics.

Yet immediately after the First World War there was a generally high regard for the press. The techniques that had so annoyed Warren and Brandeis were not yet common in England. At least that was the view of a Canadian, Stephen Leacock, who observed a difference between English and American newspapers. "With us here in America," he wrote, "the great thing is to get the news and shout it at the reader; in England they get the news and then break it to him as gently as possible. Hence the big headings, the bold type, and the double columns of the American paper, and the small headings and the general air of quiet and respectability of the English press."[19] There is no evidence of the extent of Leacock's knowledge of English newspapers. But his comments did not significantly differ from those of Winston Churchill, who in 1922 told the Press Club that the press "as a vast implement in our social life stood at a higher level in this country than in any in the world. Journalists could not claim a greater intellectual ability. But they had standards in this country which were never broken, and which were never even established in other civilized countries of the world."[20] Churchill did express surprise at the "insurance orgy" that had followed the lifting of wartime newsprint rationing; he suggested that the newspapers could devote their energies in better ways than offering free insurance to regular subscribers.

Not everyone, however, was satisfied with the standards of journalists; already there had been renewed criticism of newspaper reports of divorce cases. The severest reaction followed the reporting of a divorce trial in which the son of Lord Ampthill alleged that his wife had committed adultery with two named men and with another unnamed man who was the father of her child.[21] In the House of Commons, Sir John Baird, under secretary for the home department, promised that the home secretary would consult with the lord chancellor about implementing the prewar recommendation of the Royal Commission on Divorce and Matrimonial Causes that divorce courts be closed to prevent publication of unsuitable evidence.[22] When no action appeared to come from those consultations, twenty-four M.P.'s circulated a letter calling attention to laws prohibiting the publication of indecent matter.[23] One of the signers of the letter, Sir Evelyn Cecil, proposed a motion favoring legislation if the common law were not strong enough to limit publication.[24] Both major organizations representing newspapermen, the National Union of Journalists and the Institute of Journalists, also deplored the emphasis placed on reporting divorce trials, as did the lower house of the Convocation of Canterbury.[25]

In May 1923 Sir Evelyn Cecil was given leave, under the Ten Minute Rule, to introduce the Matrimonial Causes (Regulation of Reports) Bill.[26] Its purpose was "to regulate the publication of Reports of certain judicial proceedings in such manner as to prevent injury to public morals." After receiving a second reading, it was referred to a select committee where it was renamed the Judicial Proceedings (Regulation of Reports) Bill, but it progressed no further. Reintroduced in 1924, 1925, and 1926, it was not passed until 14 December 1926, the day before prorogation. Throughout its erratic progress the bill was presented as a measure to protect public morals against a press that was driven by commercialism to threaten public decency. Sir Evelyn Cecil explained that he had originally tried to convince the newspapers not to publish detailed reports of divorce cases but had been told that the pressures of competition compelled the publication. He had therefore concluded that "if the Press cannot put their own house in order it becomes the duty of the legislature to do it for them."[27] Opposition arose primarily from persons associated with newspapers; their arguments concentrated on the difficulty of defining public morals and the potential limitation upon freedom of the press. Supporters responded that publication of the lurid details of court cases was an abuse of that freedom.[28]

The word *privacy* was not used in the debates, but some of the distinctions central to later claims of a right to privacy were manifest. The home secretary, Sir William Joynson-Hicks, explained the government's support for the bill by distinguishing between the state's interest in criminal trials and, apparently differing from the royal commission, its lack of interest in a divorce trial:

> The criminal case is a matter of which the State takes cognisance. It is a crime against the State and an offence against the community, but a divorce case is a matter between the parties, and, except in regard to the general question of morals, a matter with which the State is not concerned. The effect of divorce proceedings on other people and on publications is a matter in which the State quite rightly takes a view.[29]

Two members of the House of Lords suggested that the public had no right to have an interest in a divorce case. The earl of Desart thought that the publication of photographs and details of the evidence was cruel to the parties.[30] Lord Buckmaster, a former Liberal lord chancellor, who two years earlier had proposed that only the result of a divorce action should be published, also thought that divorce proceedings were not a matter for the public:

> I would have far wider powers than exist at present to clear the Court and absolutely prohibit the publication of any of these cases. In whose interests are they published? If there is any matter which is a private and domestic concern it is a quarrel between a man and his wife, and the Divorce Court is merely there for the purpose of saying whether that quarrel is of such a character as entitles one of the parties to be free. What rights have the public there? What interests of the public are served by publishing the details? No theory was ever more abused than the theory that the liberty of the Press and justice require the opening of the doors of the Divorce Court to everybody who likes to enter and the publication by newspapers of everything that transpires therein.[31]

The demands to limit publication of evidence in cases before the law courts abated for only a short time after passage of the bill. In the 1930s questions were asked about the publication of salacious details included in a judge's summation at the end of a divorce trial and in the evidence at a murder trial. To both requests the home secretary of the day responded that he was not prepared to go beyond the 1926 Act.[32]

Other complaints about journalists soon superseded those that had motivated Sir Evelyn Cecil. Increasingly, newspaper photographers were criticized for intruding into privacy. In a letter to the *Times*, an M.P., Major James Despencer Robertson condemned "the practice which is growing more and more common every year, of publishing in the daily illustrated Press photographs of well-known people taken at moments of mental agony—moments which every one, except the Press photographer, would respect as too intimate for intrusion."[33] He did not place all the blame on the photographers; there was, he said, a newly created aristocracy that vied with theater personalities for publicity. Nevertheless, Major Robertson believed that "there are some moments in people's lives which are too sacred even for their most intimate friends to look into—and one cannot understand the editors of reputable papers allowing the publication of pictures so lacking in taste and in general decency."

A similar complaint provoked a lengthy correspondence through the columns of the *Times* in 1929 about "The Sneak Guests." Otherwise known as gossip writers, these guests, according to the initial letter, represented "a new and dangerous tendency in our social life."[34] The largely anonymous exchange of anecdotes was concluded by a leader in the *Times* that observed: "Intimacy and an affectation of intimacy are a feature of modern freedom of manners."[35] This feature produced some people who were eager to get their names in the paper, but it also produced an "increase of gossip in general, and a disregard for old notions of privacy and privilege."

These complaints closely resembled those anticipated in the 1888 article in the *Spectator*.[36] Writing in the same magazine, the art critic St. John Ervine voiced the 1927 version of the protest.[37] Gossip and trivia were entertaining, he admitted, but when printed they acquired "a value in the eyes of undiscerning people to which [they have] no title." He believed that the "mania for printing paragraphs about private persons" had made people afraid to speak in public and, moreover, that "club-life becomes impossible, as, indeed, does all social life, if we cannot be sure that our conversation, especially when it is indiscreet, will be considered to be private."

Possibly the most important recourse to privacy arguments came in response to a series of court decisions involving representations of a person without his permission—the use of his name, photograph, or caricature. In 1899 the Court of Appeal agreed that a doctor had no property in his own name—that he could not restrain the use of his name unless he could show some damage to his property, business, or profession.[38] Horridge J., in 1916, commented that "no one possesses a right of preventing another person photographing him any more than he has a right of preventing another person giving a description of him provided the description is not libellous or otherwise wrongful. Those rights do not exist."[39]

The belief that those rights did exist had supported many of the complaints about intrusion. In 1929 an action for unauthorized use of a caricature of a person prompted Professor Percy Winfield to suggest that there should be legal recognition of a right to privacy.[40] Cyril Tolley, an amateur golfer, brought the action against J. S. Fry and Sons, manufacturers of chocolate.[41] In an advertisement portraying Tolley with a bar of chocolate in his pocket, the caption for his caddy, who also had a bar of chocolate, had said:

> The caddy to Tolley said, "Oh, Sir!
> Good shot, sir, that ball see it go, Sir!
> My word how it flies,
> Like a cartet of Fry's
> They're handy, they're good and priced low,
> Sir!"

A jury awarded Tolley one thousand pounds for libel damages. On appeal Fry argued that the advertisement was not reasonably capable of defamatory meaning and that the damages were excessive. In the Court of Appeal, Scrutton L.J. thought that the advertisement was capable of defamatory meaning but agreed that the damages were excessive; Greer and Slesser L.JJ. said there was no evidence of the special circumstances necessary to prove the innuendo alleged by Tolley. Lord Justice Greer particularly regretted having to allow the appeal:

> I have no hesitation in saying that in my judgment the defendants in publishing the advertisement in question, without first obtaining Mr. Tolley's consent, acted in a manner inconsistent with the decencies of life, and in doing so they were guilty of an act for which there ought to be a legal remedy. But unless a man's photograph, caricature, or name be published in such a context that the publication can be said to be defamatory within the law of libel, it cannot be made the subject-matter of complaint by action at law.[42]

The House of Lords decided that the words were capable of defamatory meaning but that there must be a new trial on the amount of damages.[43]

Before the House of Lords announced its decision, Professor Winfield published his article entitled simply "Privacy." In it he argues that the legal remedy Lord Justice Greer was searching for was a right to privacy and that there was nothing to prevent the House of Lords from recognizing such a right. In his article Winfield defines an infringement of privacy as "unauthorised interference with a person's seclusion of himself or of his property from the public."[44] After evaluating the protection available for the privacy of property, Winfield concludes that the law was adequate. But, turning to the privacy of the person, he discovers that the "law probably lags behind the needs of a community in which intrusion on privacy is apt to take offensive forms owing to the modern development of instantaneous photography and of methods of advertisement which, to say the least of them, are totally indifferent to the feelings of private individuals."[45] The similarities with Warren and Brandeis are obvious and many. Like Warren and Brandeis, Winfield suggests that the "social exigencies" of the day justify the recognition by the courts of a tort of "offensive invasion of personal privacy" He considers that the word "offensive" would allow the courts to correct the defects of having truth as a defense, while at the same time limiting the scope of the tort. Unlike Warren and Brandeis, however, Winfield does not advocate the "sweeping recognition of a general 'right of personal privacy'"

Privacy was not part of the argument before the court in Cyril Tolley's case.[46] But the fact that a legal right was felt necessary is indicative of the intensity of the opposition to the conduct of the newspapers. At the same time, Parliament did not feel that the matter was serious enough to warrant action. In the only Parliamentary reference to the case, the home secretary said that, though he sympathized with the grievance, he had no reason to think that legislation was necessary.[47]

By the end of the next decade, however, a noticeable shift in opinion had occurred. The privacy complaints of the 1920s had been partially questions of privilege and manners; the complaints of the 1930s had less of a social structure. Once again the intensified complaints followed an escalation of the competition for circulation. This new battle began when J. S. Elias (later Lord Southwood) determined to increase the circulation of the *Daily Herald*. Early in 1930 he began by giving free gifts to subscribers, but the Newspaper Proprietors Association decided that the practice was against their rules. Elias therefore switched to "selling" books at nominal prices to registered subscribers; later he changed to selling clothing, then to kitchenware. The *Daily Herald* was soon joined by the *Daily Mail*, the *Daily Express*, and the *News Chronicle* in the race for increased circulation.[48]

In 1933 a letter from St. John Ervine appeared in the *Times* under the heading "Privacy and the Press."[49] "There must be many people," the letter began, "who feel dismay at the tendency, steadily increasing, of certain newspapers to invade private life, especially in times of personal grief and great distress." Ervine acknowledged that there were times when intrusions were of no consequence, such as when he was telephoned at 2:00 A.M. and asked if he knew where George Bernard Shaw was. Other instances were of consequence, such as hounding a man who had given evidence at an inquest, or the rapidity with which the announcement of a man's death was followed by a reporter's call to the widow. Ervine complained that all types of newspapers invaded the "privacy of grief."

The first published response was from a fellow of the Institute of Journalists, Gordon Robbins.[50] Representative of the arguments defending the press, the letter said that the complaints showed a lack of proportion because only a few "black sheep" caused the troubles. Robbins contended that newspapers were constantly improving their standards and that they had done so particularly since the "new journalism" of the early twentieth century. The correspondence ended after eight days, only to be resumed the next month when Lady Ellerman wrote to complain about newspaper photographers at her home and later at the cemetery when her husband was buried.[51] Both the National Union of Journalists (NUJ) and the Institute of Journalists passed resolutions instructing their members to avoid intruding.[52]

The complaints about intrusion were adopted by the Institute of Journalists to support its proposal for a register of journalists that would operate like those for the professions of law, medicine, and architecture. A deputation from the institute called on the home secretary in January 1934 to discuss the register.[53] Their suggestion was opposed by the NUJ, which favored a union-enforced code of conduct.[54] The recently enacted German press law (which required registration) also militated against the institute's plan.[55]

One response to the continuing complaints about intrusion came in June 1935 from the home secretary, Sir John Gilmour. He said that if the press did not regulate itself, he might have to consider other means of protecting the public.[56] The next month Sir Percy Hurd introduced his Journalists (Registration) Bill, which would have created a register like that advocated by the Institute of Journalists.[57] The bill was never enacted; it was introduced on three other occasions without ever having a second reading debate.

Although these sporadic attempts at legislation were unsuccessful, numerous events continued to strengthen the demands for some limitation to be placed upon the press. Two of the most poignant involved the Lindberghs and the crash of a Dutch airliner. Late in 1935 Colonel Lindbergh and his wife arrived in England, in part to evade American newspapermen. Their plight prompted St. John Ervine to write of the "social menace" of press intrusions on privacy.[58] He did not believe that the English papers had descended to the squalid depths of those in the United States, but he thought that there was a downward trend. "We have made much progress in scooping from sorrow since" a passage written in 1928, "and newshounds are no longer content to crouch under the cottage window, but leap through the window and even paw the bed where the sick are dying."[59] As part of his criticism he echoed a familiar refrain—the harms of commercialism. "It is clear that we cannot allow pressmen," he argued, "in the pretence of public interest, but really for the benefit of their own pockets, to continue in this exploitation of private trouble."[60]

Similar complaints arose after reporters telephoned the relatives of a man with the same name as one of the victims of the Dutch air crash. The reporters' conduct prompted an M.P. to ask the home secretary, Sir John Simon, whether he would "consider the introduction of legislation to put a stop to the growing tendency on the part of a section of the Press to intrude upon the affairs of private citizens."[61] Although he sympathized with the complaint, the home secretary did not think that legislation was an appropriate remedy for what he perceived as a matter of "taste and decency." He believed that the conduct of newspapers before the abdication of Edward VIII had demonstrated that they were capable of self-restraint, and he had no doubt that those responsible for the press "would be equally capable, if they were so minded, of putting a stop to inconsiderate and heartless intrusions upon private persons which are, I am sure, abhorrent to the vast majority of journalists and newspaper proprietors alike."

The most scathing criticism of the press occurred after an inquest into the suicide of Captain G. S. C. Swinton. The coroner criticized the press for intrusion, and Captain Swinton's son protested about his mother's being called at 1:00 A.M.[62] In the House of Commons, Wing Commander A. W. H. James asked the home secretary:

> Whether his attention has been called to the increasing intrusion of the Press upon the private lives of citizens, as instanced by the disclosures at an inquest held on 19th January that, failing to be given information by a harrassed family at a time of great personal sorrow and having telephoned to the elderly widow at one a.m., certain organs of the Press published untrue, sensational, and painful details of the case.[63]

The home secretary reaffirmed an earlier promise to communicate with the representatives of the press about the complaints.[64]

On 11 February 1937 the home office announced that three major newspaper organizations had passed resolutions condemning intrusions.[65] Later, the NUJ and the Institute of Journalists also announced their opposition to intrusion.[66] The institute invited the other press organizations to take part in a conference with an impartial chairman "to discuss the question of the unwarrantable intrusion by newspapers into private family affairs and other unprofessional practices in the collection of news."[67] At its annual delegate meeting, the NUJ proposed a joint committee with the proprietors to enforce the union's code of ethics.[68] But, after all the formal statements, there was no action.

The next year "A Member of Parliament" wrote to the *Times* to protest about press intrusions during the Belgian king's visit to Welbeck Abbey.[69] Significantly, the letter suggested a legal remedy: "I venture to ask lawyers to consider whether a right to privacy could not be given by statute, and infringement without reasonable excuse made actionable. Safeguards would, no doubt, be required to prevent frivolous litigation."

Another allusion to Parliamentary action appeared in the 1938 PEP *Report on the British Press.* That such a study of the newspaper industry's economic condition was made is in itself indicative of the commercial nature of the press. But the report also discussed causes for the public's lack of respect for journalists: "Perhaps the most acute cause of trouble," PEP concluded, "is the intrusion into private lives and personal affairs which has led to considerable public indignation against sections of the Press. This intrusion arises largely out of attempts to fill columns, not with news connected with public affairs, but with private matters which are of no public interest, however interesting they may be to the curiosity of members of the public, who find in them a substitute for, or addition to, personal gossip."[70] The report rejected as impractical the registration of journalists, but tentatively suggested a press tribunal to deal with the intrusion that had angered the public.[71] The tribunal would consist of three members: a chairman, "an eminent lawyer or public man of judicial ability commanding unqualified confidence," and two asssessors, "drawn from panels of representatives of proprietors and of journalists." Although it would have no powers to fine or to punish, the tribunal would build up a working code of practice. As with the parliamentary bills, no action was taken on this suggestion.

The evolving demand for legal restraints on the press was not without a counterforce. During the years after the First World War newspapers were aggrieved by the "gold-digging" libel actions brought against them. A desire to restrict these actions prompted Sir Stanley Reed to introduce the Law of Libel (Amendment) Bill.[72] Its supporters argued that the law had been brought into disrepute by those who relied upon legal uncertainties in the hope of obtaining large damages. The bill proved to be the start of bargaining between those who wanted to lessen the ambiguity of the libel laws and those who wanted to stop intrusion by the press. Sir Stanley Reed said he had been told that the bill would have no chance of success because of the resentment about intrusion.[73] And, A. R. Wise, seconding an amendment to postpone the bill for six months, thought that the press should first correct its own defects before asking for a relaxation of the libel laws.[74] The bill was withdrawn when the government announced the appointment of a royal commission under the chairmanship of Lord Porter "to consider the Law of Defamation and to report on the changes in the existing law, practice and procedure relating to the matter which are desirable."[75] The committee held only a few meetings before its sittings were suspended at the outbreak of war.

iii

Thus, before the start of the Second World War, concerns about privacy had begun increasingly to dominate the criticisms of newspapers and of population surveys, though for different reasons. The privacy claims used against survey questions were but part of a larger mistrust of increasing governmental power. Critics of newspapers, by contrast, objected to the use of a person's photograph without his permission: some said it amounted to appropriating his property; others complained about the circumstances under which the photographs were taken. Both aspects of the concern for privacy hibernated as the nation devoted its entire energy to winning the war.

An example of the subservience of privacy arguments to the war effort was the rapid passage given the National Registration Bill, which required that everyone have a registration number and carry an identity card with that number.[76] There were some expressions of discontent in the House of Commons, but the bill was quickly passed; it took little more than fifteen minutes to pass through the House of Lords. There were no protests about docketing and indexing as there had been during the debate on the 1920 Census Bill.

Although limitations on freedoms were accepted during the war, there emerged a feeling that a statement of principle was needed to counteract the propaganda from Germany, to provide a basis for the unification of Europe at the end of the war, and to ensure the permanent eradication of all that totalitarianism represented. Four debates in the House of Lords demonstrated those feelings.

In June 1942 Lord Addison, a socialist peer, called upon the government to "prepare without delay the proposals they intend to make for the world settlement after the war."[77] There were almost twenty speakers during the two-day debate built around the framework of the Atlantic Charter. Each peer had his own special cause, but together they expressed a desire that the hopes and aims of mankind should not be frustrated by a lack of planning as they had been after the First World War. Lord Davies had a similar intent in his motion of August 1942 to consider the establisment of an international authority at the end of the war.[78] The ideals of a lasting peace and the creation of a new international organization were the themes of the earl of Darnley's motion in June 1943.[79]

Near the end of the war, thoughts turned to a statement of rights as the solution to the problem of promoting European unity and deterring future wars. In December 1944 Viscount Templewood (formerly Sir Samuel Hoare) introduced a motion:

> That the unifying forces of Europe stand in urgent need of strengthening, and in particular that every European citizen

> should be ensured of certain fundamental rights and liberties without which European civilization cannot continue.[80]

Speaking for himself and for many others, he addressed the House: "Your Lordships will see that if these rights, which are the very antithesis of everything that is meant by Nazism, were once admitted . . . dictatorship in the future would become almost impossible."[81] He described the uniqueness of European civilization as its concentration "upon the sanctity of human personality and upon the development of the individual soul."[82]

Not everyone agreed with Viscount Templewood's specific suggestions, but most people accepted the need for a statement of general principles, a statement of rights. From this agreement arose the first postwar discussions of a right to privacy.

5

Privacy and Individual Rights

i

The Second World War gave a sinister sense of urgency to fears for the protection of human rights. Events in Europe and the Soviet Union provided an international demonstration for those who had warned of the evils of concentrated executive power. In the United Kingdom the postwar intermingling of national and international concerns added new vocabulary to the evolving dialogue on human rights. After an unsuccessful attempt to exploit the electorate's fears in the 1945 election, the Conservative party continually raised the specter of Hitler and Stalin whenever they criticized Labour policies.

Much of that critique was a reflection of a belief then current in the international sphere that a formal statement of human rights could thwart future growth of totalitarianism.[1] The first expression of that belief was the Universal Declaration of Human Rights, adopted by the General Assembly of the United Nations on 10 December 1948.[2] Among the principles proclaimed as "a common standard of achievement for all people and all nations" was Article 12, which said: "No one shall be subjected to arbitrary interference with his privacy, family, home or correspondence, nor to attacks upon his honour and reputation. Everyone has the right to the protection of the law against such interference or attacks."[3]

In November 1950, with the Universal Declaration as a guide, the member nations of the Council of Europe signed the European Convention on Human Rights. The European Convention also made a statement about privacy:

> 1. Everyone has the right to respect for his private and family life, his home, and his correspondence.
>
> 2. There shall be no interference by a public authority with the exercise of this right except such as is in accordance with the law and is necessary in a democratic society in the interests of national security, public safety or the economic well-being of the country, for the prevention of disorder or crime, for the protection of health or morals, or for the protection of the rights and freedom of others.[4]

As is evident from the article's wording, it was inspired by totalitarian governments and not by intrusive press behavior. Some years later, the English representative to the Council of Europe when the convention was approved, Viscount Kilmuir, confirmed that implication. He explained that the article's drafters "were aiming mainly at physical interference, such as the activities of secret police and other officers of a public authority."[5] Similar thoughts had motivated the authors of the Universal Declaration. Norman Bentwich, who had participated in the drafting of the declaration, recalled that in 1948 everyone was "full of hope and faith. The memory was still strong of Hitler's degradation of man and its disastrous consequences. The purpose of the Charter, to reaffirm the faith in fundamental human rights and human dignity, in the equal rights of men and women, and of nations large and small, was a strong motive."[6]

These two documents, though of no legal force in the United Kingdom, marked the first linking of privacy with a concept of human dignity. And though they have been the subject of little public concern, they have served as a statement of principle to which the United Kingdom is a signatory and to which proponents of privacy could point in support of their arguments.

Since United Kingdom representatives played a leading role in the formulation of both declarations, it is not surprising that assertions of rights became part of the continuation of prewar arguments about the increased powers of the executive and the loss of effective Parliamentary or judicial control. Typical of the general complaint was a letter to the *Times* from C. K. Allen, who had devoted much of his life to combating creeping bureaucratic power. Explaining an earlier letter, he wrote:

> I was referring to governmental and administrative powers, and

> I repeat unhesitatingly that in that sphere the whole present tendency is to place the executive above the law, chiefly by framing statutes in such manner that subordinate legislation is made "judge-proof" by making Ministerial "discretion" virtually absolute, and by thus paralysing the immemorial legal safeguard against executive abuses—namely, the doctrine of ultra vires.[7]

That concern found expression in four debates in the House of Lords. Those debates also exemplify the attempt to translate international efforts to protect human rights into the British idiom. Instead of advocating generalized statements of principle, the lords concentrated on ad hoc solutions to specific complaints. Among those complaints is the first evidence of privacylike concerns in the postwar years.

In the first of those debates the Marquess of Reading proposed to implement the Donoughmore Committee's Report on Ministers' Powers with a bill "for the better securing the liberty of the subject."[8] Primarily dealing with controls on ministerial powers, the bill had only one section that evidences a privacy-related concern. Had that section been enacted, before any official could enter a building, he would have had to obtain a warrant specifying the building or part of the building to be searched.

The second[9] and third[10] debates, like the first, were dominated by remarks about increasing governmental power. The influence of the international declarations was apparent during the third debate when Lord Mancroft predicted that the time was not far off "when we shall want a wider restatement of all the liberties of the subject." Later in the debate he added that "the time may shortly come for a completely new Bill of Rights to be drafted." Without revealing any details, he admitted that he had already drafted such a bill.[11]

The fourth lords' debate originated with a second attempt to implement the report of the Donoughmore Committee.[12] That debate, like the other three, was not so important in itself; it did not reveal a new concern with the increased powers of government—that concern had begun long before the Second World War. But the debate did serve to indicate that, even though international declarations, aimed primarily against wartime dictators, included privacy among their general provisions, within the United Kingdom concern with topics such as "freedom" and "liberty" was expressed in less lofty terms and with the intention of alleviating specific complaints. Moreover, the debates did mark a developing tendency, in both domestic and international affairs, to phrase arguments in terms of human rights.[13]

In the four debates the only sign of a privacy-related concern had been a clause included in the proposed bills of rights to limit the powers of officials to enter private homes or other premises. Questions and expressions of discontent about that power of entry had appeared in the official record of the House of Commons as early as February 1946. It was not until 1951, however, that a focal point was provided for this dissatisfaction: a court case that arose out of the entry of Eastern Gas Board representatives into a private home to collect money from the gas meter. Following eleven unsuccessful attempts to call the homeowner (a Mr. Charles Grove), a representative of the gas board entered the home with the assistance of a carpenter, who removed a pane of glass in the door. After the money had been collected, the door was closed and the pane replaced. Upon his return from vacation, Grove discovered the entry. His action for trespass was tried before Hilbery J. and a jury; decision for the gas board was based on powers that had been granted under the Gas Act 1948.[14]

Commenting on the case, the *Evening News* said that each man who was authorized to enter a home often had a valuable function to perform and that the officials were not Gestapo thugs (as some more excitable critics had alleged):

> Yet, it is still an unpalatable fact that these officials have an authority which is not granted to the police. . . .
>
> The right [of] access used to be a rarely granted privilege, now, we contend, it is handed out far too freely; and the citizen's *right of privacy* is thereby much diminished.[15]

The *Daily Express* held a similar view that it was objectionable for the 19,448 other inspectors to be able to enter without the warrant that was required by the police.[16]

The distrust of governmental powers brought about the bills of rights in the House of Lords and the reaction to entry into a home by a gas board official. The same feelings also influenced attitudes toward the first postwar census in 1951. Although all of the national newspapers supported the census in principle, some complained about the questions asked. The *Daily Mail* was not unlike other publications when it wrote of the draft census order that "every new census is more like Nosey Parker than the last. Bit by bit the area of inquiry is widened until questions are asked for the sake of asking. That, it seems to us, will be true of the 1951 Census."[17] The *Evening News*, by contrast, praised the census form as a "clear, . . . well-phrased, . . . comprehensible" exception to its objection to forms for the sake of forms.[18] Viscount Simon, who had been an ardent supporter of the various bills of rights in the House of Lords, wrote a special article for the *Daily Telegraph* in which he defended the census because it directed attention to problems that should concern everyone. Furthermore, he explained that the confidentiality of the data was protected by law and by the fact that the government's interest was only in impersonal totals and not in any individual return.[19]

The *Daily Express* published a short leader entitled "Age of Wariness" that epitomized the postwar doubts surrounding the census:

> Why is the 1951 census arousing so much irritation and suspicion? There was nothing like this atmosphere in 1931.
>
> As in those days, there is a guarantee that information given will never be used for any other purpose than the compiling of general statistics. Yet somehow people have their doubts.
>
> The fact is that since 1939 Governments have taken too much interest in the private affairs of the citizen.
>
> If the worthy objects of the 1951 census are suspect, blame not the suspicious but those who have created the spirit of this curious age.[20]

In another leader, the *Daily Express* suggested that the "census should have been devised with more respect to human privacy."[21]

There had been no opposition to a family survey sponsored in 1946 by the Royal Commission on Population, yet only five years later there was verbal objection to the census. True, the census was compulsory and was addressed to more people. But a more important cause of the different reaction was the revived criticism of governmental powers. As often before, the census provided an occasion for expression of views on issues of current importance. In 1951 the most frequently expressed fear was that the data would be used for purposes other than compiling statistical tables: some believed the information would be used to trace deserters from the service; others thought that knowledge of the number of rooms in a house would be used in billeting troops. A few women objected to the description of the husband as "head of household." Officials of the Housewives' League planned to burn their census forms (and their ration books) outside Parliament. And, in the only objection to the census on privacy grounds, the vice-chairman of the league described the census as an "unwarrantable interference with privacy."[22] Otherwise, there was no principled opposition to the census. The bulk of the protests had been responses to particular questions or wording. None of the objections presupposed an individual's claim to control information about himself or a right to be let alone.

Two months after the census and thirteen months after the gas board decision, there occurred a third event that further aroused the public's misgivings about increased governmental powers. In this instance the source of the objections was the identity card. First required by the National Registration Act 1939, identity cards had been continued from year to year by appeal to administrative efficiency. As with other similar explanations, the retention of identity cards was criticized as one of the appurtenances of a police state.[23] That criticism found a hero in Clarence Willcock, who refused to produce his identity card when requested to do so by a uniformed police constable. Willcock argued that the state of emergency described in the National Registration Act no longer existed and, therefore, that the requirement to carry an identity card should not be continued.[24] Although given an absolute discharge by the magistrates who had convicted him, Willcock appealed. In the divisional court, the lord chief justice criticized the use of wartime statutes for purposes other than those originally intended. Nevertheless, he upheld the conviction because there had been no order in council withdrawing the provisions of the particular act.[25]

The national newspapers opposed this decision with much the same vigor as they had opposed the gas inspector's power of entry. The *Daily Mail* commented:

> The bureaucrats will be seriously perturbed. Their system of tabling the individual by a number is threatened. They do not, and perhaps cannot, think in terms of the individual. A Briton to them is not Tom, Dick, or Harry, but a numbered unit of population. . . .

> We boast of being a free people, but the bureaucrats still have us taped as a series of numbers. A curse upon their whimstone hearts![26]

In a leader that drew upon the memories of the past and the anxieties about the future, the *Daily Mirror* asked: "Why should British people have tabs on them as if they were the subjects of a police state?" The leader concluded with the maxim that "machines must be made to fit freedom and not freedom trimmed to suit machines."[27]

The House of Lords also expressed its disapproval when in July 1951 it approved by 54 votes to 28 a motion from the Marquess of Reading "that in present conditions the use of identity cards is unnecessary and oppressive and should be discontinued without delay."[28] Introducing his motion, he explained that "many people feel that the enforced possession of an identity card is an intrusion upon their private lives and marks them out as mere planning fodder for a card-index State."[29] Those who concurred believed that an identity card robbed a person of his individuality and somehow implied that he was not trusted. They argued that administrative convenience was not acceptable justification for the card. Those who supported the retention of the card contended that the contemporary cold-war conditions (and "hot war" in Korea) made the national registration system essential for the security services as well as for compulsory military service and rationing coupons.

As he had done in the 1947 debate on ministers' powers, the Marquess of Reading exhibited a commonly held belief that equated an omnipotent state with the loss of all sense of private self. Only in that way can one understand his assertion that the identity card was an intrusion upon private life. A similar belief had also found expression through those who feared that the government would use the census data to impose some form of control. The ministerial powers, the census, and the power to enter into private homes were three topics that shared a common and persuasive theme: opposition to enlarged governmental powers. The refrain of that theme contained the first significant postwar expressions of privacy arguments. But, unlike the Warren and Brandeis article, those expressions were not directed against the conduct of individuals.

ii

There were two other postwar topics that also betokened privacy arguments. One, technological developments, shared many of the characteristics of the antigovernmental topic. The other, the reappearance of criticism of journalistic ethics, more closely resembles the concerns of Warren and Brandeis.

Immediately after the war two proposals dominated the discussions about newspapers: the establishment of a formal code of conduct for journalists, to be enforced either by a union or through a professional body similar to that in law or medicine, and an investigation of the ownership and control of newspapers. Both proposals became enmeshed in the rivalry between two organizations representing newspapermen—the Institute of Journalists and the National Union of Journalists (NUJ). The institute favored the registration of journalists who would be subject to a code enforced by a professional body; the institute opposed a union closed shop. The NUJ advocated a union-administered code in conjunction with proprietary support. After most national newspapers opposed the Labour party in the 1945 election, the NUJ intensified its efforts for an investigation into the ownership and control of the press. That proposal was supported by members of the Labour government, who felt that their policies were unfairly reported in certain newspapers. That feeling is exemplified by a speech by Sir Hartley Shawcross at a North Battersea by-election meeting: "If the public at large realised fully the present ownership and structure of the Press, the financial and other relationships between different newspapers, the way in which the policy of particular newspaper proprietors governs the presentation of news in their papers, there would be far less danger of the Press abusing the freedom which is accorded to it."[30] Other similar remarks are not important to a discussion of privacy. It is sufficient to note that on 29 October 1946 the House of Commons passed a resolution calling for a royal commission "to inquire into the finances, control, management and ownership of the Press."[31] It was not until March 1947, however, that a royal commission was appointed under the chairmanship of Sir William Ross

> with the object of furthering the free expression of opinion through the Press and the greatest practicable accuracy in the presentation of news, to inquire into the control, management and ownership of the newspaper and periodical Press and the news agencies, including the financial structure and the monopolistic tendencies in control, and to make recommendations thereon.[32]

The committee's only relevance for the development of privacy claims lay in the absence of any evidence that press intrusions had been an immediate factor in its appointment.

Soon after the war one incident had aroused critical comment. A photographer from the *Daily Mirror* attended, uninvited, the wedding reception for Captain Robert Cecil and his bride; without permission he took photographs of the newly married couple. When the photograph was taken, Captain Cecil hit the photographer and threw his camera to the ground, for which he was later fined and ordered to pay costs.

Captain Cecil pleaded guilty and was called "cowardly" and "ungentlemanly" by the judge who fined him. The periodical *Justice of the Peace* commented that those epithets were better applied to the photographer, Thomas Lea.[33] For that comment Lea initiated a libel action that was heard in March 1947. Giving judgment against Lea, Hilbery J. condemned the attitude of some photographers who believed that they could go wherever they wished and photograph whomever they pleased: "I do not think it can be too strongly emphasised," he continued, "that in this country the Press has no right to go upon private property or into private places and to intrude upon private people and into private rights, and that the standard of conduct and manners demanded of them is as high a standard as should be demanded of every citizen in a civilized community."[34] The committee itself mentioned an example of photography at a burial.[35] Otherwise, there was no indication that complaints about intrusion had again reached prewar levels.

Nevertheless, the members of the royal commission interpreted their mandate broadly and examined all aspects of the performance of the press, including allegations of intrusion. Under the heading "Triviality and Sensationalism" their report included statements reminiscent of Warren and Brandeis:

> It is no doubt legitimate for a newspaper to entertain its readers by reporting events which are in themselves entertaining; but it too easily loses the distinction between what will entertain and what is intrinsically important, and comes to judge importance solely in terms of interest to the reader.[36]

The committee found that intrusive conduct had increased since 1927. One aspect of this sensationalism was "the intrusion on the privacy of individuals necessary to satisfy the appetite for intimate personal detail about the lives and affairs of people who are, perhaps quite accidentally, in the news. In ordinary circumstances this may be no more than an annoyance to the people concerned, but if they have suffered some personal tragedy it may cause great pain."[37] The report also discussed the distress that could be caused by large numbers of reporters besieging an individual either in person or by telephone. But the committee belived that there was another aspect to the problem:

> The pain to individuals is, however, only part of the evil of this practice. The greater evil lies in the degradation of public taste which results from the gratification of morbid curiosity, and in the debasement of the professional standards of the journalists who, whether willingly or otherwise, minister to it.[38]

No additional mention of privacy was made except to comment upon suggestions that legislation should be enacted to protect the privacy of those suffering bereavement; the members of the committee felt that it would be difficult to draft legislation that could be both effective and enforceable. Instead, reminiscent of the 1938 PEP report, they favored a general council of the press that would be able to formulate journalistic principles and to act when those principles were desregarded.[39] Such a general council would be able to regulate the relations between the press and the public and to oversee the internal operations and standards of newspapers. The committee believed that the press should voluntarily establish the general council with a lay chairman and lay membership of about 20 percent of the whole. In summary, the report said:

> The objects of the General Council should be to safeguard the freedom of the Press; to encourage the growth of the sense of public responsibility and public service among all engaged in the profession of journalism—that is, in the editorial production of newspapers—whether as directors, editors, or other journalists; and to further the efficiency of the profession and the well-being of those who practice it.[40]

The residual effects of prewar criticisms of the press had also appeared in evidence to the Royal Commission on Defamation, which had resumed sittings at the end of the war. Lord Porter and his committee thought that the proposals for privacy legislation were outside their terms of reference. They did, however, comment that it would be difficult to draft a statute that could be effective and yet not seriously interfere with the freedom of the press. Like the Ross Committee, they believed that the newspapers could act together to enforce their own standards.[41]

That both committees had been presented with evidence alleging invasions of privacy by newspapermen indicated that the complaints from before the war still lingered—in particular those complaints that arose from intrusion at a time of personal grief. The recommendations of neither report were acted upon immediately. By 1952 the opposing sides had resumed their bargaining: Parliament would enact the Porter Committee's recommendation if the press formed a general council.[42] Nevertheless, Harold Lever's Defamation (Amendment) Bill[43] received the royal assent in the final days of the 1951–52 session of Parliament, even though no general council had been created. During the debate on that bill, there was some discussion of the propriety of publishing information from the past (including the example of a woman's "lapse" in her younger days); but there was no discussion in terms of a right to privacy.[44]

The failure of the newspapers to agree upon a press council prompted James Simmons to introduce a bill to compel the formation of a general council of the press.[45] Even though the national newspapers had shifted toward favoring some type of press council, they were in near unanimity in their opposition to the bill. Lord Beaverbrook's *Daily Express* and *Evening Standard* saw the bill as inspired by Herbert Morrison and as the first step toward the elimination of all freedom of speech or opinion.[46] Other newspapers opposed the bill for reasons that they were to repeat throughout the next two decades whenever there was an apparent threat to freedom of the press. The *Sunday Times* ended a second leader with this statement: "If the people want a cleaner, fairer average in the Press, it is up to them to support those papers which stand for the better rather than the worse in journalism."[47] The *Times* argued that the bill was objectionable because it was vague, because it sought to formalize a relationship between the press and the government, and because it allowed lay membership. The leader writer of the *Times* said:

> Freedom to make public the objective truth about affairs at home and abroad and to comment independently upon them is the first duty and the most important function of a newspaper. Once this freedom is invaded the electorate ceases to be informed as in a democracy it has the right to be informed. . . . Nobody who is not a professional journalist and unfettered in the exercise of his professional discretion—subject, of course, to the laws of libel—

can judge fairly and with detachment when and how news should be published.[48]

The bill received impetus from two incidents that occurred after the report of the Royal Commission on the Press. One incident involved Aneurin Bevan, a Labour M.P. who had unsuccessfully sought the party leadership. According to Barbara Castle: "Mr. Bevan was 'nearly hounded out of his wits' during the illness of his wife's father. One enterprising newspaper which shall be nameless hired a room opposite and installed a long-range camera to get shots of that home!"[49]

The other incident involved allegations of false reporting. In May 1951 two British diplomats, Donald Maclean and Guy Burgess, disappeared. The *Daily Express* was particularly energetic in its pursuit of the story and on 16 July 1952 it published a report of an interview with Mrs. Maclean with the headline "Mrs. Maclean Tells Why I'm Quitting."[50] Other newspapers printed a similar story that originated with the Press Association, but the story in the *Daily Express* purported to be a personal interview by its reporter.

The following Monday, 21 July, a letter from Lady Violet Bonham Carter, a Liberal and a member of the Royal Commission on the Press, was published in the *Times*. She called attention to what she termed a "recent and flagrant violation" of the ethics of journalism. Lady Bonham Carter wrote that Mrs. Maclean had signed a declaration denying that the interview had ever taken place; a reporter from the *Daily Express* had telephoned, but Mrs. Maclean's only remark had been that she had nothing to say. Lady Bonham Carter could understand the attention that the disappearances had received in the press. "But," she wrote, "the repeated invasion of the privacy of their families—an invasion amounting at times to persecution—by some members of the Press is surely indefensible." The letter ended with the question: "Is there no method by which the honourable profession of journalism can safeguard its standards?"[51]

The next day, her letter was answered by a letter from the general secretary of the Institute of Journalists, who emphasized that his organization had strongly condemned intrusion into private family affairs. W. L. Andrews, editor of the *Yorkshire Post* and a leading British newspaperman, also wrote that there had been conscientious negotiations for a press council but that there was a fear of censorship under the pretext of ethics. Other letters followed, but the dispute over the authenticity soon resolved itself into one between the *Observer* and the *Daily Express.*

On 25 July the editor of the *Daily Express* wrote a front-page reply to the criticism. He defended the reporter and concluded with this promise: "The *Daily Express* does not propose to be deflected from the publication of news because it causes displeasure."[52] Two days later, the *Observer* printed a report detailing the inaccuracies in the story and reporting Mrs. Maclean's denial of the interview. The incident was never investigated—a press council had not then been formed and the NUJ refused to act because the journalist was not a member. In November the *Observer* concluded its part in the dispute with the remark that the "vendetta" carried on by the Beaverbrook newspapers had been expected and with the pledge that it would not be deterred "from attacking such 'yellow press' practices as the ruthless invasion of privacy, the distortion of fact, and the persecution of selected individuals by a 'smear technique,' without even according the victims or their spokesmen any right of reply."[53]

The Bevan and the Maclean events provoked renewed criticism of newspapers for intrusions into the private sphere at a time of intense personal emotion or concern. The critics did not suggest that the public should remain ignorant of the facts; the Press Association story of Mrs. Maclean's departure was not the subject of adverse comment. In the case of Aneurin Bevan's father-in-law, the criticism was of the number of reporters who tried to get an interview and of the use of long-range photography. Mrs. Maclean's case essentially involved only allegations of inaccurate reporting, but there was also criticism of the continued attempts to interview any member of the family.

The Press Council Bill did not receive sufficient assistance from the two incidents to be given a second reading. It was revived in May 1953 only to be withdrawn after the announcement of the formation of a voluntary press council.

iii

The postwar years saw the beginning of a third stream of events that was later to appear especially threatening to those concerned about privacy. Military requirements had stimulated development of miniaturized electronics and transistors; the need to control sophisticated weapons had provided greater impetus to the development of computers.

In 1946 computers were known by a variety of terms: electronic brains or mechanical brains or automatic computing engines. That an electronic brain might actually be practicable came to the public's attention with the report of a speech by Admiral Lord Mountbatten of Burma, president of the British Institution of Radio Engineers, in which he described a machine at the University of Pennsylvania that had 18,000 tubes. There were machines in use that had a degree of memory and even one that could play a mediocre game of chess. Toward the end of his speech, as reported in the *Times*, he said that "the stage was now set for 'the most Wellsian development of all.' It was considered possible to evolve an electronic brain, which would perform functions analogous to those at present undertaken by the semi-automatic portions of the human brain."[54]

Less than a year later, further developments prompted the *Times* to comment in a light leader: "All who are prone to come to grief over the simplest sum will be cheered to learn that there has just been invented an electronic computer which can work about 100,000 times faster than man's mind." The writer foresaw machines that could digest all the state papers, documents, and literature and, upon demand, eject a printed slip with a decisive answer to any problem. The comment concluded: "Some might feel the existence of such machines as a derogation of human dignity. There would seem to be no alternative."[55]

Thus, from the first stages in computer development there was apprehension; a suspicion existed that the new devices would somehow compete with man. Before 1952, however, this fear did not advance beyond an incipient stage. In February of that year, there was even some evidence that the fear might be misdirected. Lord Halsbury, managing director of the National Research Development Corporation, mentioned that the latest achievement for the world's most powerful electronic digital computer was to be taught to play "God Save the Queen" through a loudspeaker.[56] Presumably, this was to allow it time to practice for the coronation in June 1953.

Whatever the purpose in so instructing a computer, it was but one indication that by the end of 1952 the fears engendered by the war were fading. In many respects 1952 was the last of the postwar years. With a new, young queen on the throne, with the Conservatives back in power, and with a truce in Korea, however uneasy, there were fewer major threats to the security of the world. Both the United Nations and the Council of Europe had proclaimed statements of human rights that had been accepted by the United Kingdom (though the government would not allow individual appeals to the court established to rule on disputes arising under the European Convention). Identity cards had been abolished as an economy measure, and an agreement seemed imminent on a voluntary press council that would be able to remedy any complaints about the press. For concern with privacy, at least, the traumas of Hitler and Stalin had faded, and, even though there had been need to chastise some newspapers, there was little reason to doubt that the press would soon reform itself.

6

Privacy and the Press

i

Not all of the privacy-related expectations of 1952 were to be fulfilled. During the next eight years a number of otherwise dissimilar events compounded concern for protection of privacy. Some of the events that aroused that concern had precedents before the war; others were without previous parallel. But each generated recurrent resorts to the postwar vocabulary of rights and liberties. Following the war, government had been seen as the dominant threat, but that fear subsided after 1952. Correspondingly, technology, once viewed with curiosity, caused greater disquiet. Automation and a belief that machines would make man obsolete provoked the first concerns. It was not until the end of the decade that particular uses of technology aroused privacy complaints. The third major institution, the press, did not appear as a threat to privacy in the years immediately after the war. Whatever threats there might have been were dormant for the moment. That dormancy was short-lived. By the end of the decade the public had come to perceive the press, more than either government or technology, as the greatest threat to privacy.

The two events that contributed most to the emergence of the press as the dominant perceived threat to privacy were the formation of the Press Council and the ending of newsprint rationing. The General Council of the Press, as it was formally named, had no lay representatives; all twenty-five members were to be full-time newspapermen. Once established, it provided a body to which complaints could be made and from which authoritative decisions were expected. Thus, its formation meant that allegations of intrusion would receive dual publicity, both when the complaint was made and later when the council issued its ruling. The second event, the ending of rationing, prompted a series of circulation battles and financial crises in the newspaper industry. Together the two events created an industry collectively hypersensitive to any criticisms yet individually reluctant to take any action that might decrease circulation.

Even though newspaper organizations had agreed to create the Press Council, it soon became clear that they were not going to accept its strictures contritely. The first complaints to the council were the consequence of a story that also provided one of the most frequent themes for the council's decisions during the 1950s. The basis for the story was conjecture that Princess Margaret might marry Group Captain Peter Townsend, a divorced man whose former wife was still living. Rumors had first appeared in 1952 shortly after the coronation of Elizabeth. But the newspapers did not initiate daily coverage until after the announcement of Group Captain Townsend's reassignment from the royal household (where he had been equerry to the queen) to Brussels (where he would be air attaché to the embassy). The *Daily Mirror*'s headline for the story read: "Princess Margaret's Friend Posted Abroad."[1]

Of all newspapers, the *Daily Mirror* was the most severely criticized for reporting the events; thus, its reports deserve special attention as examples of the type of comment that provoked reaction. One photograph of Princess Margaret, then in Rhodesia, was published in the *Daily Mirror* with the headline "The Sad Princess."[2] As speculation about her plans increased, other newspapers—the *Evening Standard* for example—reported that the letters it had received were overwhelmingly in favor of Princess Margaret's marrying whomever she chose.[3] The *Daily Mirror* was not content to rely upon readers' letters. On 7 July a box on its front page contained an announcement: "The *Daily Mirror* is about to conduct two national polls of public opinion. See tomorrow's *Daily Mirror*." The first poll began on 8 July and asked the readers to select a successor for Churchill; the results were published on Saturday, 11 July. The next Monday, while Princess Margaret was still in Rhodesia, the second poll appeared under the heading "Princess Margaret and the Gallant Pilot" and with this comment: "The *Daily Mirror* believes that the time has come for the voice of the British people to be heard in the problem of Princess Margaret and her friend, Group Captain Peter Townsend." The question posed by the poll was: "If Princess Margaret, now 22, so desires, should she be allowed to marry him?"[4]

Reaction was immediate and almost unanimously censorious. Dr. Donald Soper, president of the Methodist Conference then in progress, called the poll an "unwarrantable and disgusting intrusion into the affairs of that royal personage."[5] The following day, the editor of the *Daily Sketch* agreed with Dr. Soper. In a leader entitled "Private Lives" he wrote: "If the *Daily Sketch* launched a ballot on Never's [editor of the *Daily Mirror*] private life he would be furious. And rightly so. He would be justified in howling blue murder against intrusion into private lives."[6]

The *Daily Mirror* refused to retreat. It printed Dr. Soper's comment in a box on its front page along with the poll question and the query, "Have you sent in your vote yet?"[7] On Thursday of that week it announced that the poll had broken the "world record entry" for newspaper polls (previously held by the *Daily Mirror*). And on Friday, by a vote of 67,907 to 2,235, implicit approval of the marriage was given. The *Daily Mirror* explained that it had "launched the poll in the belief that the views and feelings of the British people on the problem confronting a beloved Princess should be given expression. The amazing response of our readers indicates their deep interest in the subject, and more than justifies the holding of the poll."[8]

Publication of the results coincided with Princess Margaret's return from Rhodesia. The *Sunday Graphic* and the *Sunday Times* both published leaders welcoming the queen mother and the princess on their return. Both newspapers were critical of the speculation about the princess, and both argued that the private life of someone who contributed so much to the nation should be respected. The *Sunday Graphic* said that most of the speculation was groundless and termed it "blatant nonsense" and "ill-formed and ignorant tittle-tattle."[9] The *Sunday Times* had a different style but was equally scathing:

> The marriage of the Queen's sister, third in succession to the throne, is indeed a matter of public moment; but its consideration is safely left to those who have the experience, wisdom and discretion to deal with it, and have certainly no less concern for the interests of the persons involved and the nation and Commonwealth than have the sensation-mongers of Grub Street.[10]

On 22 July the Press Council announced its initial two resolutions. The first said that newspapers had the right to refuse advertisements—specifically Dr. Marie Stopes's birth-control advertisements. The second resolution concerned the *Daily Mirror*'s poll:

> This meeting of the Press Council, while conscious of the great interest of the public in the lives of members of the Royal Family, strongly deprecates as contrary to the best traditions of British journalism the holding by the *Daily Mirror* of a public poll in the matter of Princess Margaret and Group-Captain Townsend.[11]

Of the ten London daily newspapers, only the *Evening Standard*, the *Daily Express*, the *Daily Mirror*, and the *Times* commented upon the resolution, though all the newspapers reported it. The *Evening Standard*, which had not given as much space to the speculations as had some of the morning newspapers, criticized the Press Council and said that it should be ashamed of "a smug pompous resolution containing an entirely unwarranted attack."[12] The *Daily Express* said that the council should reveal that its members had not been unanimous in reaching their decision.[13] And the *Daily Mirror*, after reprinting the *Evening Standard*'s comment, added its own:

> The Press Council has introduced a new concept into British justice.
>
> The *Mirror* was "condemned" by the representatives of rival (and less successful) newspapers.
>
> The editor of this newspaper was not informed of the date of the "trial." He was not invited to give evidence.
>
> He was sentenced in his absence. And he was denied the right to appeal.[14]

Only the *Times* supported the Press Council, though obliquely. In a long first leader it acknowledged that the gossip that had surrounded Princess Margaret had gone beyond affectionate concern, but there was no ready remedy: "Only public opinion can impose a check upon the cruel business of prying into private lives 'that small and sickly eyes may glare and gloat.' The personal affairs of the Royal Family are private no less than others; the matters which have lately been canvassed so loudly are matters for them to decide."[15]

In its search for increased circulation, the *Daily Mirror* had aroused the wrath of many. When criticized by the Press Council, its defense was that the large number of responses justified the poll. To the *Daily Mirror*, circulation statistics were an appropriate measure of journalistic propriety. More closely related to privacy was the evident lack of agreement on a distinction between public and private life. The national newspapers were almost equally divided over whether Princess Margaret's marriage was a public or a private matter. The Press Council's resolution did not use the word "privacy"; it merely said that the possible marriage of Princess Margaret was not an appropriate subject for a newspaper poll. There was no attempt to formulate guidelines for future newspaper conduct. The matter disappeared from the pages of the newspapers without a satisfactory conclusion.

Just over two years later Princess Margaret and Peter Townsend were again in the headlines. The *Sunday People* began this episode with a headline on 6 March 1955: "Princess Margaret Marriage Rumours." The next week it had a special edition entitled "The Royal Love Drama," complete with a leader that discussed the vital distinction between public and private life:

> If the Princess, who is third in succession to the throne, is romantically attached to a divorced man—and that is undeniable—then it is a matter of gravest consequence to the throne and to the state.
>
> In matters of this kind the Royal Family have no private life. They are the symbols of our way of life and they belong to the people of the Commonwealth.[16]

The leader also said that the people should be informed "of the principles that are at stake." In other words, the statement that the royal family had no private life really meant that the *issues* were not private; it did not mean that they must allow photographers and reporters into Buckingham Palace and other royal residences to observe and to record every action.

Other members of the journalistic profession did not act as if they accepted that qualification to the *Sunday People*'s statement. In October, a journey by Group Captain Townsend was again the signal to begin regular newspaper articles about the couple. Unlike 1953, the two were together, and newspapers responded with daily status reports accompanied by photographs. Group Captain Townsend had already returned from Brussels to London when Princess Margaret arrived there on 13 October. On the fourteenth a statement was issued from Clarence House (Princess Margaret's official residence):

> In view of the varied reports which have been published, the Press Secretary to the Queen is authorized to say that no announcement concerning Princess Margaret's personal future is at present contemplated.
>
> The Princess Margaret has asked the Press Secretary to express

> the hope that the Press and public will extend to her Royal Highness their customary courtesy and cooperation in respecting her privacy.[17]

Peterborough of the *Daily Telegraph* foretold the result of this statement and the refusal of the press secretary to clarify the "enigmatic phrases": "If a more comprehensible statement does not quickly follow the wish that the Princess's customary privacy should be respected is certain to be stifled."[18] No exceptional prescience was involved in that prediction, for what the *Daily Mail* described as "the most romantic of situations—the age-old love story of Princess and commoner"[19] sold newspapers, and sold many newspapers. Front-page headlines told the story:

"Come on Margaret" "Please Make up Your Mind"
Daily Mirror, 19 August[20]
"For Pete's Sake . . . Put Him Out of His Misery!"
Sunday Pictorial, 9 October
"Now They Meet in the Country"
Daily Mail, 15 October
"No Ring Yet!"
Daily Mirror and *Daily Sketch*, 17 October
"Princess Dines at Kensington"
Daily Telegraph, 18 October
"Midnight . . . and Another Evening Together is Over"
Daily Express, 18 October
"Margaret Goes Home Without a Smile"
Daily Herald, 20 October
"They Dine Again—By Candlelight"
Daily Express, 22 October
"Princess: Her Decision is Likely Soon"
News Chronicle, 22 October
"Princess Sees the Primate"
Daily Express, 28 October
"Margaret: The World is Discussing—The Cruel Plan"
Daily Mirror, 29 October
"The Romance is Off"
Daily Express, 1 November
"Margaret Decides: Duty Before Love"
Daily Mirror, 1 November

Lost amid the fury of sixty-point type was a statement by the Press Council critical of "certain papers" that had "offended against good taste and have done a considerable ill-service to the reputation of the Press."[21]

That Princess Margaret might marry was of special interest to the people who recognized her sister as queen and head of the Church. Without doubt, the Church of England, and at least some of those people, would not have recognized her marriage to a man whose former wife was still living. And, there could be little doubt that it would be better for the press to inform and to discuss the issues involved rather than to maintain a silence reminiscent of the abdication of 1936. But granting the propriety of public discussion of Princess Margaret's marriage plans did not imply approval of the fortnight of crisis-toned reporting. The seige conditions created by the reporters and photographers were not necessary to inform the public of the issues involved; nor did photographs of the couple taken from a distance aid in making a decision—one that would have been difficult under the most placid conditions. The sense of urgency created by the newspapers could not have contributed to a proper and rational decision. Moreover, the urgency would not seem justified in 1955 with a monarchy that had survived nearly a thousand years and that had no apparent source of danger. Nor did the urgency and sensationalism provide the public with a discussion of the matters of state involved. The methods adopted by most newspapers served only to obscure or to distract from those issues . . . and to sell newspapers.

In 1955, though not in 1953, there existed an epitome of invasion of privacy—privacy considered as necessary to make important decisions. Insofar as Princess Margaret's possible marriage would affect constitutional matters, the press was justified in calling attention to those matters. But there was also a personal aspect even to a princess's marriage; and her decision-making process, if it may be so formally described, ought to have been respected and not invaded by reporters or photographers. As Cecil King said on the BBC in response to a question about Peter Townsend: "If one newspaper sends one discreet sympathetic reporter to make enquiries, fair enough. If fifty newspapers send one discreet sympathetic reporter to make enquiries, that's persecution."[22]

In the aftermath of these three weeks in October there was no attempt by the press seriously to reexamine the role of the Church or of the monarchy in mid-twentieth century Britain; nor was there any attempt by the press as a whole to reach a consensus about a possible distinction between the private lives of public figures and their public careers. The extensive criticism from outside the newspaper industry moved the *Times* to warn of three contemporary threats to the freedom of the press: industrial disputes, direct or subtle government intervention, and loss of public confidence through dishonest presentation of news, offending the sense of decency, or triviality.[23] The *Times*'s warning was not heeded; during the next five years newspaper conduct provoked a growing public mistrust.

The publicity surrounding Princess Margaret was only the most blatant of a series of incidents involving relations between the royal family and the press. Twice the Press Council issued statements asking that articles by former members of the royal household not be published.[24] On another occasion the editor of the *Daily Sketch* was rebuked for publishing an article about the duke of Kent's twenty-first birthday party in spite of a request from the palace that the party be private.[25]

Although members of the royal family were the ones most frequently involved in alleged press intrusions, others also found themselves the objects of intense press coverage. The four occasions that provoked the greatest controversy were all like the prewar instances, times of extreme emotional trauma for the persons involved. As with the coverage of the royal family, the newspapers were criticized not for reporting the story but for the manner of the reporting. When privacy was mentioned, it usually reflected a sense of propriety and not a legal right.

The first occasion involved Siamese twins whose birth had at first been kept secret; when they were brought to London for an operation to separate them, however, their existence was discovered and they received widespread publicity. The demands from newspapermen necessitated a change in the site of the operation; according to the administrator and secretary of University College Hospital, "The publicity that followed [the original decision to operate] and the behaviour of the Press caused great distress and for this reason only it was considered inadvisable to proceed."[26] This criticism of the reporters' conduct was reiterated in a long letter to the *Times* from the secretary of the Medical Defence Union, Robert Forbes, who deplored "the unseemly behaviour of certain representatives of the Press" in seeking information about the twins. Basing his complaint upon the doctor-patient relationship, Forbes contended that "every fair-minded person will surely agree that it is wholly improper for representatives of the Press to exploit the medical misfortunes of others and especially when the methods employed to collect information create impossible situations for the medical and nursing staffs of our hospitals. Clearly something ought to be done to prevent the recurrence of this distressing and unjustifiable interference with the private affairs of patients and doctors."[27] Forbes endorsed a suggestion that the newspapers and the medical profession should discuss possible solutions. This proposal was also supported in a letter from the editor of the *Yorkshire Post*, Linton Andrews, who wrote that the Guild of British Newspaper Editors had in the past made suggestions "to deal with all aspects of privacy."[28] He suggested that there were really three problems involved: the pestering caused by numbers of news-hunters, the problems caused by free-lance reporters and photographers, and most difficult, the problem of separating matters of public interest from matters not of public interest. "The dividing line between loutish, gaping curiosity and a sympathetic interest in the troubles of others is not always too easy to draw." For the first two problems he proposed solutions; for the last, his only suggestion was that the press should consider solutions.

The Press Council felt that the complaints were exaggerated, and repudiated the contention that the conduct was common among reporters. The council did, however, welcome the invitation of the British Medical Association (BMA) for a joint meeting.[29] In October, amid the publicity surrounding Princess Margaret, the Press Council and the BMA announced agreement on a recommended procedure to be followed by hospitals in releasing information about patients.[30]

The third major event of the decade occurred less than two years later when newspapers were severely criticized for their actions in attempting to report about the murder of a Dutch girl, Mary Kriek, whose body was found in Essex early in January 1958. Few national newspapers published photographs of Kriek's father and sister, who came to England from Holland, but the conduct of reporters and photographers irritated R. St. C. Fearon, a friend of the Kriеks. In a letter to the *Times*, Fearon alleged that within five minutes after the parents were informed of the death, reporters from well-known British newspapers "swarmed" into the parents' flat in Holland. He said that in England there had been a "ceaseless stream" of reporters looking for "scraps of gossip." One reporter, according to the letter, "even threatened to make up some news if I did not give him any, and this he did two days later." And, among other things, he complained that a cameraman wanted a photograph of the Krieks when they first saw the body.[31]

Linton Andrews, chairman of the Press Council, responded, also in a letter to the *Times*, that the Press Council readily investigated such complaints.[32] Discussion of the incident continued throughout January in the correspondence columns of the *Times*. The writers were divided into two groups: journalists who defended their colleagues but who were unable to agree on a remedy, and non-journalists who evidenced a pervasive mistrust of "the Press." Thus, newspapermen suffered from a double disadvantage: from within they were divided into factions, while from without they were viewed and condemned as a single unit.

The *Daily Mirror*, which had not published pictures of the Krieks, replied to the criticism with a statement of principle that took the form of an answer to the question "Does the Press, on occasion, intrude into private grief?"

> The *Daily Mirror* has conducted a thorough inquiry into the work of its staff in reporting this tragedy.
>
> The Editor is satisfied that none of the allegations made applies to any photographer or journalist on this newspaper. This does not cause any surprise in this office.
>
> The *Daily Mirror* has always tried to observe the accepted standards of decent behaviour, and to treat all citizens with consideration and respect.
>
> We do not claim haloes for ourselves.
>
> This is a vigorous, outspoken newspaper.
>
> We will not hesitate to expose the buffooneries of public personalities when it is in the public interest to do so.
>
> Nor, through fear of criticism or accusation of "bad taste", will we flatter fools in high places or shield wrongdoers.
>
> But we believe in the dignity of human beings. We believe that news obtained at the cost of personal distress is not worth printing.
>
> The *Daily Mirror* pledge that its staff will always act as responsible men and women in their pursuit of news.[33]

The statement concluded with an invitation for anyone who felt that the pledge had been broken to write to the editor. A month later Cecil King said that during the first fortnight ten letters had been received in response to the invitation: one referred to another newspaper and nine were "either frivolous or trivial."[34] Since then, he added, they had received only one complaint that appeared to have any merit.

The letters in the *Times* had shown both the rapidity with which a part of the public responded to allegations of press misconduct and the sensitivity of journalists to such complaints. The controversy had only just waned when a British European Airways (BEA) airplane carrying the Manchester United football team crashed; twenty-one people were killed, seven of them members of the team. News of the crash was first published in the morning newspapers of Friday, 7 February 1958. Saturday's newspapers included photographs of the injured in a Munich hospital. The *Daily Mirror*, *Daily Mail*, *News Chronicle*, and *Evening Standard* had the photographs on their front pages; the *Daily Sketch*, *Daily Express*, and *Evening News* had photographs on inside pages. Included among the photographs was one of United's manager, Matt Busby, whose survival was in doubt at the time.

Following the publication of the photographs, complaints were expressed in two traditional forums—the correspondence columns of the *Times* and the House of Commons. Anthony Milward, chief executive of BEA, wrote to the *Times* about the "hordes of British cameramen who were gathered in the corridor" of the Munich hospital; he contended that it was time for the Press Council to take action to stop the "scandal of our time."[35] The same day a motion was tabled in the House of Commons by Lieutenant Commander Lynch Maydon "deploring the conduct of a section of the press in violating the privacy of the victims."[36] Milward had been in the Munich hospital; Lieutenant Commander Maydon received his information from a BBC news bulletin.

Press reaction to Milward's accusations began with a letter to the *Times* from Max Aitken of the *Daily Express*, who termed Milward's letter "a disgraceful document" because it had been sent before the burial of newspapermen who had died in the air crash.[37] Cecil King, chairman and managing director of the Daily Mirror Newspapers, wrote that he had investigated the allegations and had found Milward's letter to be misleading: of the thirty photographers at the hospital, only six had been British. Of those six, two represented his newspaper and they, according to him, had behaved with complete propriety.[38] Arthur Christiansen, of Beaverbrook Newspapers, wrote that in his experience people welcomed a reporter into their home; he suggested that the public men who denigrated the press were "inspired by a desire to impose totalitarian legal curbs on newspapers for the purpose of preventing the free and full dissemination of news."[39]

At the end of the week, thirty-two M.P.'s had signed Lieutenant

Commander Maydon's motion; the letters to the *Times* continued to criticize the press. Two newspapers explained their publication of the photographs. The *Daily Mail* said that no pictures had been taken without permission and suggested that the publication of photographs could have been reassuring to friends and relatives.[40] The *News Chronicle*'s editor explained that before publishing the photographs he had ensured that they had been taken only with the full cooperation of the hospital and without any intrusion "The only thing remaining to be said," he concluded, "is that the *News Chronicle* does not allow its staff to commit intrusion into private grief, but that it believes the British public has a right to hear about and see for itself what is being done in such tragic circumstances as the Munich air disaster in caring for the injured."[41]

Not until April did the Press Council publish its decisions about the Kriek case and about the Munich hospital.[42] In the former, the council merely condemned those charges that could be substantiated. In the latter, the council initially said that the charge of intrusion failed; generally, the question of publication of the pictures was a matter of taste, but they should not have been printed if "likely to cause needless distress and pain to relatives."[43] Anthony Milward was not satisfied and refused to retract his statements. Instead, he suggested that the council should publish its evidence. Before it reached a promised decision, an official of an aviation trade union disclosed the evidence of Dr. Maurer, the German doctor who was head of the Munich hospital. His testimony seemed to support Milward's allegation that the great number of photographers had finally forced the doctor to admit them to the wards [44] In an interview published in the *Observer* soon after the crash, Dr. Maurer had said much the same thing: "They wore me down, though most of them were very nice fellows and I saw their side of it."[45] The Press Council's response to the publication of Dr. Maurer's evidence was probably the most accurate analysis of what must have been a very confused hospital ward: the council suggested that language difficulties had been the cause of some misunderstanding.[46] That belated response did little to enhance the council's reputation, and neither ruling encouraged those who had hoped that the Press Council would formulate a general statement of the proper ethics of journalism.

The Essex murder and the Munich air crash produced the decade's severest sustained criticism of the conduct of newspapers. Although the volume of criticism declined, discontent lingered—to reappear two years later when Aneurin Bevan was in the hospital for a major operation. The Labour party felt compelled to assume the responsibility for issuing bulletins about Bevan because of the pressure of reporters at the hospital and their attempts to enter his room.[47] A Labour M.P., Charles Pannell, wrote to the *Times*:

> We remember Munich—Manchester United and that terrible photograph of Mr. Matt Busby almost at the point of death. We remember the charges and counter-charges and the whitewashing by the Press Council that convinced no one. And now we have this new threat to the privacy and perhaps to the very life of a public man about whom there is widespread anxiety.[48]

Eight months later the Press Council issued a statement that criticized both the Labour party and the newspapers for their handling of Bevan's illness.[49]

There were other complaints about intrusion during the first eight years of the Press Council's existence, but none produced a public outcry to compare with that which followed the murder of Mary Kriek and the air crash near Munich. In fact, by 1958 the Press Council reported that the number of complaints of intrusion into private life had decreased. This decline was attributed to the threat of censure by the council and to the attention drawn to such intrusion in the correspondence columns of "some of our leading papers."[50] Not everyone, however, concurred with this conclusion. The standards of journalists remained a prominent subject for comment and discussion. For example, Lord Justice Denning chose a speech to the American Bar Association to express his concern that some "newspapers, pandering to sensationalism in order to increase their circulations, had invaded the privacy of individuals and had prejudiced the outcome of trials by comment on cases which were *sub judice*."[51]

After the formation of the Press Council, the first legislative attempt to remedy the complaints about intrusion was a bill introduced in the House of Lords by Lord Selborne.[52] The bill would have established a press authority to license newspapers and news agencies and to evaluate newspapers according to the standard of the *Times* of May 1956. The Press Council unanimously condemned it as "misguided and reactionary."[53] Most newspapers thought that the bill was a joke. The *Daily Mirror*, on the one hand, felt that Lord Selborne had given the lords their "biggest chuckle for years."[54]

The *News Chronicle*, on the other hand, in seriously opposing the bill anticipated future press opposition to similar measures. Its argument was that the bill would impose shackles on the innocent as well as on the guilty and that it could be only the first step toward a more general limitation of the freedom of expression. To the *News Chronicle*, the remedy lay in the hands of those who purchased the newspapers.[55]

The second of Lord Denning's criticisms was of the publication of matters properly *sub judice*. This criticism became most severe after the reporting of the charges against Dr. John Bodkin Adams in 1957. Dr. Adams was acquitted, but there was concern over the amount of publicity given to the proceedings before the examining magistrates. Lord Tucker was appointed to chair a committee to inquire into such proceedings. Another aspect of the reporting of trials was the power of a court to hold a newspaper in contempt. These two related matters were of some importance to the continuing expressions of criticism for intrusions into privacy because each criticism tended to reinforce the argument for the next and to aggravate the general sense of grievance against the newspaper industry as a whole. In the second half of the decade of the 1950s, along with a critical reappraisal of the function of the press, there developed an atmosphere amenable to limiting the freedom of the press.

Lord Selborne's bill was an early product of this atmosphere.[56] Another result, arising from a different impetus, was a trio of bills introduced to restrict the publication of wills. The first such bill was introduced in 1955 but failed to receive a second reading. The *Times* opposed the bill as an attempt to restrict the freedom of the press. The argument was predicated upon the fact that anyone could inspect a will that was a public document, and, if anyone could inspect the document, newspapers should be able to publish it. To the *Times*, the two arguments for the bill—that publication was an intrusion into private life and that the newspapers distorted the wills—were but questions of manners and were not proper subjects for legislation. Typical of the *Times*'s opposition to attempts to regulate the press was the final sentence in its leader: "But experience over the years, and not least in the last generation, has shown that a healthy society cannot afford to allow even the thinnest of wedges to be insinuated into the fabric of freedom."[57]

In 1956 Nigel Fisher introduced a second bill to restrict the publication of wills;[58] Marcus Kimball proposed a similar measure in 1958.[59] Fisher said that the purpose of his bill was "to spare beneficiaries and relatives the very considerable distress and embarrassment which many people do now suffer as the result of the publication of the details of wills in the Press. The effect of the bill would be to protect them and to respect their privacy."[60] To him a will was a personal document and its publication was "a quite unwarranted intrusion into a man's private affairs" at a moment of great distress for the family.[61] C. I. Orr-Ewing supported the bill because it would "protect the freedom and privacy of individuals after they are dead in the same way as we protect their privacy when they are alive."[62] Sir Leslie Plummer was representative of the M.P.'s who opposed the bill, and, as a member of the Council of Newspaper Proprietors, a spokesman for the press. He saw the bill as an attempt "to encroach on the freedom of the Press" and a limit upon the "freedom of every ordinary citizen in this country to know what is going on." He believed it was of social importance that the changes in wealth and economic conditions be made known.[63] The bill was lost because of a procedural rule during the second reading debate.

Marcus Kimball's bill reached its committee stage before stalling. An individual would have been given the option to state in his will his desire that it not be published; previous bills had simply proposed a prohibition upon the publication of wills. Kimball hoped "to give to the individual the same right of privacy in regard to his own private affairs when he is dead as he enjoyed during his lifetime."[64] Other supporters compared the proposal with the limits that had been placed on the reporting of divorce trials. But Niall MacDermot, who opposed the bill, rightly rejected that analogy because the limitation upon publication of certain facts in a divorce case had been enacted to protect public decency and "not in order to protect the privacy of the persons concerned."[65] MacDermot agreed that newspapers did invade privacy, but, in his opinion, the correction of that fault was the function of the Press Council and not of the law.

A very different cause of the reexamination of the role of the press was the precarious economic situation in the newspaper industry. Lord Northcliffe had warned in 1920 that the increasing costs to the industry posed a serious threat to the freedom of the press.[66] Through the circulation battles of the 1930s and the newsprint rationing during and after the war, the newspapers were aware of their own difficulties but took no action. After the Second World War the

Ross Committee had considered the decline in the number of newspapers in terms of a reduction of outlets for different opinions and had concluded:

> We do not therefore see cause for alarm in the decrease of the number of national morning newspapers from 12 in 1921 to 9 in 1948; but while the number is not alarmingly inadequate it is not so large that any further decrease could not be contemplated without anxiety.[67]

When the 1955 newspaper strike ended, both the *Times* and the *Daily Express* published leaders defending the necessity for free and independent newspapers in a democracy.[68] But neither the strike nor the fact that fifty newspapers had closed in forty years was thought worthy of more than a short, fourth leader in the *Times* in January 1957.[69]

The complacency abruptly ended four months later when the *Picture Post* announced that it would cease publication after 1 June. The next day, a Friday, the House of Commons spent five hours discussing the condition of the press; the *Daily Herald*, the *News Chronicle*, the *Star*, and *Reynolds News* were all in financial difficulty. The possibility existed that there would be no national popular newspaper of the Left. Francis Williams wrote a series of articles based upon the theme that "Fleet Street to-day faces a crisis which could rock to its foundations the whole conception of the Freedom of the Press."[70]

Unabated, the trend continued, and on 18 October 1960 the *News Chronicle* and the *Star* ceased to exist. As had happened in the years immediately after the Second World War, Labour M.P.'s led the call for a royal commission to examine newspaper ownership. The House of Commons agreed without a division to a motion calling for an inquiry, but, as in 1946, the government did not act immediately.[71]

The press of 1960 differed in one very crucial way from the press of 1946: in 1960 it had to defend itself from the cumulative effects of the criticisms for intruding into private lives. Immediately after the war the critics of newspapers had concentrated upon the treatment of public topics, such as whether there was an anti-Labour bias, whether Lord Beaverbrook's newspapers had unfairly emphasized objections to bread rationing, and whether Lord Kemsley dictated the editorial policy of the members of his chain of newspapers.

No one suggested that bread rationing, or Labour candidates for Parliament, or nationalization was not a proper subject for publication, as had been suggested about Princess Margaret's engagement, about the hospital photographs of football players, or about wills admitted to probate. Newspapers in 1960 were in a more tenuous position than they had been in 1946, both economically and in the eyes of the public.

Not all the criticism during the 1950s had come from outside the newspaper profession. The *Observer* had criticized the *Daily Express* "interview" with Mrs. Maclean; the *Daily Sketch* had depricated the *Daily Mirror*'s poll on Princess Margaret. The bulk of the criticism of the standards of newspapers had come from the *Times*, which feared the gradual erosion of the freedom of the press that might occur if the trust of the public was forfeited. Commenting upon a report by the Commonwealth Press Union on the status of the freedom of the press, the *Times* had written:

> Sometimes freedom is directly assaulted, more often it is nibbled at piecemeal with some specious show of reason or public interest. The truth which has to be constantly reasserted is that there is a still higher public interest in the people being sure that the consent they give to acts of government derives from a confidence that they have been correctly informed of the issues and the facts.[72]

Although the *Times* felt that there were reasons for fearing governmental limitations of press freedom, to it the more disturbing trend was "the growing apathy towards" encroachments on freedom. "It is necessary to fight not only for the continued freedom of the Press but also for the continuance of a Press that is worth keeping free."

The *Times* had assumed for itself the leading role in the struggle to keep the press worthy. To commemorate the centenary of the repeal of the stamp duty on newspapers, it published a leader entitled "Second Chance."[73] It criticized certain tendencies that had followed the repeal:

> The race for mammoth circulations has led in some cases to a disgraceful lowering of values. The baser instincts are being pandered to, not only in lasciviousness—the influence of this can be overrated—but in social attitudes and conduct as well. Envy, jealousy, intolerance, suspicion are all too often being indirectly fostered. Irresponsibility is rife. The tone of voice is a perpetual shriek.

The economic weakness of newspapers caused the *Times* to return to the importance of newspapers that were worth preserving:

> Printed circuses have no abiding future. There is still, and always will be, a public demand for information, which is the bread of public life. The challenge is to devise a twenty-first century way of presenting it, while preserving its true values for this new generation.[74]

The temptation would have been to respond to the phrase "the bread of public life" with a comment patterned after "but man does not live by bread alone." Cecil King resisted that glib response but did disagree with the *Times* when he asserted that "you cannot sell nothing but education, instruction, propaganda and get twopence ha'penny for it. It's got to be carried on a bandwagon of entertainment, any newspaper has."[75] Arthur Christiansen voiced a similar view when he recalled his twenty-five years as editor of the *Daily Express*: "What I tried to do was to present a fair amount of entertaining news which needed to be recorded and I did it quite prominently for the purpose of getting the whole of my newspaper read."[76] These two views were not, in fact, identical. As PEP's *Report on the British Press* had discussed in 1938, the *Daily Express* attempted to extract the entertainment from the news itself—thus Christiansen's mention of "news which needed to be recorded." The *Daily Mirror*, by contrast, believed that the news was intrinsically dull and in need of extra entertainment to carry the news content.

These differing views of the proper attitude of newspapers were emphasized after the editor of the *Times*, Sir William Haley, had repeated his "bread and circus" metaphor when speaking to the Commonwealth Press Union. The *Daily Sketch* responded:

> We say Sir William takes too solemn a view of modern journalism. He wags his head at the tabloids for having made the wrong choice, as he puts it, between bread and circuses. As circuses, he warns us darkly, we shall die.
>
> Fie on you, Sir William! Can you name one British newspaper that has gone bankrupt because it made itself too entertaining?[77]

So reappeared the economic justification for the actions of newspapermen—like the *Daily Mirror*, which had justified its poll on Princess Margaret by appealing to the number of responses. Remnants of the circulation battles of prewar years, such arguments were used in the years after the Second World War to defend newspapers against all forms of criticism. Massive circulations were to prove nothing about respect for the freedom of the press: a public accustomed to being entertained or titillated was not a public easily aroused by cries of danger to press freedom. Daily emphasis upon the unimportant and the trivial was to prove inadequate to support claims of the importance that such publication continue unregulated.

When the decade of the sixties began, newspapers were divided about their purpose and the means to attain that purpose. Neither the Press Council nor the newspapers themselves had evolved a coherent explanation of the necessity for a free press. This lack became critical because it coincided with a period of economic threats to the existence of certain newspapers. When economic success was equated with a proper course of action, then economic failure could only be equated with the wrong course. Economic failure should be no cause for alarm.

For those who traced their concept of the freedom of the press from Milton, the economic argument was an injurious distortion of the true function of any outlet for expression. If freedom of expression truly meant the right of anyone to test his ideas against those of another, then there had to be sufficient outlets for ideas independent of other considerations. But, if economic success were made the criterion of judgment, then only those ideas that succeeded were guaranteed freedom of expression. No one recognized that economic success could also be used to justify censorship.

Almost alone among daily newspapers, the *Times* had campaigned for higher standards, but without results. At the end of 1960, in spite of rising circulations, there remained a latent public discontent with the press.

ii

The press was not the only institution subject to questions about its proper role. During the 1950s the function of the government was also the object of much discussion. Two aspects of this discussion involved privacy-related issues: the role of the government in protecting the security of the state, and the relationship between the government and concepts of morality. Each aspect was usually discussed independently of the other, but there were some who linked the two by arguing that the security of the state depended upon a public morality. Although the arguments were not often expressed in the privacy idiom, both questioned the extent to which the state should regulate an individual's conduct. In the most general terms, the issue, as with the press, was whether, and where, a line should be drawn to separate a public sphere from a private sphere.

In the decade after the Second World War, the manifestations of the government's national-security role had changed. But the public's awareness of the importance of that role had not. Thus, when a series of incidents in the mid-1950s reflected somewhat lax security precautions, the public demanded more stringent protective measures.[78] At other times during this period of increased consciousness about security, there were incidents that provoked adverse reaction against excessive measures. But even then the moderation of the critics was evidence of the receding fear of government. For example, reports that the Post Office had opened private letters elicited only two questions in Parliament.[79]

The single exception to the otherwise temperate critique of governmental actions occurred because a security weapon, telephone tapping, appeared to have been misused. The controversy erupted on the eve of Parliament's Whitsun recess when Marcus Lipton asked the home secretary, R. A. Butler, about reports that a barrister's telephone conversations had been monitored and a transcript given to the Bar Council. Butler replied somewhat ambiguously that the power to intercept telephone calls was never used except "in the interests of public order"; he also emphasized the importance of ensuring that persons connected with the administration of justice should not associate with criminals in their criminal activities.[80]

Although the facts of the case were never definitely stated, their outline was clear. The conversations were between Patrick Marrinan, a barrister, and his client Billy Hill, a self-described leader of the underworld. While monitoring Hill's telephone, the police had recorded conversations between him and Marrinan that seemed to indicate that Marrinan was acting improperly.[81] Somehow the Bar Council, which had received a complaint about Marrinan's conduct from the attorney general, discovered that the police had information relevant to the council's investigation of Marrinan. In response to the Bar Council's request, Butler's predecessor as home secretary, Major Gwilym Lloyd-George, agreed that the police could furnish the information learned from the wiretaps. The chronology of the events and the source of the Bar Council's information were among the facts never conclusively determined. Other than the question about the sanctity of lawyer-client communications, two issues were raised by the wiretapping: whether it was a method of gaining evidence that should be used at all, and, if it were used, what restrictions should be placed on its use and on the information so gained.

Before Parliament adjourned, there was a short but inconclusive discussion of the incident.[82] The speakers were primarily critical of the decision to communicate the information to the Bar Council. There was little evidence of a more general concern about the wiretapping itself. Butler's only concession was a promise not to use the events as a precedent. When Parliament reassembled, the prime minister offered to consult with party leaders about telephone tapping, but the Opposition insisted upon a full inquiry. Shortly thereafter, Sir Norman Birkett was appointed to head an inquiry along with two other privy councillors.

Outside Parliament there was equal difficulty in focusing objections to the telephone tapping. The spectrum of press opinion ranged from the *News Chronicle*'s acceptance that telephone tapping was necessary to the outright condemnation in the *Times*. The *Sunday Times* and the *News Chronicle* used similar analogies, in intermediate positions, to defend wiretapping for security or criminal investigations. To the *News Chronicle* there was "very little difference between having a man trailed by detectives and having his telephone tapped."[83] The *Sunday Times* thought that there was "nothing sacred about a conversation merely because it is conducted over a telephone line, and if a policeman may hide in a cupboard or lurk in a shadow a detective may tap a wire."[84] Illustrating a less permissive position, the *Manchester Guardian* wrote: "The practice would be tolerable if it was confined to suspect spies or traitors and to the organisers of the traffic in drugs or prostitution, who may be hard to detect by other means."[85]

The *Evening Standard* and the *Times* were most restrictive; both felt that the practice should not be allowed. The *Evening Standard* conceded that in time of war wiretapping might be excused, but not in time of peace.[86] In another leader the *Evening Standard* was explicit:

> But a weapon which can legitimately be used against the enemy should not be turned against the nation's own citizens in time of peace. It then becomes treason against freedom: a betrayal of the country's traditions of liberty. Its use undermines trust, spreads suspicion and destroys faith in the integrity of government.

> MPs have a duty to smash the Government powers which allow the State to invade the privacy of individuals. Only when they have done so will people feel that the wings of freedom are spread around them.[87]

The *Times* was not certain that even war would be sufficient justification:

> Telephone tapping is so odious, it is so repugnant to every idea of what constitutes freedom within a society, it has attached to it so much the aura of the police state that the question has to be asked whether even in this highest cause [security of the state] it should be allowed.[88]

Although there was a great diversity of opinion, few would have concurred with the abolitionist view. Most expressions of opinion admitted, however grudgingly, that there might be circumstances that would justify the use of wiretapping. But even those who were willing to countenance the practice thought that it should be done only under the strictest supervision and that the information gained should be limited to police channels and not disclosed to anyone else. As in the Commons, the greatest outrage was caused by the disclosure of the information to the Bar Council. The *Daily Mail*, for example, was disturbed because this "was a case of an unofficial body being supplied for its own purposes with unsworn evidence secretly obtained on Ministerial authority."[89] Likewise, the *Daily Telegraph* questioned the "propriety of communicating the record to a non-official body," though it did not doubt that there might be certain conditions under which telephone tapping would be appropriate.[90]

Amidst all the shock headlines, the protestations about loss of liberty, and the allegations of police-state tactics there was a notable lack of attention paid to the reasons for the repugnance felt about wiretapping. That lack was evidenced by the focus on the disclosure of information rather than upon the method of gathering the information. A similar balance had been evident in the debate over press intrusions; rarely had anyone said that the reporters should not have been present. Instead, the most common complaint concerned the manner of the reporting. In neither the instances involving the press nor those involving the government were there considered, principled objections. All instances had more emotive than rational content. To be sure, there were complaints of threats to liberty and ominous comparisons between wiretapping and a police state. But they were more of the nature of bugbears than coherent discussions of philosophical principle. The character of the entire debate was reflected in the use of privacy concepts. Although participants readily appealed to the notion of privacy, few used it as more than a convenient label. It was a concept with instrumental, not intrinsic, value. For example, the *Manchester Guardian* objected to wiretapping because it feared that the police would compile dossiers from the information so collected. And that information might, in time of crisis, prove useful to silence political opponents.[91]

Nearly absent from the list of objections to the practice of wiretapping was a suggestion that it violated a right to privacy. The *Manchester Guardian*'s argument about uses of information was the type that later became a privacy argument, but, in 1957 it was not such an argument. The claim of a right to privacy had not yet become part of the lexicon of phrases to be used when opposing governmental acts. The Birkett Committee's report, issued at the end of October 1957, added little to the already meager normative discussion. Instead of considering whether wiretapping ought to be practiced, the committee related the history of governmental interception of communications. Having traced to 1663 the practice of the secretary of state's issuing warrants to authorize the opening of letters, the committee formulated this expression of the law:

> (a) The power to intercept letters has been exercised from the earliest times, and has been recognised in successive Acts of Parliament.
> (b) This power extends to telegrams.
> (c) It is difficult to resist the view that if there is a lawful power to intercept communications in the form of letters and telegrams, then it is wide enough to cover telephone communications as well.[92]

The report received little public attention because in the two months taken to prepare the report other events had captured the public's attention: British forces had intervened in Oman, federal troops had been sent to enforce school desegregation in Little Rock, Arkansas, and the Soviet Union had launched the first space satellite. The furor over wiretapping had lost its impetus. The *Times*, however, was critical of the Birkett Committee; a leader entitled "Not Far Enough" said of telephone tapping:

> With good reason it is popularly associated with the worst excesses of the police state. It flies in the face of the free man's right to

> pursue his lawful affairs in privacy; and of all the means of detection it is the most open to sinister and corrupt abuse. . . . The line should be drawn only at the point where the odiousness of the procedure is manifestly outweighed by the advantage which the community will derive from it—and only very rarely will that condition be satisfied.[93]

The secrecy and the indiscriminate nature of the interception remained as indictments against the practice. No amount of historical documentation could cleanse the image of wiretapping as a characteristic part of any police state. The committee's recommendation that "it would be wrong for figures [showing the number of warrants issued] to be disclosed by the Secretary of State at regular or irregular intervals in the future" did nothing to allay the public's fears.[94]

The failure of the Birkett Committee to examine the principles involved rather than the technical precedents for wiretapping created difficulties when, in November 1959, it was revealed that evidence obtained by police listening to a telephone conversation had been subpoenaed by the General Medical Council (GMC) for proceedings against Dr. Kenneth Fox. The doctor was accused of having had an affair with a woman patient who later committed suicide. At the request of the deputy coroner, the police had made investigations but had brought no charges. During their investigation they listened (over an extension telephone) to a conversation between Dr. Fox and a neighbor, who Dr. Fox later said was very hostile toward him. In that conversation Dr. Fox admitted that he was the father of a child born to the deceased woman. After investigation by the GMC, Dr. Fox's name was struck off the register.

In the House of Commons, Marcus Lipton asked the home secretary, still R. A. Butler, about the incident. Butler said that a subscriber's permission to listen made the issue different from wiretapping, which was done only on the authority of the home secretary. According to his information, the woman had merely complied with a police suggestion that she make the call.[95]

That response failed to satisfy the critics. And shortly thereafter, Patrick Gordon Walker opened the debate on an Opposition censure motion for the government's handling of the events.[96] According to Walker, who had been the only dissenting member of the Birkett Committee: "The argument between us here is not about whether or not the police should have the sort of power they used in this case. We are saying they should not use the power off their own bat, that they should have applied for a warrant to the Secretary of State."[97] He had particular reasons for thinking that the disclosure to the GMC was worse even than the original interception:

> It means that the words of a man were secretly taken down by the police, without his being warned and without his knowledge at all, and they were then used in evidence where he was in jeopardy. . . . Since the conversation was instigated by the police, it is very difficult not to make the assumption that the conversation was meant to incriminate the man who was being listened to secretly.[98]

In reply, Butler reiterated his earlier position. He argued that there was the "clearest possible distinction" between listening "to a single conversation with the agreement of one of the parties" and "the secret interception by the Post Office of all the telephone calls of a particular individual on the warrant of the Secretary of State." He relied upon that distinction to support his contention that the Birkett Committee's report and recommendation were inapplicable since they involved only the latter situation.[99]

That not one of the twelve M.P.'s who spoke mentioned privacy should be no surprise. The debate was not about the question of whether telephone calls should be intercepted but about a narrower issue of the propriety of disclosing the information to professional bodies. When broader issues were considered, they were likely not to be privacy matters. For example, Peter Rawlinson, later a Conservative attorney general, illustrated the ease with which the question could be expanded into an issue of state security when he suggested that the "security of the State can be endangered not only by outside enemies or internal political enemies but, of course, by criminals."[100]

Defeat of the censure motion marked the end of public discussion of this instance of wiretapping. The debate purged the choler from the nation but without apparent change in governmental policy. During the same years that saw the Marrinan and Fox incidents, however, there was another debate that did, eventually, bring about a change in policy. At the heart of this debate was the report of the Committee on Homosexual Offences and Prostitution—the Wolfenden Report.[101] As in the wiretapping debate, the problem faced by the Wolfenden Committee was to define the proper role of the state in its relations with individuals. The debates were also alike in two other important ways: in each set of debates, "security of the state" was used to justify use of the law to regulate individual conduct, and in neither of these late 1950s debates were claims of a right to privacy a prominent factor.

The appointment of a committee to inquire into homosexual offences and prostitution was announced in 1954.[102] A leader in the *Times* defined the task facing the committee:

> The crucial question before the Committee is not whether homosexual relationships are sinful, but whether the law should punish them as such. . . .
> However deplorable some of these types of behaviour may be [different expressions of the sexual impulse] it is in general agreed that they belong to the realm of private conduct and are outside the domain of the criminal law. Even the prostitute is not now punished for being a prostitute, but only for annoying other people.[103]

Published in September 1957, the committee's report recommended an end to criminal punishment for homosexual activities committed in private between consenting adults. Even though a right to privacy was not mentioned, privacy-related arguments were an integral part of the jurisprudence of the report. Several times the theme was repeated—once when the committee concluded that it was not "proper for the law to concern itself with what a man does in private unless it can be shown to be so contrary to the public good that the law ought to intervene in its function as the guardian of that public good."[104] And later the committee echoed the *Times* when it explained that unless "a deliberate attempt is to be made by society acting through the agency of the law, to equate the sphere of crime with that of sin, there must remain a realm of private morality and immorality which is, in brief and crude terms, not the law's business."[105]

The committee's investigation of the laws concerning homosexual conduct led it to conclude that one basis for those laws was revulsion against conduct considered to be unnatural or sinful. "But moral conviction or instinctive feeling, however strong," the committee thought, "is not a valid basis for over-riding the individual's privacy and for bringing within the ambit of the criminal law private sexual behaviour of this kind."[106] In several ways, the committee reiterated its belief that an individual must be allowed to retain some separation from society and the state. But the members of the committee did not suggest that there existed a *right* to privacy that could be relied upon to exclude regulation by the criminal law. Nor did they argue that all conduct committed in private (physical seclusion) should be free from the purview of the criminal law: some such conduct was properly the subject of criminal sanctions, murder being a readily apparent example. The committee's primary argument was that moral conviction was not a sufficient justification for engaging the criminal law to regulate conduct. The terms *private* and *privacy* were used to describe conduct that was not done in public and that therefore necessitated proof of its deleterious effect upon the community before regulation could be justified. Public conduct, such as solicitation by prostitutes, was prima facie liable to regulation; private conduct required some special proof of harm before it could be regulated.

The committee's thesis was not new; Mill and others had proposed similar arguments. Nevertheless, the committee's application of the argument to homosexual conduct spawned both an academic and a political debate. The academic debate centered around Lord Devlin's 1958 Maccabaean Lecture, "The Enforcement of Morals," and Professor H. L. A. Hart's 1962 Harry Camp Lectures at Stanford University.[107] This debate extended over a decade and thus out of the period under consideration, but it was instructive for the arguments about the justification necessary for interference with conduct in private. Both of the major protagonists agreed that the onus was upon those who would interfere with private conduct. They disagreed about the kinds of arguments that would be acceptable to justify this interference.

For his part, Lord Devlin thought that the function of law was to protect society; society, in turn, was "entitled by means of its laws to protect itself from dangers, whether from within or without."[108] One of those internal dangers against which he believed that society could protect itself was the disintegration of its fundamental moral code. To him, that moral code was best expressed as that "about which any twelve men or women drawn at random [that is, a jury] might after discussion be expected to be unanimous."[109] He was not, however, prepared to argue that only society's interests should be considered; the individual must also receive consideration and not always be subservient to society. Lord Devlin proposed four general principles to guide the balancing of societal interests against those of the individual:

> There must be toleration of the maximum individual freedom that is consistent with the integrity of society.
> The limits of tolerance shift.
> As far as possible privacy should be respected.
> The law is concerned with the minimum and not with the maximum.[110]

Lord Devlin thought that there was a "general sentiment that the right to privacy is something to be put in the balance against the enforcement of the law."[111] But he thought that the right could have only a very limited effect upon determining the formation of the law: "When the help of the law is invoked by an injured citizen, privacy must be irrelevant."[112] In cases where there was no complaint about an act committed in private between consenting adults, the inevitably haphazard enforcement was "an additional reason for moderation."

Professor Hart did not quarrel with Lord Devlin's general principles; rather, he disagreed with his belief that society was justified in using the law to enforce morality. Professor Hart's argumentative method was to show that some laws, those against bigamy for example, could be supported on grounds other than morality even though morality seemed to be their only justification. In making his distinction "between the immorality of a practice and its aspect as a public offensive act or nuisance" he spoke in terms of individual liberty:

> Recognition of individual liberty as a value involves, as a minimum, acceptance of the principle that the individual may do what he wants, even if others are distressed when they learn what it is that he does—unless, of course, there are other good grounds for forbidding it.[113]

Professor Hart appealed to liberty; he had no need for the concept of a right to privacy. In fact, neither privacy nor liberty was at issue in the debate between the two men. Each judged the propriety of regulation of private conduct by its effect upon the society; Lord Devlin said that a strong feeling of moral repugnance agreed upon by twelve persons justified the regulation; Professor Hart said that it did not.

The political debate on the Wolfenden Report concentrated upon the committee's recommendations rather than its philosophy. Introducing the debate in the House of Lords, Lord Pakenham paraphrased the report's principle:

> If a man (and the same is true of a woman) is doing wrong the law must not intervene to stop him unless he is harming someone else; and if two or more men are doing wrong together, neither coercing the other nor taking advantage of his weakness, they must not be interfered with by the law unless their behaviour is harmful to a third party or parties.[114]

That principle could be accepted, not because it would be morally wrong to do otherwise, but because experience had shown that the law could not intervene "without interfering with private life and human liberty so drastically as to undermine the whole growth of moral responsibility."[115]

The Archbishop of Canterbury and the Bishop of Rochester agreed about the benefits of an individual's formulating his own moral code based upon his belief in God, but they disagreed about the use of criminal sanctions against homosexual conduct. The Archbishop of Canterbury concurred with Lord Pakenham that the criminal law should not regulate homosexual behavior between consenting adults in private.[116] To the Bishop of Rochester homosexuality was a vice and unnatural and a proper subject of the criminal laws. He denied that private conduct had no effect on third parties because "it is our private conduct and behaviour which make us, which develop character, and so make us either a baneful or a healthful influence among our fellows."[117]

Lord Mathers also disagreed with the committee's conclusions, particularly with the emphasis placed on the site of the act. Stressing "too much the point about whether the offensive act is committed in private or in a place where it could be more easily detected" would only encourage "the better organisation of facilities for the carrying on of practices which are liable to penalties."[118]

The House of Commons did not debate the Wolfenden Report until over a year after its publication.[119] The home secretary, R. A. Butler, confirmed what the lord chancellor had said during the lords' debate—namely, that the government could not immediately adopt the recommendations because much education was needed to alter the views of the public. The remainder of the debate evidenced a divergence of opinion similar to that demonstrated in the House of Lords. There was a consensus that some areas of life should be unregulated by the government, but there was disagreement over whether homosexuality or prostitution should be part of this unregulated area.

Three M.P.'s expressed opinions representative of this diversity. Dr. A. D. D. Broughton, a psychiatrist, thought that the private acts of homosexuals and prostitutes should not be regulated. He wished that both types of sexual urge could be "cured," but until they were, he believed that they should be kept covered, like a festering sore, and out of the sight of the general public.[120] He believed that the public should not be unwillingly exposed to practices that they found offensive. This argument viewed the problem from a perspective different from the Wolfenden Report, which had taken the regulation as a given factor in its equation and looked into the private sphere to determine the effect; Dr. Broughton looked into the public sphere and saw harmful results if such acts were revealed to the public and concluded that the acts should be confined out of the sight of the public.

Peter Rawlinson held a different view. Disputing the report's conclusion, he argued that there were "private realms in which the State should intrude." As examples he listed the prohibition upon two people battering "themselves to pieces in a prize fight" and upon incest being "committed in privacy."[121] Even so, he did not think "a term of imprisonment should ever be imposed for offences between consenting adults in private."[122] Instead, he thought that the offense should be retained to mark society's disapproval of the conduct—a fine would be sufficient punishment.

Still another view was expressed by Kenneth Younger, who commented upon the capricious enforcement of the law. After conceding the difficulty of the issue, he concluded that homosexual conduct was immoral but not criminal. He believed that society was corrupted more from the blackmail accompanying homosexual conduct than by the acts themselves.[123]

The word *private* was used in two ways in the debate on the Wolfenden Report: to mean not open to general view or participation, and to mean not warranting intervention by the state. The first meaning was descriptive of a physical state; the second sense was the conclusion of a reasoning process. The debate was about the extent to which the first physical description influenced the reasoning toward the second. Distinction between the two was not always maintained. That an action was unobserved by any nonparticipant was not sufficient justification for insisting that the state not interfere. The fact that an act was performed in private was, however, a signal that there was less likelihood of an effect upon the public and that there was a need to ask additional questions before the public interfered.

Because the perceived problem of homosexual conduct arose primarily from acts not committed in the sight of the public, the argument about descriptive privacy being justification for freedom from interference assumed primary importance. But even then there were different facets to the argument: some considered the effect of "private" acts upon society, while others thought in terms of the effect upon the individual if the "private" acts were regulated. There was agreement that there should be a line separating a private sphere from the public sphere; the dispute concerned where that line should be drawn with regard to homosexual conduct. Only the group who considered the problem from its effect upon the individual advanced arguments that resembled later claims of a right to privacy.

The debate about prostitution was different because the perceived problem arose from the presence of the prostitutes in the public sphere. The question was not whether prostitutes should be allowed to pursue their activities in private but whether their public activities constituted such a nuisance that they should be compelled to practice their profession out of the sight of the public.

In neither the debates on intercepted communications nor those on the Wolfenden Report was the right to privacy a factor.[124] The absence of a privacy notion thus set the discussions about the proper role of the government apart from those about the role of the press. In a similar way, the concerns about technology could also be distinguished. One use of technology, to intercept telephone calls, had already called attention to the potential threat. But, in general, during the years from 1953 to 1960 privacy was not seen to be greatly endangered by technology. Instead, the threat was a loss of jobs. Nevertheless, there were many indications that the more pervasive the impact on society by technology, the greater the danger to freedom.

iii

The much-prophesied link between technological innovation and loss of freedom was a favorite subject for "shock" or sensationalistic newspaper articles. Prompted by the discussion about Patrick Marrinan, the *Sunday Graphic* published a photograph of a man with a "shotgun" microphone that could receive sounds from a great distance.[125] Three weeks later an article was published in the same newspaper under the boastful headline "No Private Conversation Left in Great Britain That Cannot Be Overheard." The claim was made that even Prime Minister Macmillan's security screen could be pierced.[126]

A leader in the *News Chronicle* had equally sensational content, though it received less impassioned presentation. Based on a report from Washington, the leader urged that the time had come to consider limitations on electronic devices.[127] An accompanying article by the Washington correspondent reported the investigations of a committee of the California state senate and observed: "Science has got privacy on the run." He described a device that could be placed twenty feet from a wire and receive both sides of a conversation, a "hearing aide" that would pick up conversations, and, "most alarming," a parabolic microphone that could receive conversations at a distance of three hundred yards.[128]

These uses of technology meant that the threat of intrusion was no longer solely physical; traditional safeguards for the sanctity of the home were possibly no longer adequate. This sense of insecurity was reinforced by both governmental and private uses of technology. By 1952 the Post Office had developed and put into use a device to detect unlicensed television sets.[129] In 1956 there was a five-day experiment using television cameras to watch Durham's traffic.[130] After the success of that experiment, television cameras were installed for permanent use.[131] Elsewhere, police experimented with the use of radar to determine vehicle speeds.[132]

Not all of the governmental usages of technology were in the law-enforcement field. Some innovations appeared to be friendly—the premium bond winners were selected by a computer reassuringly named ERNIE. And ERNIE even had good manners: he would not reveal the names of the winners.[133] Changes were initiated to prepare for increased utilization of available and expected technology. To allow nationwide dialing, a new telephone numbering system was required; the first trial of the all-number dialing was conducted in Bristol in early 1959.[134] Likewise, to automate the postal system, there was a proposed experiment with the use of postal codes in November.[135] But the experiment was to take place only after the Post Office had conducted a survey of public attitudes—itself an increasingly prominent preliminary to any action.

When attitude surveys became part of advertising techniques, however, fears of manipulation of the purchaser's desires were aroused. The publication in 1957 of Vance Packard's *Hidden Persuaders*[136] triggered suspicions that subliminal messages were being used on television to influence purchasing habits.[137] The Institute of Practitioners in Advertising appointed a subcommittee to consider subliminal advertising. But the subcommittee could find no evidence to support the allegations that such methods were effective in selling or persuading. Although it suggested that the institute should continue to study possible effects of subliminal communications, the subcommittee was unanimous in its opinion that "irrespective of developments that might or might not prove effective, the use of subliminal communication in whatever form for advertising or sales promotion is professionally unacceptable. The free choice by the public to accept or reject is an integral part of all forms of professionally acceptable advertising, and does not appear to be available to recipients of subliminal communications."[138]

Sociologists also were concerned that the use of research techniques to affect purchasing habits was unethical and, more important, might make the public distrust the surveys taken for "legitimate" sociological research. According to Terrence Morris of the London School of Economics, sociologists were concerned that motivational research and subliminal advertising were but "one of the long shadows of the Admass society of 1984." Before any similar methods should be used, he wrote, "The question which needs to be asked is whether we can regard as wholly acceptable, in a moral sense, methods of inquiry which invade the privacy of the individual. Is it legitimate to discover, for example, hidden anxieties, and then play upon them for commercial gain?"[139]

Such misgivings were expressed by a small group of people; the public was not disturbed about either motivational research or subliminal advertising. Among the public, much greater fear was aroused by the possible loss of income arising from automation of production.

Little concern had been expressed when computers were developed. In fact, for the first decade after the Second World War there had been no reason to develop qualms about devices that were confined to the scientific laboratory. But by 1955 the situation had altered; the word *automation* suddenly appeared in the mid-fifties when the prospect of machines that could perform the jobs of humans became real. The Amalgamated Engineering Union expressed fears of a press-button era; both the Trades Union Congress and the British Association discussed the subject at their annual meetings.[140] In

May 1956 an all-party subcommittee on automation and its effects was established by the House of Commons.

By this time new developments in machinery and control mechanisms had ceased to be amusing. A new assembly line might not be able to play "God Save the Queen" or defeat anyone at chess, but it could take away a man's job. The computer too was progressing beyond the harmless innocence of ERNIE. Indicative of the growth of the industry was the announcement in 1957 of plans for the formation of the British Computer Society. University College, London, planned to build by the end of 1960 a computer that would resemble the nervous system of animals and that might be able to recognize human faces.[141] At the National Physical Laboratory a symposium was held on the "Mechanization of Thought Processes." It was hoped to develop machines able to do the tedious work of man. A computer to provide weather forecasts was installed at Dunstable. And, when a machine was developed that would say "thank you" when a coin was inserted into its slot, the *Times* commented:

> Man is everywhere being put in his place by the forces he has himself released, the mechanical monsters he has himself created. . . .
> Generally speaking, humans have good cause to mistrust machines, but here they can, with profit, learn from one.[142]

At the end of the decade the Independent Television Network was able to predict the Conservative majority accurately after only fifteen results were known. In 1960 still more computers were injected into the daily life of the citizen when the Board of Internal Revenue announced a test of using a computer for the Pay As You Earn (PAYE) system in Scotland.

Other events were but forecasts of future trepidations. Tape recordings were admitted as evidence in court for the first time in the early 1950s: recordings were of officials apparently asking for a bribe,[143] and served as evidence in divorce cases.[144] In the credit field, a plan to give everyone a credit rating provoked a brief but intense reaction. Much of the protest arose from aversion to a "black list" and from fears that banks would provide personal information for inclusion in the credit register.[145] A final example of imaginable intrusion came from the report of the Citizens Advice Bureau that in the first six months of 1959 it had received over twenty thousand questions about doorstep salesmen, only three thousand fewer than in the whole of 1958.[146]

These miscellaneous events, and those involving technology, were but omens for the future. In the years after the Second World War, technological innovations had only begun to affect the daily lives of individuals. The first indication of an adverse effect appeared in the anxieties about automation. By then the expanded role of the government that resulted from the "welfare state" had been generally accepted. But before the acceptance had come harsh criticism, much of which had been phrased in terms of human rights. Yet this tendency, and the postwar declarations of human rights, had not broadened the concept of a right to privacy. In the first fifteen years after the Second World War the concept's use had returned to much the same position that it had attained during the 1930s: privacy was appealed to primarily in conjunction with complaints about newspaper reporters or photographers. Demands that privacy be respected were used as a counterpoise to assertions of freedom of the press. The discussions of economic regulation by the state, and later, of the enforcement of morality, had sharpened the awareness of a distinction between the public sphere and the private sphere, but there had not developed a coherent claim of a right to privacy.

7

First Attempt at Legislation

i

Insofar as claims to privacy were concerned, the years from 1961 to 1966 marked a transition from the emphasis upon the press that had identified the postwar years to the emphasis upon computers and other technology that was to be characteristic of the years after 1966. In this period the three categories of government, press, and technology, though still analytically useful, were no longer discrete. In addition, during these years there occurred an increasing number of events that did not easily fit into any of the three categories. The transition years divide almost equally into two periods: between 1961 and 1963 the rancor that had built up against the press was given expression; from 1964 to 1966 the increased use of computers foreshadowed the reaction against technology that took place after 1966.

At the end of 1960 there was an underlying rancor against newspapers that had grown from incidents surrounding Princess Margaret, the Essex murder, the Manchester United football team, and Aneurin Bevan. One manifestation of those feelings occurred when a jury awarded damages of one thousand pounds against a photographer who sold a wedding picture to newspapers after the father of the bride had been murdered. The trial judge's acerb comments reflected public opinion:

> The fact is that the defendant was only paid £15 which (having regard to the decreased value of money since the time of Judas Iscariot) makes the thirty pieces of silver for which the latter betrayed his Master a sum comparable to that for which the

> defendant sold intimate pictures of his former school fellow's wedding.[1]

The photographer appealed, alleging that the damages were excessive. Sellers L.J. thought that the award was not excessive. In his opinion, the sale of the picture "was a flagrant infringement of the right of the plaintiff, and it was scandalous conduct and in total disregard not only of the legal rights of the plaintiff regarding copyright but his feelings and his sense of family dignity and pride. It was an intrusion into his life, deeper and graver than an intrusion into a man's property."[2]

When Princess Margaret married in May 1960 she managed to avoid most of the harrassment that had followed her in 1953 and 1955, but her activities were still certain to attract reporters and photographers. After her marriage a lone letter to the *Times* questioned the use of a helicopter by a newspaper photographer to circle the royal yacht before it sailed.[3] On a private visit to the Republic of Ireland at the beginning of 1961 she and her husband, Lord Snowdon, were not so fortunate; the number of journalists led the press secretary to the Queen Mother to request that "Princess Margaret's privacy be respected and reporters and photographers be withdrawn from Birr Castle."[4]

The conduct of the press prompted Lord Windlesham to raise the issue in the House of Lords. Viscount Hailsham, lord president of the council, responded by explaining the government's view that such matters were "essentially questions of taste and good judgment and are best left to the influence of public opinion."[5] The issue of intrusions by the press was left to simmer.

Complaints about reporters and photographers were not the only source of difficulty for the newspaper industry. Once again there were concerns that economic considerations, rather than the public interest, controlled the actions of the industry. The foremost cause of that concern was the competition between Thomson Newspapers and the Daily Mirror Newspapers for Odhams Press, which controlled the labour-oriented *Daily Herald*. Indicative of the industry's economic imbalance as well as its tendency toward concentration of ownership, the acquisition of Odhams by the Daily Mirror group inspired renewed calls for an investigation of the newspaper industry. No action had been taken on the 1960 Commons' motion, but this new event caused the prime minister to announce the appointment of a royal commission, under the chairmanship of Lord Shawcross

> to examine the economic and financial factors affecting the production and sale of newspapers, magazines and other periodicals in the United Kingdom, including (a) manufacturing, printing, distribution and other costs; (b) efficiency of production; and (c) advertising and other revenue, including any revenue derived from interests in television; to consider whether these factors tend to diminish diversity of ownership and control or the number or variety of such publications, having regard to the importance, in the public interest, of the accurate presentation of news and the free expression of opinion.[6]

Even before the full membership of the committee was announced, the press's second source of difficulty, complaints about intrusion, produced other Parliamentary action. Lord Mancroft had become so dissatisfied with journalistic standards that he introduced a Right of Privacy Bill—the first attempt to provide legislative protection for the concept.[7] The explanatory memorandum for the bill said that its object was "to give every individual such further protection against invasion of his privacy as may be desirable for the maintenance of human dignity while protecting the right of the public to be kept informed in all matters in which the public may be reasonably concerned."[8] The language of "human dignity" was reminiscent of the debates on individual liberties after the Second World War. In 1950 Lord Mancroft himself had suggested the need for a new Bill of Rights. A decade later he proposed to protect one of those rights. But he did not attempt to define privacy; instead, he included this statement:

> A person shall have a right of action against any other person who without his consent publishes of or concerning him in any newspaper or by means of any cinematograph exhibition or any television or sound broadcast any words relating to his personal affairs or conduct if such publication is calculated to cause him distress or embarrassment.[9]

In fact, the only use of the word *privacy* was in the bill's proposed short title.

Four defenses were provided to protect the public's right to be kept informed. The defendant would have a defense if he proved that he did not intend to refer to the plaintiff or if the words were published on an occasion of absolute or qualified privilege. It would also be a defense to prove that the plaintiff, by virtue of his office, position, or conduct, "was the subject of reasonable public interest" and that the words published related only to that office, position, or conduct. Fourth, it would be a defense to prove

> that at the time of the publication the plaintiff was the subject of reasonable public interest by reason of some contemporary event directly involving the plaintiff personally, and
>
> (i) that it was reasonably necessary to disclose the identity of the plaintiff, and
>
> (ii) that the words published related solely to matters which having regard to the event and the position of the plaintiff were the subject of reasonable public interest, or were fair comment thereon.[10]

The defenses clearly marked the acceptable paths for journalists to follow. In addition, certain paths were forbidden: none of the defenses would be available if the material had been gathered "by force or threats or by any means calculated to cause distress or embarrassment to the plaintiff or any member of the family or household of the plaintiff."[11]

Lord Mancroft explained his purpose in a radio interview. "All I'm trying to do by my Bill is to extend the age-old right of the citizen against Peeping Toms and Paul Pry's and eavesdroppers. I'm trying to do something very narrow indeed. I'm trying to develop this right in the age, the modern sophisticated age, of highly skilled newspapers, television cameramen, photographers, and so on."[12] Like Warren and Brandeis over seventy years before, Lord Mancroft perceived the use of a traditional concept, such as privacy, against newspapermen as a logical and necessary development in a complex world. But unlike Warren and Brandeis, Lord Mancroft did not argue that privacy could be protected by the common law; to him a new statute was needed to fill a gap in the existing law.[13]

Somewhat unexpectedly, the newspapers paid little attention to Lord Mancroft's bill. The *Times*, the *Daily Mail*, and the *Evening Standard* thought that the bill itself was unsatisfactory but acknowledged that there was need for the concept to be further considered; the *Daily Express*, the *Daily Telegraph*, the *Daily Sketch*, and the *Evening News* did not comment. The only comment from the *Daily Mirror* was a repeat of its 1958 pledge on "Private Lives."[14]

The *Daily Mail* reacted to the introduction of the bill with a leader entitled "Rogue's Charter." It accused the bill of attacking the freedom of the press by making an illusory distinction between what should be private and what should be public. The newspaper feared that if the bill were enacted it would be used by those who wished to evade other laws to prohibit publication of information.[15]

Before the second reading debate the *Times* criticized the bill for being excessively vague and lacking sufficient justification. The leader suggested that if the bill became law it "would make a lawyer's mouth water, and fill anyone else with dismay."[16] At the same time the *Guardian* thought that there was one aspect of privacy that should be protected: a person's name or voice should not be used without his permission. Even so, the *Guardian* opposed the bill and wrote: "It is a cardinal principle, and one of our most precious freedoms, that anyone should be free to tell the truth, however unpalatable. If anyone is to be penalised for stating the truth there must be some very compelling reason."[17]

The Sunday newspapers also had little comment. The *Observer* thought, like the *Guardian*, that there should be a select committee to consider the subject.[18] The only other national Sunday newspapers that commented on the bill's introduction and second reading, the *Sunday Times* and the *Sunday People*, were both opposed to it.[19] In general the newspapers seemed to sense no real threat from the bill. In part this was because there had been no recent incident to arouse public opinion against journalists, and in part because the government offered no support for the bill.

In the House of Lords the primary opposition came from the earl of Arran. The crux of his argument was that terms such as *public interest* and *consent* could not be defined. Like the *Times*, he thought that the vagueness of those terms would make the bill a "lawyers' banquet" and would be a serious limitation on the press, perhaps delaying the publication of news.[20] His final warning was a suggestion that the bill was the kind a dictator would introduce as his first step toward control of the press.[21]

The lord chancellor, Viscount Kilmuir, also opposed the bill. He did not disagree with its principle, but thought it unworkable because of its imprecise terminology. He suggested that it would be better to accept certain actions that were admittedly in bad taste rather than to create a legal sanction that might restrict the real interests of the legislature—ensuring that the people knew as much as possible about the issues facing them.[22]

Eleven other peers endorsed the bill with varying degrees of enthusiasm; they belived that it should at least advance to the committee stage. There was little real argument, more a listing of grievances and possible remedies. Lord Silkin thought that a press council with lay members would help. Lord Saltoun feared that the bill was primarily aimed at free-lance journalists. Lord Taylor tried to explain the need for privacy; he thought that everyone had a need for "off-duty times." The bill was given a second reading by seventy-four votes to twenty-one, but it was withdrawn during the committee stage for lack of government support.[23]

Nine years later a letter to the *Daily Telegraph* explained part of the strategy behind the dropping of the bill. J. L. T. Guise, of Lincoln's Inn, wrote that he had been a participant in its preparation and presentation.[24] Although procedural difficulties were part of the reason for not pressing the bill, he said that its backers had believed that "sufficient had been done to arouse public opinion to the need for some increased curb on the activities of certain sections of the Press and other media of publicity." The failure of the bill indicated, at least at the time, that the public did not feel that there was a need for legislative action to limit the publication given to certain facts.

Lord Mancroft's bill marks the beginning of serious discussion of a right to privacy in the United Kingdom. Certain comparisons with the Warren and Brandeis article have already been mentioned. But one key difference remains: Warren and Brandeis had complained of publication and had directed their proposals to remedy that problem. Lord Mancroft complained of conduct while gathering news. Among the examples he gave of the conduct that had engendered his bill were the treatment of Princess Margaret when she was in Ireland, the attempted entry by photographers into Aneurin Bevan's hospital room, the harrassment of the relatives of Mary Kriek, and the impersonation of policemen by photographers to persuade a man to open his door in order to photograph him. Yet his bill was directed at publication; it would not have offered secure protection against the events that he listed.

Newspapers had not seen Lord Mancroft's bill as a serious threat. Another indication of dissatisfaction with the standards of journalists did, however, provoke a significant response. In July 1961 libel damages amounting to £217,000 were awarded against the *Daily Mail* and the *Daily Telegraph*.[25] The facts of the case were not important, nor even the knowledge that the House of Lords decided in March 1963 that a new trial would be necessary because the damages were excessive. What was important, and vitally important, was that for at least two years the fear of a jury's award of crippling damages hung over the newspaper industry with less support than Damocles' sword. The impact of the jury's decision was greater because of the fragile financial condition of the industry (which had led to the appointment of the Shawcross Committee). Cecil King's comment in the 1962 annual report of the Press Council epitomized the beleaguered and highly uncertain position sensed by editors. King complained of legal restrictions that effected censorship of the press: "Not directly: not openly by decree. But by the arbitrary operation of a series of loosely drawn laws which make it hazardous in the extreme for newspapers to comment or even report on a number of issues of vital public importance."[26]

One other privacy-related event occurred in the six-month period that ended when Lord Mancroft's bill lapsed in June 1961: the census.[27] The census of 1951 had been the first for twenty years. Then it had been an unfamiliar procedure to many people after the interval necessitated by the war. The public reaction had also been influenced by contemporaneous events—the order had been approved early in 1950, but the census itself was taken during the intensified political acrimony between the general elections of January 1950 and of October 1951. Thus the census had provided an opportunity to attack the Labour government for interfering with private lives. Yet, as though still promoting the wartime spirit of national unity, most newspapers had urged their readers to comply with the census regulations to ensure the maximum of accurate information for the nation.

In the early months of 1961 the situation was very different. On Census Sunday, the Conservatives were nearing the end of a decade in control of the government. The first man had been launched into space less than a fortnight before. The headlines were dominated by Adolph Eichmann's trial in Israel and by the failure of an American-supported invasion of Castro's Cuba. South Africa had left the Commonwealth and in Southeast Asia attempts were being made to secure a cease-fire in Laos.

Reflecting the lack of public concern, newspapers devoted significantly less editorial comment to the 1961 census than they did to the census of 1951. There was some discontent, but none of it was serious. The *Daily Express* reported that West Indians in Paddington were tearing up their forms after hearing rumors about deportation. A special article began: "The Uninvited Callers will be ringing England's doorbells today asking people to reveal secrets they wouldn't tell their friends, their employers, or, in many cases, their own children."[28] A longer census form, sent to 10 percent of the population, aroused the greatest suspicion; the *Daily Express* foresaw an unintentional possibility of the answers revealing whether a bride was pregnant on her wedding day. But those objections were minor, and the *Daily Express* itself was the leading proponent of the contented state of the nation. A leader the day after Census Sunday mentioned the various statistics that would come from the census and then commented that one fact could be established without waiting for the returns—the last ten years had been the best ever for Britain.[29]

The *Times* devoted one article to the census itself, another to its history, and published a short leader praising the principle that only essential information was sought and hoping that the results would be available rapidly.[30] Other than the *Daily Express*, the *Times*, and a short article in the *Daily Mail*, the national newspapers treated the census as an event that produced amusing anecdotes or humorous cartoons. The *Daily Mail* told of a woman who dialed the emergency "999" when the census enumerator called.[31] The *Daily Sketch* reported that Scotland's only cave dweller had been properly enumerated.[32] And Grandma, in Giles's cartoon for the *Sunday Express*, wondered: "What did he put in the damn census form that makes them go 'Cor!' every time they come to a bit about me?"[33] This lack of anxiety about the census was confirmed by the small increase in number of persons who were prosecuted;[34] in 1961 the number was less than 90.[35] Thus, in ten years there was a marked shift in the events that caused concern about privacy. The government had been replaced by the press as the chief protagonist.

Even though the stimuli changed, the concept of privacy remained a narrow one. In 1961 the only significant use of the concept was an attempt to alter some of the information-gathering practices of journalists. At the end of this half year no one had offered an analysis of a right to privacy; no one had suggested that a right to privacy might be claimed to defend against anything other than representatives of the press. Lord Mancroft's bill was evidence that not everyone was complacent about the performance of newspapers, but it was also an indicator of the circumscribed nature of the concept. As with James Simmons's Press Council Bill in 1952, Lord Mancroft's bill should have indicated to the newspapers that there was discontent with the use of "freedom of the press" to defend harrassment of individuals. Both the press and its opponents were without a considered philosophy, but the opponents had shown the direction in which they planned to move.

ii

The next two years were but a hiatus in the development of the concept of a right to privacy. But then in June 1963, at the end of the first half of this transitional period, the resignation of John Profumo once again concentrated the public's attention on privacy issues. Before that, however, a number of apparently unrelated events occurred that were to create the atmosphere in which privacy arguments were later to thrive.

The Royal Commission on the Press (Shawcross Committee) published its report in 1962. Building on the recommendations of its predecessor (the Ross Committee), the Shawcross Committee's report contained a thorough analysis of the economic trends within the newspaper industry in the intervening years. Very little was said of the standards of journalism other than in the context of comments on the variety of available opinion. The committee noted the failure of the Press Council to have lay membership as suggested by the Ross Committee. The Press Council was also criticized for not taking full advantage of its existence as a representative of the press as a whole "to enlarge public knowledge of the problems which the Press have to face"[36] Primarily as a possible solution to some of the economic problems, the committee thought that the Press Council should be reconstituted to resemble more closely the originally suggested form and that the government should consider legislation if the reorganization did not occur voluntarily.

The review of the economic problems of the newspapers temporarily silenced the critics of the mergers. But new criticisms for "sensationalism" developed almost the day the Shawcross Committee's report was published. The arrest of Gordon Lonsdale, the Krogers, and two others on official-secrets charges raised again the specter of widespread security gaps. Shortly thereafter, another lapse of security was revealed when, following a trial *in camera*, George Blake was sentenced to forty-two years for spying for Russia. Into this atmosphere of seemingly inept security arrangements was thrust the announcement that an Admiralty clerk named William Vassall had been committed for trial on secrets charges; he pleaded guilty and received a prison sentence of eighteen years.

Without the repeated security breaches, the internal civil service investigation announced by the prime minister would probably have concluded the matter. But security had again become a matter for great anxiety, and several newspaper reporters believed that they had evidence to substantiate allegations of incompetence in the security organization. While the newspapers multiplied their speculations, from the public and members of the government came accusations of irresponsibility. Finally, Macmillan submitted to pressure from the newspapers and an Opposition censure motion and announced a larger inquiry: Lord Radcliffe was appointed to head an independent tribunal under the Tribunals of Inquiry (Evidence) Act of 1921. According to the prime minister, the tribunal was to be a "trial of the truth."

The appointment of the tribunal, which began *in camera* sessions almost immediately, stopped the public comment, rumor, and gossip. But the hostility that had developed between the press and Macmillan and other members of the Conservative party remained. For the first time the most vocal criticism of the press came from the Conservative party.

For six weeks the tribunal sat *in camera*, and the confrontation between the press and the government retained its explosive potential. Then, early in 1963, the Vassall tribunal returned to the center of public controversy. When public hearings were resumed, Louis Kirby, chief reporter for the *Daily Sketch*, and William Foster, a *Daily Sketch* free-lance reporter, refused to reveal their sources of information about Vassall. By the end of the week five journalists had refused to reveal their sources, including Brendon Mulholland of the *Daily Mail.* The first reporter to be cited for contempt appealed to the Queen's Bench Division, where the lord chief justice, Lord Parker of Waddington, saw no special reason for the claimed privilege and confirmed the six-month sentence.[27] But that reporter did not go to prison because his source volunteered to testify.

Only two journalists actually went to prison, Brendon Mulholland and William Foster. The Court of Appeal unanimously denied their appeal. After hearing the arguments, Lord Denning M.R. concluded that the tribunal had a duty to determine the origins of the newspaper reports that had caused the inquiry. Those who argued that journalists were privileged not to reveal their sources misconceived the nature of privileges. According to Lord Denning the legal profession was the only one that was accorded a privilege from disclosing its information—and that privilege was the client's and not the lawyer's.[38] In all other cases the court would require a professional man to testify if the question was relevant and necessary. So, concluded Lord Denning: "There is no privilege known to the law by which a journalist can refuse to answer a question which is relevant to the inquiry and is one which, in the opinion of the judge, it is proper for him to be asked."[39]

When leave to appeal from the Court of Appeal's decision was refused, the matter was no longer *sub judice*, and the leader columns filled with condemnation of the jailing of the journalists. Yet the newspapers that had been so critical of Lord Mancroft's bill for its vague terms were no more adept at defending their own representatives. As a group, the newspapers failed to establish a reason for concealing sources. And for a group that had argued in near unison for the right of the public to know everything, there was a noticeable lack of explanation for why the public had no right to know the sources from which a journalist had acquired information. The same suspicions that those who claimed privacy did so only to conceal something also haunted the newspaper spokesmen who claimed the privilege not to reveal their sources.

The *Daily Express* and the *Daily Mirror* printed constructive leaders that suggested the need for an authoritative ruling by the House of Lords or a debate in Parliament. But there was no hint of the basis for the newspapermen's claim. The *Daily Express*, for example, said:

> Respectable men are being sent to prison because they are loyal to their professional code of conduct.
>
> Is that code wrong? It is devised in the public interest. . . .
>
> They believe—every newspaperman in Britain believes—that this right is essential to the efficient working of a democracy.[40]

The *Daily Mail* could not view the matter so calmly. Its leader, "We Humble Men," began by asserting that there was a serious constitutional crisis striking at the liberty of the subject.[41] This crisis arose out of the two journalists' refusing to reveal their sources: "To do so would have been a stain on their journalistic integrity." The leader continued:

> But this refusal involves a matter beyond personal honour. The liberty of the Press, which means the freedom to publish anything (within legal limits), is a well-recognised part of our unwritten constitution.

> But this freedom cannot be exercised unless the sources of information remain inviolate. If such protection cannot be given, truth withers and dies. . . .
>
> [In the High Court Gorman J. had commented that the public policy to discover the truth was overriding.]
>
> That is, in fact, the public policy which guides the production of newspapers. They exist to discover, and disseminate the truth. They cannot do this if the law decides that its interpretation of public policy is the only permissable one. . . .
>
> . . . a Government could employ it [the new rule of contempt] to exercise tyrannous powers over the Press in all matters in which their interests would be affected by public disclosure.

For the *Observer* the most important facet of the controversy was that the government should not deliberately place journalists in the position of having to betray a confidence. But if a journalist did find himself in that position, he had to decide for himself; he should claim no special privilege. In the words of the *Observer*: "It is the duty of the Press to print any evidence they can discover of inefficiency or corruption in high places. But no one would give them that evidence if they thought they might be betrayed to the police or to the Government."[42] The *Daily Telegraph* and the *Times* agreed that the law required that the journalists be imprisoned. But to the *Times* the judgment imprisoning the journalists was "against the public interest."[43]

As the newspaper with the largest number of reporters who initially refused to reveal their sources, the *Daily Sketch* might have been expected to have the most emotional reaction. It did. In a front-page leader the editor exalted the position of the press:

> Democracy as we know it depends on a series of delicate checks and balances; the excesses of government are checked by a free Press representing the people and free to inquire, to probe inefficiency and injustice. The Press, in turn, is checked by severe laws of libel.
>
> Once this delicate balance has been thrown out, it is time for everyone who values freedom to watch out.
>
> If newspapers revealed their sources no one would even dare hint at any abuse of government or point the way to any disclosure which might embarrass Whitehall. Such is the path to dictatorship.[44]

To ensure that its readers were aware of the path to dictatorship, the *Daily Sketch* began a three-part series: "The Road to 1984." The first headline included the quotation from the lord chief justice that had most incensed the newspapermen: "How can you say there is any dishonour on you if you do what is your duty in the ordinary way as a citizen to put the interests of the State above everything." For the *Daily Sketch*, "1984" described what would result if the state's interests were put above all else.[45] The series was a list of grievances against bureaucracy and against the lack of certain civil liberties. There was no mention of privacy but there were familiar complaints (powers of entry without a warrant) combined with newer ones (electronic devices used to track motorists entering a city).

All of the circumstances surrounding the Vassall tribunal were unsatisfactory; the animosity between the government and the newspapers led the editors to identify the rulings of the courts with "the Government." But this was no more accurate than those who criticized "the Press" for the actions of a single photographer. The most unsatisfactory aspect of the episode was the inability of the newspapers to explain the need for freedom of the press—and especially for a special privilege for journalists. As editors had noted about Lord Mancroft's bill, *public interest* was an all-too-nebulous concept upon which to base a specific claim; yet they had no better to offer. The newspapers asserted that freedom of the press meant the freedom to disclose, while they argued before the courts that they should be allowed secrecy for their sources.

These inconsistencies and apparent double standards were important for their contribution to an understanding of the public's reaction to the jailing of the journalists. Instead of mirroring the indignation expressed by the press, the public did not understand the arguments espoused and tended to think that the journalists had been properly jailed. Whenever, in the past, someone had wanted to prevent a newspaper from disclosing some fact, the press had wrapped the public spokesman's cloak of righteousness about itself and wondered what that person had to hide. In the case of the two journalists, the public spoke for itself and wondered what the press had to hide.

Both the *Daily Telegraph* and the *Times* commented upon this adverse public reaction.[46] The *Times*'s classic leader "It *Is* Happening Here" began:

> The predominant note in the letters *The Times* has received about the two imprisoned journalists has been that of hostility to

> the Press. The bitterness has gone far beyond what could be justified by a reasonable reading of the published proceedings of the Vassall Tribunal. It has overflowed and at times sought to sweep away the principle at stake in these cases. They have broken the dam to a long pent-up, ever rising, flood of resentment against the practices of some newspapers. Intrusion, triviality, distortion, muckraking, the inversion of values—the list of offences is long. The newspapers were warned years ago that if they went on the way they were going they would end by alienating those very sections of society upon whose good will the freedom and the working conventions depend. This has now happened.

The question at the heart of the controversy was the same one that had engrossed the press since before the Second World War: Who was to judge the standards of journalism? Was it to be the press itself, or was it to be the courts? The formation of the Press Council had been a first move away from the self-regulation that the newspapers preferred. But there was still a vast distance between a permanent jury of journalists that could not impose sanctions and a temporary jury of twelve persons that could. Without lay members on the Press Council, the press was still seen to sit as judge in its own cause. The continuing call for lay membership symbolized the discontent over the balance of judgment. But not until November 1963 did the first lay members join the Press Council.

Before the report of the Vassall tribunal was written, the newspapers had another opportunity to publish evidence of alleged improprieties. But the response of the public to the jailing of the journalists and the specific response of the jury in the *Daily Telegraph* libel case had convinced the newspapers that they lacked the requisite public support to publish their information.

Brendon Mulholland and William Foster went to prison on 7 March 1963; at the end of the week, under the headline "War Minister Shock," the *Daily Express* reported that John Profumo had wanted to resign for personal reasons but that Macmillan had asked him to stay. Accompanying the main headline was a photograph of Christine Keeler with the headline "Vanished Old Bailey Witness."[47] Profumo denied that he had offered his resignation, and a week later he told the House of Commons that he had no knowledge of Keeler's whereabouts. During the next ten weeks reporters made repeated attempts to ferret out the truth and to inform the public of the innumerable rumors by juxtaposing stories. In the Vassall case, some newspapers had succumbed to printing gossip and rumor; with Profumo they did not. It is impossible to determine whether the Vassall inquiry had a chastening effect or whether Profumo's successful libel action against Continental Publishers caused the apparent change in behavior.[48] For whatever reason, the newspapers were noticeably restrained in their comments and news reports prior to Profumo's resignation. Afterward, there was harsh criticism of the reporting of the trials of others involved in the affair and of the publication of the "memoirs" of Christine Keeler. Once again the newspapers were accused of perverting the doctrine of freedom of the press.

Profumo's resignation concentrated the discussion that had arisen from the Vassall affair on the need to distinguish between public and private life. That distinction was at the core of the conflict between assertions of freedom of the press and claims of a right to privacy. The opportunities were present for a discussion of both the gathering and the publishing of news, but little advantage was taken of the situation. The question involved in Profumo's resignation was whether there had been a lapse in the security procedures. But since it could only be answered by reference to the fact that Christine Keeler had shared herself with both Profumo and a suspected Russian spy, Profumo's private life became inextricably involved. The *Times* disagreed with those who suggested that the issue was solely one of security; one of its leaders asserted: "It *Is* a Moral Issue."[49]

Profumo's case was possibly the most difficult that could be constructed for the exercise of distinguishing between public and private life. If he had had no access to secret information relating to national defense—had he been the minister of public buildings and works, for example—the claim exerted by the public over his private life would not have been so great. But the implications of any possible indiscretion by a minister of defense were of the greatest concern. As had been evident during the wars, when matters of the survival of the nation were involved, traditional liberties were temporarily of secondary importance. It would be unrealistic to expect such a difficult set of circumstances to produce a reliable rule for the future conduct of newspapers when the private lives of public individuals are concerned. Nevertheless, in general terms some leader writers attempted to define the proper areas of private and public concern. The *Daily Sketch*'s attitude toward the public Profumo and toward the private Profumo was informative. In a leader agreeing with the *Times* that the issue was a moral one, the *Daily Sketch* said: "No good will come of pretending that how a Cabinet Minister behaves in private can be separated from his job as one of the country's leaders. For a man's character does not change when he comes out of one door and goes into another."[50] A week later, when the Profumos had returned to England, the paper declared:

> It is only humane to leave them alone to their misery. That is what the *Daily Sketch* will do.
>
> It they have public statements to make we will print them. If they wish to be photographed, we will photograph them. Otherwise we will give them privacy to pick up the broken pieces of their lives.[51]

The *Daily Telegraph* was equally certian that public men could not expect their private lives to be free from scrutiny:

> The standards of conduct expected from a Minister, and, indeed, from a Member of Parliament must be different from those expected from a private individual . . . it would not be right that all actions considered legally venial in a private person should be similarly treated as of no account when committed by public men. . . . For their private reputation is not a matter concerning themselves alone.[52]

It was the duty of the press, according to the *Daily Telegraph*, to inquire into all rumors and to give them publicity "if it judged them to affect the public interest."[53] There was no suggestion that newspapers should publish only those rumors that had some minimal element of truth. It was the duty of the press "to tell the people everything they wish to know, not only what Ministers, politicians, or even judges find it convenient to have revealed." And this was true of anything that the public wished to know, including information about the lives of sinners and saints; the supply was dependent upon the demand and the demand was dependent upon the popular tastes of the contemporary world.[54]

Normally one would not expect to find the *Daily Telegraph* and the *News of the World* in agreement on the ethics of the press. But in this instance they were. The *News of the World* explained that it had offered a large sum of money for Christine Keeler's memoirs because the British public wanted to know what was happening.[55] And when severely criticized by the Press Council for printing the memoirs, the *News of the World* resorted to an economic justification similar to that of the *Daily Mirror* after its poll on Princess Margaret: "In the belief that the public is entitled to know what is going on, and to know authentically, we have discharged our prime duty of giving the news. A prodigious and mounting readership tacitly acknowledges the rightness of the course we have followed."[56]

Likewise, after Profumo's resignation the *Observer* had commented that the real issue was "whether Mr. Profumo's sexual pecadillo was relevant to his duties as Secretary of State for War—and, if so, whether the Prime Minister ought to have been informed of it and acted?"[57] After Lord Denning's report on the entire Profumo matter, the *Observer* said of the opinion that the trafficking in scandal for reward should be stopped:

> There are strong arguments against allowing any body, whether Press Council or Parliament, to lay down the law to newspapers in this way. The line between material which satisfies a legitimate public interest, and that which only promotes the circulation of the newspaper concerned, is extremely difficult to draw. And the risk of stifling controversy seems to outweigh any possible advantage that might result.
>
> Ultimately it is the public which decides what newspapers print.[58]

From neither the press nor Parliament came a thoughtful suggestion to remedy the apparent problems. The newspapers were so concerned with the economics of their industry—the rising circulations that became the justification for any series or gimmick—that they were unable to look without prejudice upon the justification for the freedom they enjoyed. Most of the newspapers felt that the journalists in the Vassall case should never have been judged for any abuse of the freedom; in the Profumo case the sympathies were similarly opposed not only to prior restraint but also to any restraint other than that imposed by the public who voted with their coins. Yet even this latter justification had been belied by the clamor when the *News Chronicle* and the *Star* died and the *Daily Herald* tottered. The press appeared to desire the optimum from all possibilities: for those newspapers that were successful, whatever they printed was justified if people continued to buy the daily or Sunday issues; for those in financial difficulty, special care was warranted to prevent a crisis for the freedom of the press.

As had happened with previous instances of serious conflict between the freedom of the press and other claims, especially that to some private life, there was no resolution. With the report of Lord Denning the matter was considered ended. But like the earlier accusations of newspaper misconduct, the Vassal and Profumo affairs left a distasteful residue.

Almost as though the newspapers and their critics were emotionally exhausted by the Vassall and Profumo events, there was no major clash between 1963 and 1966.[59] In November 1963 the Press Council did change its constitution to provide for lay members and a lay chairman. And in the spring of 1964 a joint working party was set up by JUSTICE (the British Section of the International Commission of Jurists) and the British Committee of the International Press Institute under the chairmanship of Lord Shawcross. This working party evolved from a symposium organized by the two groups "to explore the issues arising out of the imprisonment of two journalists for refusing to disclose to the Vassal tribunal their sources of information."[60] Their report, published in June 1965, was valuable not only for the recommendations it made for changes in the law relating to contempt of court, official secrets, and libel, but also for its explanations of the anxiety felt by newspapers with regard to each of the three areas.

In particular, the summary of the newspapers' view of intrusion on privacy revealed some of the interrelationships that existed in the early part of the decade. Witnesses before the working party acknowledged that the excesses of some newspapers had created a climate hostile to the press, and from that climate had come the large damages awarded in cases such as *Lewis* v. *Daily Telegraph*. As a result, the press had become aware of a need "to avoid injury to its own image by unwarranted attacks on individuals and groups, or by injurious gossip about matters which could not conceivably be regarded as affecting the public interest, or by intrusions on privacy."[61] The report also said that the witnesses felt that the Press Council had been strengthened in dealing with such matters by the appointment of lay members and a lay chairman.

In its conclusion the working party said that it was satisfied that the press was "generally aware that its present unfavourable image has arisen in some measure from its own lapses, in particular those involving intrusions on privacy."[62] It felt that the strengthened Press Council was the best possible remedy since legislation such as Lord Mancroft had suggested would unduly restrict the press. "Moreover, the borderline between that which the public has a legitimate right to know, and that which constitutes an unnecessary intrusion on privacy, is in practice hard to define."[63] After the extremes of the Vassall and Profumo episodes, the report was a useful synthesis of the position of the press at the end of this transitional period in the development of claims of a right to privacy.

iii

Although in the early 1960s concern about privacy arose almost entirely in conjunction with criticisms of newspapers, there were other events that were auguries of future sources of anxiety. Primarily involving applications of technologies, these other events showed the increasing involvement of computers in everyday life.

The 1961 census, the first to use computers to process the data, was but one instance of the new uses for computers. A special article in the *Times* traced the phenomenal sales growth in the computer industry from one hundred thousand pounds in 1953 (the first year of any significance according to the article) to one million pounds in 1956 and to nearly 10 million pounds in 1960.[64] The article also described the birth of a second generation of computers, with transistors rather than tubes, which could work faster and store more information and thus reduce the cost to the operator. The results of a survey by the Privacy and Public Welfare Committee of the British Computer Society confirmed that the early 1960s saw the beginning of widespread use of computers. According to the survey, only 26 percent of computer-users first used computer-based data processing prior to 1963 (eleven out of forty-three responses, with five of the eleven first using computers in 1961–62), 58 percent between 1963 and 1968, and 17 percent in later years.[65]

Those increases meant more frequent routine contact between computers and humans; computers were no longer confined to industrial works and laboratories. Scandinavian Airlines boasted that it was the first airline to have an international seat reservation system.[66] Computers were used to ask diagnostic questions of patients when they attended a doctor's surgery.[67] Nationalized industries also made greater use of computers: British Rail first used a computer for its timetables in 1963, and the Midlands Electricity Board announced that it would place the accounts of more than 1.5 million customers onto a computer.[68] In January 1963, International Computers and Tabulators, Ltd., advertised: "Computers No Longer an Experiment—but a necessary tool. . . ."[69]

But along with the innovations came complaints. In the correspondence columns of the *Times*, banks were criticized for no longer sending current account statements with the names of payers and sources of payments. The Westminster Bank responded with an advertisement theme: "Not too many numbers."[70] The *Daily Sketch* revealed a similar critical reaction when it wrote of proposals to control London's traffic by a computer: "Motorists are to be controlled by Big Brother traffic computers."[71]

This rapid increase in computer utilization during the mid-sixties added a new dimension to the automation problems that had existed for a decade. The title and key statement in a special article in the *Times* typified the ambivalent feelings toward computers: the title was "Robots Will Set us Free to Serve"; the statement was: "There is much anxiety about automation. It may replace the Bomb as the focus of our pervasive disquiet. It impinges on the most secret area of our being, the mind itself. Little is known and much is rumored."[72] There was a marked difference between that somber comment and the almost cheery tone of the *Times* in 1947 when it had announced a new computer.

Yet another use for computers was projected in 1965: the computerization of the criminal records of almost two million sets of fingerprints.[73] Six months after that announcement, the president of the Forensic Science Society wrote a letter to the *Times* asking if the time had not "come when the fingerprints of every citizen should be registered with the authorities? Such registration would be of the greatest value to the police, not only in the apprehension of criminals but also in dealing with the problem of unidentified bodies."[74] The absence of significant adverse reaction to this suggestion indicated that the public had not yet developed strong antipathies toward computers. It specifically indicated that claims of a right to privacy had not been extended to encompass computers. An article in the *Times* discussed the matter without mention of any definite rights that might be violated. Nevertheless, computers were beginning to tread on civil libertarian toes; the article mentioned that the secretary of the National Council for Civil Liberties foresaw dangers and a possible conflict with individual rights.[75]

By 1966 science had gone beyond the fingerprint as a means of identification and had developed voiceprints. The *Times*'s Diary reported the first use of voiceprints in a United States court and commented that their wider use "could mean the wholesale introduction of listening-in-devices which have never captured the imagination of the British public. Whatever may happen on fingerprinting, compulsory voiceprinting seems a long way off."[76]

Unmindful of minor objections, computer-users inexorably increased their reliance on computers. In the middle of 1966 computers were first used to match couples for marriage potential, and just before Christmas the computer announced its first success.[77] Early in 1966 the Board of Inland Revenue proposed to transfer all PAYE work from seven hundred local taxation offices to seven central computer points by 1974.[78] And, at almost the same time, Barclays Bank announced that it would be the first bank in the United Kingdom to issue credit cards—a service not possible without computers.[79]

Possibly the single use of computers that affected the largest number of people was the census of 1966. Publication of the data from 1961 had been delayed because of its complexity and the number of people.[80] Nevertheless, that experience was expected to help with the processing of the first-ever quinquennial census. The questions on the fertility of marriage that had aroused opposition in 1961 were not repeated. Even though a 10 percent random sample was asked very detailed questions, there was no organized opposition, and only a few individuals refused to complete the form.

Not all of the technological developments involved computers. Some recalled memories of the security issues that had arisen with William Vassall and John Profumo: hidden microphones were discovered in Western embassies (in the United States embassies in Czechoslovakia and in Moscow, and in the British embassy in Warsaw).[81] Other uses of technology encouraged different fears. The ogre "Big Brother" had cast his shadow over the pages of the *Daily Sketch* when computers were introduced for London traffic control, he darkened the pages of the *Daily Express* when radar was first introduced to detect traffic speed,[82] and he appeared on Sunday when the *News of the World* reported the use of closed-circuit television cameras to catch shoplifters in a Northampton supermarket.[83] The *Sunday Times* was criticized by the Press Council for publishing a photograph of Lord Denning reading a letter during his inquiry into the Profumo affair. The photograph had been taken through a window from outside the building and was enlarged to allow the letter to be read.[84]

Miniaturization was another cause for anxieties. Pocket-sized radios had been exhibited at the National Radio Show as early as 1959, and many had been sold without apparent concern.[85] When

King's Tele-Service Company began its sales of minute radio transmitters (described by some as a pocket spy), however, controversy erupted. King's then agreed to sell the devices only to those with licenses from the Post Office.[86] The devices prompted Leo Abse to ask Sir Eric Fletcher, minister without portfolio, the following questions:

> . . . whether he is aware of public concern at the inadequacy of the law to protect the rights of privacy of individuals; whether he is aware that technical devices now on sale, such as micro-bug transmitters, constitute an invasion of the privacy of the citizen; and whether, in view of present ambiguities concerning remedies for infringement of privacy, he would cause the Law Commissioners to review the existing law.[87]

Sir Eric responded that the matter would be difficult for the law commissioners because a "proposal to create a general statutory right to privacy would raise wide and controversial issues, including the liberty of the Press."[88] Two days later, the postmaster general, Anthony Wedgwood Benn, said that he was considering what action he might take; in the interim, he promised that there would be no new licenses without his permission.[89] Private members' bills were introduced in the next week, but not one dealt with electronic devices. The next year, the postmaster general forbade the showing of telephone-bugging devices at the United States Trade Fair.[90]

Twice during the period there were allegations of wiretapping. In August 1965 one telephone girl resigned and another was suspended pending an investigation into allegations by the *Wiltshire Echo* that telephone calls had been tapped. The subsequent investigation cleared both girls of any wrongdoing and explained that they had to listen to the opening of conversations to ensure that the call had been properly connected. The owner of the newspaper, Woodrow Wyatt, M.P., said that the investigation was a whitewash and promised to raise the matter in the Commons.[91]

The other instance of alleged wiretapping arose in November 1964 when a Labour M.P., Russell Kerr, asked about the tapping of M.P.'s telephones. No details were published about the background to Kerr's question, but it did produce a momentary controversy. The complaint was not that telephone tapping was inherently evil but that M.P.'s should be privileged in their communications with constituents. Prime Minister Harold Wilson adhered to the traditional position and refused comment on the general question, but he did say that no M.P.'s telephone had been tapped.[92] The *Times* Diary noted that Wilson had referred to "members."[93] The House of Lords then wondered whether its telephones had been tapped, but the lord privy seal, the earl of Longford, assured the peers that their telephones, too, were sacrosanct.[94]

In the United States a committee of the House of Representatives, under Congressman Cornelius Gallagher, had been investigating technological threats to privacy since late 1964. There was also an open dispute about wiretapping between Attorney General Robert Kennedy and the director of the Federal Bureau of Investigation at that time, J. Edgar Hoover. The effect of events in the United States and in the United Kingdom was summarized by a leader in the *Times*:

> Wiretapping and electronic eavesdropping are becoming an increasingly sensitive issue in most advanced countries, particularly in the United States. It poses in very acute form the conflict between the individual's right to privacy and the state's need for weapons to fight crime.[95]

There were two other series of events continuing from the 1950s, that presented potential privacy issues: tests to determine the amount of alcohol in a driver's body and fluoridation of water supplies. Initially, "breathalysers" had been rejected because of their inaccuracy and their high cost.[96] But the testing program continued, and in 1961 it was predicted that breathalysers would be in use in twelve to eighteen months.[97] Four years later Graham Page introduced a private member's bill that would have established penalties for driving with more than a prescribed amount of alcohol in the blood.[98] The bill was withdrawn when the minister of transport said that the government planned to introduce one of its own. In December 1965 a white paper recommended random breath tests by the police.[99] The police criticized the proposal because there were too few police, the Automobile Association's opposition mentioned the "public indignity of a breath test," and the Royal Automobile Club termed random tests an "unjustified interference with the rights of the overwhelming majority of drivers who did not drink heavily."[100] Letters to the *Times* objected to the random tests for numerous reasons: Lord Watkinson wrote that the tests were "a serious interference with the liberty of the subject" and suggested that they would worsen relations between the police and the public.[101] Others objected to the inaccuracies of the devices. Supporters of the proposal said that they were willing to give up some of their liberty if it meant that the roads would be safer; it was suggested that only criminals objected to being stopped by the police. The arguments covered a wide spectrum of opinion, but they did not include mention of a right to privacy.

When finally introduced, the Labour government's Road Safety Bill included a clause giving the police the power to make random checks.[102] But the bill was one of many lost when Parliament was dissolved for the 1966 general election. The bill was reintroduced in the new session, but the random-test provision was omitted.[103]

Fluoridation was a final subject with potential for privacy-oriented arguments.[104] The National Public Water Association's president, Lord Douglas of Barloch, contended in 1963 that opposition to the fluoridation of water was growing. His principal objections were that fluoridation was unscientific and unethical.[105] A letter to the *Times* signed by thirteen M.P's said:

> We believe that every citizen has certain rights which must be regarded as inviolable and inalienable. Among these is the right, when there is no risk of the spread of disease by contagion or from pollution, for every individual to be free to decide for himself what shall go into his body and the bodies of his children, and what shall be kept out of them. Fluoridation breaches this right and sets a dangerous precedent.[106]

Again, though the potential existed to claim a right to privacy and thereby the right to control one's own body, the privacy claim was not made.

At the end of the transitional period, as at the beginning, there was an underlying current of opinion in favor of some legislation to protect "privacy." But the similarity ended with the vocabulary; the object of the legislation had changed. Early in the period the concept of *privacy* was part of expressions of opposition to the conduct of newspapers; later it was part of the budding complaints about electronic surveillance devices.

Lord Mancroft had proposed a right to privacy to protect individuals from harrassment by newspaper photographers and reporters. He wanted to impose a test of "public interest" on the publication of information that caused distress to an individual. But discussion of his bill left unresolved the extent to which freedom of the press meant freedom to collect information, as well as freedom of unrestrained publication.

There was no such counterbalancing claim for those, such as Leo Abse, who suggested that the use of miniature listening devices was an invasion of privacy. Other than the applicability of arguments for freedom of the press, the two uses of the concept of privacy were at this time similar. Both relied upon the traditional value attached to an individual's maintaining his seclusion. Lord Mancroft supported the value because of the distress caused if it were denied; Abse supported it because it was intrinsically valuable. Thus at the end of the transitional period, the notion of *privacy* remained closely linked with the private-sphere definitional concept.

8

The Lyon and Walden Bills

i

After Lord Mancroft's bill in 1961, there was not another privacy bill until 1967. Thereafter, however, bills to protect concepts of privacy were proposed with increasing frequency. Bounding this period of renewed interest in privacy legislation were the two most general of the bills. The first was introduced in 1967 by Alexander Lyon, who saw it as but the initial skirmish in a long campaign.[1] The second, introduced in 1969 by Brian Walden, marked the peak intensity of the campaign.[2] Common to all the bills was a rhetoric that Warren and Brandeis would have found familiar. For example, Alexander Lyon asserted that "there ought to be in the law a right to be left alone if one wishes to be left alone."[3] In the Commons he explained: "In a civilised community, where we are living on top of each other, there must be an area of life which an individual has the right to keep to himself."[4]

Beyond the vocabulary, little else retained any likeness to the earlier proposals. Lord Mancroft had proposed a narrowly defined cause of action that, as with Warren and Brandeis, was directed against the press. His bill would have limited the courts' role to determining if publication of personal information had occurred and if it were "calculated to cause [one] distress or embarrassment." Since the judicial role was to be so limited, he had not even thought it necessary to define *privacy*. In contrast, Alexander Lyon's bill defined the right to privacy as "the right of any person to preserve the seclusion of himself, his family or his property from any person."[5] Correspondingly, there was a disparity between the role envisioned for the courts by the two men. In place of Lord Mancroft's restricted role, Lyon advocated setting out "a principle with reasonable defences," which would "then allow the courts to interpret them in practical instances."[6]

These differences arose because the aims of the two bills were different. Like Warren and Brandeis, Lord Mancroft had focused on the press as the primary threat to privacy. But for Lyon the press was of secondary importance. To him technology (represented in particular by electronic surveillance devices) posed the greatest threat to privacy. To be sure, Warren and Brandeis do write in their article that "modern devices afford abundant opportunities" for taking photographs without an individual's permission. But those comments are little more than embellishments of their discussion of property rights for personal characteristics. Their dominant concern remains the press.

The examples utilized by Lyon illustrated both the different aims and the broader concept of privacy that had developed since 1961. He referred to two instances of intrusion by journalists (when Aneurin Bevan was in the hospital and when Vietnamese children arrived at East Grinstead Hospital for plastic surgery) and to one instance of intrusion by television (when cameras were present as Mrs. Donald Campbell received the news of her husband's death). He also mentioned topics not considered by Lord Mancroft: a divorce case in which inquiry agents had "bugged" a hotel bedroom to obtain evidence, "numerous cases" of telephone tapping, and doorstep salesmen. Finally, Lyon suggested that the most important part of the bill was "the protection it affords against forms of industrial espionage, which have become all too common in recent months."[7]

No action was taken on Lyon's bill. Even so, by bringing a number of previously unrelated concerns under the privacy rubric, it clearly marked a new phase in the development of the concept of privacy. One proposal that illustrated privacy's fresh popularity was introduced soon after Lyon's bill. Unlike the more general approach, Peter Bessell's Unauthorised Telephone Monitoring Bill was tailored to a specific problem.[8] Its purpose was "to prohibit monitoring of private telephone conversations by unauthorised persons." He appealed for support because his measure was "designed to protect something which is at the foundation of our national heritage, namely, the right of every honest citizen to security and privacy."[9] Three areas were suggested in which additional protection was required: trade and industrial secrets, divorce cases, and espionage. Bessell's bill suffered the same fate as Lyon's—the second reading debate was deferred. Nevertheless, they evinced growing concern about privacy and two possible responses to that concern.

Another indication of that growth was the decision of the National Council for Civil Liberties (NCCL) to investigate privacy. "Civil Liberty," the bulletin of the NCCL, reported in 1965:

> The Executive Committee has decided to undertake a comprehensive study on the subject of privacy. Plans are now being prepared and will be decided upon at the September meeting. It is envisaged that the study will include all aspects of the subject, including the use of modern Police methods and old-fashioned Press methods. With technological development, increased legislation and new Police methods, there is nowhere a definition of privacy, and no safeguards or controls provided against intrusions.[10]

Furthermore, in numerous other forums attempts were being made to formulate definitions of and protection for privacy. As Tom Sargant, the secretary of JUSTICE, explained, "The subject was very much in the air both nationally and internationally."[11] One of the earliest and most influential studies was sponsored by the Association of the Bar of the City of New York. The result of that study was Alan Westin's *Privacy and Freedom*, published in the United States in 1967.[12] In the same year, the Nordic Conference of Jurists recommended a law on privacy,[13] and JUSTICE itself established a committee to study the topic. A seminar was also held in Oxford under the sponsorship of the Law Commission.

Commenting upon these 1967 attempts to grapple with the concept, the *Times* returned to the Warren and Brandeis theme that the complexities of modern society make privacy even more necessary:

> The advancing density and complexity of social organisation make privacy at once more difficult and more necessary to have. At the same time it is threatened by new techniques of mass communication and concealed observation, such as bugging devices, electronic surveillance, and subliminal persuasion.[14]

According to the leader, a general statute, such as Lyon's bill, was not the best response to those threats. Instead, it "would be more consonant with the development of English law . . . to fasten upon particular abuses by means of new legislation and to leave to the common law the evolution of remedies against less easily definable invasions of privacy."

ii

Neither the two privacy bills nor the NCCL's announcement mentioned computers. Between 1967 and 1969, however, apprehensions about computers increased so dramatically that some legislation seemed essential. The principal reason for these anxieties was the rapidly growing use of computers by the government. To many, government computers meant government control and all the ramifications of "1984." An early focal point for the apprehensions was a bill introduced by the postmaster general at that time, Edward Short, to enable the Post Office to provide data processing services to private customers.[15] Reflecting concerns expressed by Alexander Lyon, Short contended that electronic storage was inherently safer than document storage and that new safeguards would better protect against industrial espionage than any other information-storage method.[16] Opponents of the bill doubted that any safeguards could guarantee that the information would be securely stored in the computer. While the bill was in standing committee, Dr. Jeremy Bray, joint parliamentary secretary to the minister of technology, introduced a new clause that he said ensured "an absolutely confidential service."[17] Among those who expressed doubts about the clause was John Osborne, who referred to the problems in the United States.[18] Fearful of the uses made of computers for central planning in Russia and of industry's lack of awareness of the possible conflict between the new data-transmission services and privacy, he suggested that there should be a committee to assess confidentiality.[19] Dr. Bray agreed that there was a need for a confidentiality council to cover all computer bureaus; he promised that the government would find some means of discussing the matter. The amendment placated most of the opponents, and the bill was enacted without additional difficulty.[20]

The nascent fears about computers had other reasons for their emergence between 1967 and 1969. It soon became apparent that the "modern Police methods" referred to by the NCCL relied to a significant extent upon computers. In January 1967 three home office working parties included among their recommendations a suggestion that a national computer network for criminal records be established.[21] In February, Scotland Yard announced that it was reclassifying its records so that two million sets of fingerprints could be put onto a computer.[22] Near the end of the year the home office revealed its plans for "a national computer with a store of criminal statistics greater than any comparable project in the world."[23] This computer would include the names of criminals, their previous convictions, fingerprints, and methods used to commit crimes. By allowing data to be linked, it would enable the police to reach conclusions that they might not otherwise have discovered. One example given by the home office suggested that the computer would record that a suspect had lunch with a man who had no previous criminal record.[24] In other words, persons convicted of crimes, persons suspected of crimes, and persons completely innocent could all find their names included in the computer's memory.

Other attempts to deal with lawbreakers affected the public more immediately. Since 1952 the Post Office had used technology to trace television-license evaders, but without much success. In 1967 Edward Short included in the Wireless Telegraphy Bill a clause to require dealers to disclose the names of customers or hirers.[25] The *Times* saw no reason to oppose the provision:

> But considering the extent and the demoralizing effects of the present evasion the demands being made upon them [dealers] are not excessive. Nor can the provisions of the Bill be convincingly represented as a significant encroachment on civil liberties, or ushering in a snooper's paradise, or anything of that sort.[26]

Apparently the House of Commons agreed, for, though there were a few who were not content, the bill passed easily. The Post Office also proposed to have a computer compare a list of those houses that once had a television license with a current list and to dispatch letters asking for an explanation to those of the former group not in the latter.[27] Later the Post Office devised a plan to use postal codes to assist its searches.[28]

Postal codes in themselves were another of the computer-related innovations that caused irritation. During a discussion of the influence of computers that took place on the BBC Third Program, Malcolm Warner, one of the authors of *The Data Bank Society*, suggested that "the most important consequence [of widespread computer use] may be the loss of identity; if not personally, then certainly politically. The reduction of the address to a postal zone digit seems to be the forerunner of the universal identity number."[29]

Speaking for many people in addition to himself, the Labour minister of technology, Anthony Wedgwood Benn, explained some of the fears about computers:

> People were becoming aware that far from men interrogating computers the computers interrogated men and fed all the information they gathered into the central machine. There would be few corners of life free from the probings of Government, the local council, credit agencies, bank managers, employers and possibly, fiancee or spouse.[30]

As though to show that the concerns transcended party boundaries, the Society of Conservative Lawyers published a pamphlet that traced the reasons for concern to the computer's ability to store and manipulate large quantities of data.[31] That pamphlet became the basis for Kenneth Baker's Data Surveillance Bill, which was designed "to prevent the invasion of privacy through the misuse of computer information."[32] The proposal, applicable to government and private computers alike, would have required the registration of every computer in which personal information was stored and the provision of a printout (of the information about each person) to everyone whose name was in the computer. The bill was not given a second reading.

iii

As the unease felt about computers was coalescing around the concept of privacy, there were still other contexts in which a similar argumentative shift was taking place. One of the more broadly based contexts was a reemerging critique of governmental activity. Kenneth Baker summarized that critique and revealed the shift toward use of the concept of privacy when he said that the widespread support for his bill showed an "increasing recognition of the need for some new protection of individual rights and protection against an over-zealous State intruding too much into individual people's privacy."[33]

In a lecture entitled "Erosions of Personal Freedom in a Modern Society," Lord Goodman, a Labour peer, detailed some of the complaints. The theme of his comments was that "encroachments on personal liberty are becoming a built-in vice of Government."[34] In particular, he referred to a quartet of erosions that had occurred in 1967: the Land Commission, the breathalyser test, wage restraint, and obscure acts (much the same heterogeneous collection of grievances that had been made after the Second World War by Viscount Samuel). Yet Lord Goodman's only comment about privacy was in an allusion to Lord Denning's investigation of the Profumo affair.

Unlike the discussions of the effects of computers, criticisms of governmental activity sounded an audible political tone. There were specific complaints about procedural devices that the government used in the House of Commons. Unique support for these complaints came from Dame Irene Ward, who protested against the steady loss of public freedom. She said: "Socialist legislation which erodes continually the freedom of the individual is being pushed through and backbenchers are given no opportunities to express their points of view."[35]

But others perceived an importance to the issues that went beyond political disputes. The *Times*, for example, thought that a constitutional change might be required:

> Too much power is centralized in Westminster and, of that power, too much is centralized in the Prime Minister, who is subject to too few restrictions on his freedom of action so long as he can maintain the support of his own party. The existence of general elections, of a free press and television and of free judges and of free law still makes this a democratic system of government and in many ways an admirable one. But there is an urgent need to change some parts of our constitution and these reforms ought to include stronger safeguards for the liberties we possess and a greater opportunity for local and national democratic action.[36]

After the queen's speech had announced the decision to establish a commission to examine the constitution, the *Times* repeated its argument that the "essential problem of the constitution is the growth of the power of government and the significance of bureaucratic administration in peoples lives."[37] The commission was urged to "examine the provision of more secure legal rights for citizens."

Although few proposed a right to privacy, there was a growing call for a Bill of Rights to protect against governmental excesses. Lord Shawcross, chairman of JUSTICE, advocated a Bill of Rights in a speech to the organization's annual meeting. As the

Times had done, he suggested new formal institutions to replace worn ones that seemed no longer effective:

> "A growing authoritarianism characterizes Government policies," he said, "and because of the stress of the party battle, M.P.s have become, as a rule, quite unable to fulfil their task of protecting the rights and freedoms of the individual citizen."[38]

The Society for Individual Freedom also announced that it had drafted a Bill of Rights, which it anticipated that Lord Lambton would introduce.[39] At the end of the Conservative Conference of 1968, Quintin Hogg spoke of the tyranny of Whitehall and suggested a Bill of Rights that would, except in emergencies, limit Parliament's power to legislate adversely on individual or regional rights.[40] The Liberal Conference of 1969 carried a resolution calling for a Bill of Rights. And Anthony Lester said in a Fabian Society lecture: "The individual citizen should have the protection of a Bill of Rights and a new system of courts dealing with maladministration to protect him against injustice by private and public institutions."[41]

Some of these arguments had arisen because of the Conservatives' tactic of portraying a Labour government as anxious to interfere in the daily lives of individuals. Other arguments had arisen from the speed with which the government attempted to enact its proposals. Still others had come from reaction to specific acts that aroused a section of the public. The result was a cacophony of cross-party complaints that had gradually found some harmony with the suggestion for a Bill of Rights.[42]

Out of this process of harmonizing came a series of Parliamentary actions. Dame Irene Ward introduced a motion criticizing the government for eroding "traditional rights and liberties."[43] During the debate Alexander Lyon (who had attended the Law Commission's privacy seminar the previous weekend) returned to his privacy theme. "It seems to me," he observed, "that the real threat to liberty in our highly complicated, civilised, modern society, is the invasion of privacy by all who have the apparatus to do so without in any way trespassing on the property of the person, which is about the only right that the English citizen has to defend."[44]

In December 1967 a second motion was introduced by another Conservative, Norman St. John Stevas.[45] During this debate the positions taken by the government and by the Opposition were epitomized: Labour members defended the economic advantages that they had secured, Conservatives alleged a loss of liberty. For example, Charles Pannell, a Labour member, said that full employment was the greatest liberty there was, while Bernard Weatherill's warnings of the danger of becoming a form-filling society were reminiscent of Conservative complaints after the Second World War. Included among the catalogue of grievances was William Wells's warning of the dangers inherent in a centralized computer system to handle the records of all government departments.[46]

After those two Conservative motions, the topic of a Bill of Rights lay dormant in Parliament throughout 1968, which had been designated International Human Rights Year by the United Nations. In 1969, however, Lord Lambton attempted to introduce the bill that the Society for Individual Freedom had announced previously.[47] He warned: "Almost without realisation we are approaching that time which is so often written about in literature of the all-powerful State."[48] Essentially a collection of protests against the power of government, the bill contained no reference to a right to privacy, though it had a section to require a warrant to enter private premises. Alexander Lyon's objection to the bill was indicative of a split among M.P.'s. Even though he had introduced a bill to protect privacy, he opposed Lord Lambton's bill because it "would put a fetter on the right of this House to change the law."[49] The bill was refused a first reading.

Three months later a bill that was introduced by Emlyn Hooson did include a privacy clause.[50] His proposal was a combination of the familiar freedoms (speech, opinion, religion) with grievances against the government (judicial review of legislation no compulsion to join trade unions). Reminiscent of the Universal Declaration of Human Rights, the "Right to Privacy" section said: "Every person is entitled to protection from arbitrary interference in his personal, family or other private affairs."

Introducing the bill, Mr. Hooson explained that there was "a deep-seated feeling, which I think is entirely justified by the facts, that individual liberty is gradually being eroded, and that there is an increasing invasion of privacy, aided by technological development, for which our law, as at present defined, does not appear to provide adequate remedies."[51] He gave four reasons for his bill: the growth of administrative power, the need to assert an individual right of privacy, the role of the Crown in daily affairs, and the potential misuse of computers.[52] There was no debate.

Before the end of 1969 no Bill of Rights was introduced in the House of Lords. Many of the same topics, however, were discussed during the debate on a motion by Lord Wade:

> To call attention to the need for protection of human rights and fundamental freedoms, to the increasing power of the State in relation to the individual, to the threat to personal privacy resulting from technological advance; and to possible measures including the enactment of a Bill of Rights.[53]

Like Emlyn Hooson, Lord Wade combined well-worn protests against the executive with new anxieties concerning technology. He spoke about concentration of power and about the influence that such power had over every aspect of human life, about the speed with which rights could be taken away, and about the growth of administrative acts and tribunals. With these he combined two newer topics: the growing evidence of infringement of personal privacy, and the possibilities for misuse of computer-stored personal information.[54]

Lord Wade suggested that there were two possible solutions: either the courts could adapt the common law or Parliament could enact a Bill of Rights. He doubted that the common-law doctrines would prove adequate "in view of the new kind of threats and the complexity of modern society."[55] To Lord Wade the courts were most effective in protecting property rights and rights such as freedom from arbitrary arrest; they were not so successful with "the less easily definable rights of privacy and the right to be protected from intrusion into one's private life."[56] Therefore he opted for the legislature to assist the courts by enacting certain rights.

The lord chancellor, Lord Gardiner, asserted that many of the arguments were but political propaganda. He contended that the government had expanded the rights of the individual in some areas: legal aid, the ombudsman, and the right to sue the government. The difficulty that he saw with every Bill of Rights was that it either restated the existing law or was too general to be predictable. The law of privacy, however, was one of five areas that he conceded might merit future consideration.[57]

Privacy received attention in other speeches; four of the ten peers who spoke after Lord Wade, including the lord chancellor, devoted attention to the subject. Baroness Gaitskell agreed with the lord chancellor that extra study should be given to privacy. Two other speakers with special expertise mentioned the topic. The earl of Arran, a director of the Daily Mail and General Trust, defended the press against privacy legislation and contended that the newspapers had improved since 1961.[58] Lord Ritchie-Calder, a specialist on computers, compared the growing fear of computers and technology with the wartime fear of Nazism:

> I am more and more alarmed every day at the degree to which we are becoming ciphers. To me, who saw Belsen immediately after the liberation and who also went to Auschwitz, to all the other unspeakable horrors of those places was added the anonymity of imprisonment and death—anonymity, the complete disappearance of the individual; just a tattooed number on the skins of the victims. But to-day, in the same way—less horrifying, but just as reprehensible, in my opinion—we ourselves are liable to become statistics and, from the point of view of authorities, cease to be names and faces. In statistical anonymity we will have no names, no faces, no personalities. We shall just become the code numbers in a computer.[59]

The fears expressed in two groups of debates—on computers and on a Bill of Rights—were not the result of rigorous analysis. Instead, they were the instinctive reactions of people who felt themselves unable to control their government and its technology. In groping for a means of control, they reasserted an unassailable claim—the claim to privacy. A detached observer with philosophical leanings might have perceived two different fears in the debates: a fear that computer-stored information could enable an individual's life to be controlled by someone else, and a fear of being treated as a unit in a sequence of numbers—unique but no different from all the rest—rather than as an individual with personal characteristics. But such distinctions were not made by the participants in the debates. Instead, with increasing frequency, they resorted to the comfortably familiar right to privacy.

iv

The intensity of the concerns aroused by the government and by the growing use of computers was reinforced by uses of a variety of technological devices that were seen to pose different threats.

For convenience, these various technological devices can be discussed in relation to the three groups mentioned by Alexander Lyon: wire-tapping, electronic eavesdropping ("bugs"), and industrial espionage.

Inclusion of industrial espionage in the catalogue of invasions of privacy attested to the expanding definitional boundary of privacy claims. No indefinite notion of personality was involved here; instead, industries were concerned about the practical effects of thefts of information that would be valuable to competitors. Books published at about this time documented the growth of the anxieties. Peter Hamilton, in his *Espionage and Subversion in an Industrial Society*, contended that industrial spying posed a grave threat to privacy and would soon become more significant than military espionage.[60] To provide instructions for countering the theft of industrial information, Philip Hickson wrote *Industrial Counter-Espionage*. The book was described as "the most complete, almost frightening, guide to the operations of the business spy—and, more important, what to do about it."[61] Yet, as an example of the breadth of the concept of privacy, one of Hickson's techniques was itself potentially an invasion of privacy. He suggested that careful screening of employees could reduce theft:

> Screening simply means getting the facts right and getting *all* the facts, including those personal details that most people leave out because they think them irrelevant or an intrusion into their private affairs. But a reasonable person, with a clear conscience, is unlikely to object to scrutiny if the need for precautions in relation to his particular job is made clear to him at the outset.[62]

Industrial espionage was an emotive problem both because it involved the taking of information (which was not classed as property for the purposes of the law of theft) and because it often involved the use of electronic listening devices. In March 1967, only a month after the introduction of Peter Bessell's Unauthorised Telephone Monitoring Bill, an instance of "bugging" was discovered in Reading. The incident began when a man asked permission to park his car and to pitch his tent behind a bungalow. During his stay he asked to use the bungalow's telephone. Later, after a microphone had been found in the telephone's receiver, the police announced that they were interviewing the man, who had since admitted that he was an industrial spy.[63] Elsewhere, in what the solicitor for the Post Office said was the first prosecution for telephone tapping in Britain, two men were fined after a trial before Newbury magistrates.[64]

When Sir Edward Boyle drew twelfth position in the ballot for private members' bills, he proposed to introduce a measure to prevent industrial espionage.[65] During the second reading debate he said that one of the unwelcome by-products of technological advances was "the emergence of the menace of industrial spying."[66] But he did not consider that the problem existed in isolation; to him: "The whole topic of industrial espionage is only one aspect of the more general topic of the invasion of privacy which the Legal Committee [of the Council of Europe] is also studying."[67] Alexander Lyon welcomed the debate in principle but opposed the manner of dealing with the problem because the bill "illustrates the fallacy of trying to tackle the problem of privacy in a piecemeal fashion."[68] Instead, he suggested a remedy such as he had previously proposed: "We should try to bring about a new statutory tort, something akin to the tort of negligence which has such a widespread application in all areas of society."[69]

Edmund Dell, the minister of state for the Board of Trade, disputed the evidence introduced by Sir Edward. Dell thought that because the problem was actually small and because there had been no significant damage, there were dangers of making the cure worse than the problem. But he did admit that an increasing use of electronic devices "could lead to an incursion into privacy."[70] The bill did not progress beyond the second reading stage.

Other reports of telephone tapping and electronic eavesdropping gave credence to suspicions that the devices were not confined to industrial espionage. Lord Russell of Liverpool alleged that his telephone had been tapped during the campaign to secure a public inquiry into the hanging of James Hanratty.[71] A bookmaker was fined after the person whom he had hired to tap someone's telephone sabotaged the attempt and the device was easily discovered.[72] And the lord chief justice, Lord Parker of Waddington, approved the admission, in a divorce trial, of evidence gathered by wiretapping.[73] Other examples included the use, also in a divorce case, of evidence that a husband obtained by fixing a microphone in the sitting room of his own home and recording conversations between his wife and another man.[74]

When the BBC used a hidden device to record a conversation between a woman and Hammersmith Council's welfare officer, questions were asked in the House of Commons by a Labour M.P.,

Frank Tomney.[75] The next day the BBC ordered that such "bugs" not be used unless prior permission had been obtained from "the highest level."[76] Even that order did not satisfy the *Times*, which drew a distinction between television's clandestine recording and a newspaperman who had to declare himself and could not hide a device on someone. The leader went on to warn that "if a line is not drawn that is clear to news gatherers and the public alike then the development of these new gadgets will increase the fear of invasion of individual privacy. This is of course a far wider question, involving industrial espionage, private detectives, and individuals with an excessive bump of curiosity."[77]

Within two years the *Times* apparently changed its mind about the use of secret recording devices because its reporters utilized them to record evidence about corruption and bribery involving at least three London detectives. The newspaper's report said that the policeman "was not aware that microphones under Mr. Smith's shirt and taped to his wrist were monitoring his words on a pocket recorder and by radio receiver in a car we had parked near by."[78]

V

Although the *Times* did in that one instance rely upon secret recording devices, newspapers generally were criticized for invading privacy in ways that relied less on technological expertise. From 1967 to 1969 the themes were much the same as those that had developed before the Second World War: questions involving the private life of a public figure and questions involving the publicity given to an incident in the life of an otherwise private individual. And, as had also developed before the war, the issues were raised against a background of the economic insecurity of the newspaper industry.

Newspaper photographs of one public figure, George Brown, provoked him to complain about the men who photographed him dancing with his wife at a Labour party conference and also at a party on board the *Queen Mary*. The *Times* published two letters that represented alternative responses to Brown's complaint. One letter criticized Brown, who, because he was a paid servant of the electorate, was "answerable for his conduct—both public and private if it so impinges on the efficient execution of his duties."[79] The other letter defended Brown and recalled that he had not been "dancing in his capacity as Foreign Secretary and, as such, ought to have been left alone."[80]

More vociferous complaints resulted from two other events: the first human heart transplant and the *News of the World*'s announcement that it would republish Christine Keeler's memoirs. Even before the first British heart transplant, Lord Brock, a past president of the Royal College of Surgeons, wrote an article for the *Times* entitled "A Plea for Anonymity in Heart Transplants."[81] He proposed that, as in other transplants, there should be no contact between the donor of a heart and the recipient, especially not through the press. His plea for special consideration received little attention after the first British heart transplant. The *Times* described the scene this way: "Rumours that the operation had begun started to leak out during the afternoon and the hospital was besieged by reporters and photographers."[82] The hospital promised not to reveal the names of either of the patients involved, and there were no complaints about the press conduct in this instance.

The second British transplant was in July 1968; fifty-seven hours after the operation the recipient died. Even though the recipient and his wife had asked that their names be withheld, their names were published. In its statement rejecting complaints about the publication, the Press Council said that the questions raised by heart transplants were not merely scientific or medical; the public also had an interest in the use of the National Health Service. The council suggested that privacy claims would have more weight if public opinion became settled, but until then it was "not practicable to arouse interest over anonymous cases."[83]

Professor Roy Calne, a pioneer in liver transplants in Britain, criticized the "ballyhoo" over the heart transplants. He said that both the press and television had demonstrated a lack of responsibility and had intruded on privacy by revealing the names and publishing photographs taken at funerals. Because of those acts, he thought that there inevitably would be a loss of confidence in the operation.[84]

A third transplant, in May 1969, followed much the same course: both families requested that their names be withheld (the wife of the recipient was also in the hospital, and it was suggested that the news might delay her recovery). The *Daily Telegraph*, however, thought that it had discovered a plot to conceal all information about the transplant. Because it believed that there were legitimate doubts about the procedures followed prior to removing the heart from the donor, it published both sets of names.[85] The Press Council followed its previous decision and ruled that the decision to publish the names was within the discretion of the editor.[86]

The announcement that the *News of the World* intended to republish Christine Keeler's memoirs was the other major event involving complaints about intrusion by newspapers. At a luncheon to mark his retirement as the Press Council's first lay chairman, Lord Devlin indirectly criticized the newspaper. His remarks also contained an attempt to resolve the difficult question of distinguishing public life from private life:

> When a man is in public life there are things about his private life which the public is entitled to know. But when his public life ceases, he becomes entitled to all the protection that can be claimed by the private citizen; and this is that his sins, his follies and his misfortunes are not used for the mere purpose of making money.[87]

Others also protested about the Keeler story, among them, Alexander Lyon, who said that he would complain to the Press Council about the "offensive intrusion into the privacy of a man who is not now in public life."[88] Even before these reactions, the *Times* had received letters of protest, and even Christine Keeler had written to explain her actions.[89] A leader in the *Times* said of the republication: "The public interest is served in no conceivable way so as to compensate for the unpleasantness caused by the publication of these articles in the largest circulating newspaper. It amounts to an unjustified intrusion on privacy."[90] Even so, the *Times* believed that the damage done by a law to protect privacy would be greater than that done by any abuse of the freedom to disclose information in the public interest.

Three days after Lyon complained, the Press Council censured the *News of the World*. The newspaper, which had reportedly increased its circulation by 150,000, rejected the censure as a prejudgment and as not having been conducted according to the ordinary rules of justice.[91]

vi

Hence, when Parliament met for the 1969–70 session, the fresh complaints about the *News of the World* were added to the accumulation of anxieties about computers and electronic listening devices.

Two other influences were also important in the consideration soon to be given to privacy: the studies by JUSTICE and the NCCL. JUSTICE's report was not published until early 1970, but the year before that the NCCL had publicly launched a campaign for legislation to protect privacy. Announcing the campaign's start, Tony Smythe, the NCCL's general secretary, had said that "people had a right to be left alone in their own homes without arbitrary interference from the Government, private agencies or their neighbours."[92]

To the NCCL, privacy was more than an issue that concerned large numbers of people. For it the campaign was also a way of publicizing itself and of ensuring its financial stability by making the general public aware of the breadth of the NCCL's activities. The NCCL Bulletin explained the privacy campaign's dual purpose:

> Here is an issue with which the whole community can identify—and through which the NCCL can make its identity and purpose known. Within the issue of the right to privacy are many of the matters of continuing concern to the NCCL. Our campaign will therefore help to create a better and wider understanding of civil liberties and, at the same time, increase public support for our work.[93]

The NCCL claimed as its first victory the refusal of Birmingham magistrates to grant the bulk application of the Midlands Electricity Board for warrants.[94] As its second victory, it claimed the growth of a serious public debate about privacy. More realistically, both "victories" were the result of the combined influences of all of the issues that had contributed to the growing public discussion of privacy. Since Alexander Lyon's 1967 bill, the pendulum of public opinion had begun to swing in favor of some form of protection for privacy. The NCCL's campaign was an additional weight that ensured that the swing continued.

Although the NCCL thought that the controversy over the *News of the World* and Christine Keeler's memoirs was "beneficial in focusing public attention on the privacy issue," it did not consider that there was a need for statutory controls on the press. It did believe, however, that "the developing technology of surveillance, the frantic collection and storage of easily accessible personal information and the absence of safeguards for preserving confidentiality" made a general law on privacy an urgent need.[95]

The crescendolike quality of discussions about privacy reached their peak in the fall of 1969. When Parliament met, Alexander Lyon tabled a motion, signed by 139 M.P.'s, calling for legislation to protect privacy.[96] After drawing fifth place in the ballot for private members' bills, Brian Walden announced that he would introduce a Right of Privacy Bill. Both JUSTICE and the NCCL circulated draft bills, but, initially, Walden selected neither. The first reading, on 26 November 1969, was given to a blank sheet of paper. By introducing the bill, however, Walden placed it and himself at the center of the vortex of concern about privacy. He emphasized that the bill would not be directed against the press: its main object would be to prevent information given for a specific purpose from being used for some other purpose. He said that he was especially concerned about the possibility of computer-based dossiers being compiled without the knowledge of the individual.[97]

The events of the last five weeks of 1969 showed how pervasive was the privacy issue. On 28 November the *Times* handed to Scotland Yard its evidence of police corruption; on 3 December Lord Windlesham introduced a motion to call attention to the problems of storage of information. The Law Commission's fourth annual report, published on 4 December, said: "An early examination of the law relating to privacy is essential." Reports were published on 20 December that the government would propose a royal commission to investigate privacy. Two days later the *Times* published a leader commenting that the distribution through the mail of obscene or offensive publications was an invasion of privacy. And, on 31 December Sir John Foster, chairman of the executive committee of JUSTICE, announced that he hoped to have its report on privacy published before Parliament reassembled.[98]

The debate on Lord Windlesham's motion was instructive both as an indicator of the sensed conflict between computers and privacy and as a preview of the debate on Brian Walden's bill. The motion was introduced "to call attention to the need to reconcile the more efficient handling of personal records by means of computers with individual freedom and privacy."[99] A total of thirteen peers spoke in the debate, which lasted just over four hours. Lord Windlesham was not certain about the definition of privacy; he thought that the right was "a somewhat ephemeral one and hard to define satisfactorily." Nevertheless, he suggested that "in its essential elements it consists of the right of the individual to select the time, circumstance, and extent to which knowledge, attitudes, beliefs, behaviour or opinions should be disclosed to or withheld from others."[100] But at another point in his remarks Lord Windlesham indicated that he did not think that control of information was an exhaustive definition of privacy:

> To me, the guiding principle should surely be that the individual has a right to know of and to limit the circulation of information about himself. This, I suggest, is the most practical way of considering the relationship between personal information and the right of the individual to privacy. It is in this sense an ingredient of the individual's right to privacy and one that shouuld not be infringed without the showing of an overriding social need and that protective safeguards have been established in the first instance and satisfied thereafter.[101]

The motion was approved by all who spoke, but, as in similar previous debates, the pet concern of each speaker revealed the diverse nature of the concept of privacy. Lord Annan commented on computers used by the universities' central record system, Lord Donaldson of Kingsbridge discussed credit bureaus, Lord Platt remarked about the medical field, and Lord Carron said that trade unions had fears of the records that would be maintained. The core of the issue was identified by Lord Ritchie-Calder:

> In the old days one had some comfort in the thought that, however thorough the collection of information for a dossier might be, there were certain inescapable limitations. Walls still gave some privacy in the home; distance was still some protection, and size made methods of acquiring and storing information either conspicuous or excessive. Those safeguards of privacy and human rights no longer exist. Miniaturization has now reduced electronic devices to concealable proportions.[102]

Shortly before Parliament reassembled after Christmas, Brian Walden's Bill was published—with one small exception, it was the JUSTICE proposal.[103] Its purpose was "to establish a right of privacy, to make consequential amendments to the law of evidence, and for connected purposes." The vital portions of the bill included Clause 1, which provided a right of action for "any substantial and unreasonable infringement of a right of privacy," and Clause 3, which set out six defenses that were based on the defendant's intent, the consent of the plaintiff, the public interest, absolute or qualified privilege, an authority of statute, or an act done to protect property or the person. In addition, rather than attempt to define privacy, the bill suggested the content of the proposed right by an amalgam of examples:

> "Right of privacy" means the right of any person to be protected from intrusion upon himself, his home, his family, his relationships and communications with others, his property and his buisness affairs, including intrusion by—
> (a) spying, prying, watching or besetting;
> (b) the unauthorised overhearing or recording of spoken words;
> (c) the unauthorised making of visual images;
> (d) the unauthorised reading or copying of documents;
> (e) the unauthorised use or disclosure of confidential information, or of facts (including his name, identity, or likeness) calculated to cause him distress, annoyance or embarrassment, or to place him in a false light;
> (f) the unauthorised appropriation of his name, identity or likeness for another's gain.

The defenses and the examples of violations of the right made it clear that, in spite of his professed preferences, Walden's bill would have affected the press as well as users of electronic surveillance devices. And yet it would not have stopped the compiling of dossiers from information given with the permission of the individual, who would have had no additional power to refuse to disclose information.

The next day both the report from JUSTICE and the Press Council's reaction were published. The JUSTICE report consisted of a concise statement of the law and a proposed remedy—as perceived by lawyers. (It was criticized for not hearing evidence from newspapers and other interested bodies.) The committee summarized its recommendations in this way:

> In short, they amount to a finding that English law is seriously defective as it now stands, and that there is an urgent need for legislation. Such legislation could take a variety of possible forms, but on balance we think that the best method would be to create a new statutory tort of "infringement of privacy."[104]

The committee thought that no purpose would be served by attempting to define privacy. Instead, it was content to discuss a topic with vague boundaries, which was described as

> a notion about whose precise boundaries there will always be a

> variety of opinions, but about whose central area there will always be a large measure of agreement. At any given time, there will be certain things which almost everyone will agree ought to be part of the "private" area which people should be allowed to preserve from the intrusion of others, subject only to the overriding interest of the community as a whole where this plainly outweighs the private right. Surrounding this central area there will always be a "grey area" on which opinions will differ, and the extent of this grey area, as also that of the central one, is bound to vary from time to time.[105]

The JUSTICE report was very much what one would have expected from Warren and Brandeis had they written in 1969; at the heart of the report was the often repeated belief that protection for privacy was necessitated by the rapid changes in society and technology.

The weakest part of the report was its attempt to quantify the problem that was being considered. It described three areas of concern: collation, collection, and publication of private material. Although an appendix was attached for each of those areas, the amount of actual harm done was never established. This was the same problem that had plagued all the previous suggestions for legislation, and it was one of the primary arguments for the committee that was appointed by the government.

The Press Council's reaction was not unexpected. It announced that it was not against legislation to limit the use of electronic listening devices, but it felt that there was first a need for a proper inquiry. The council was opposed, however, to Walden's bill, which it thought would limit the right of the press to print the truth.[106]

Allied with the Press Council, the national daily newspapers were also against the bill. The *Daily Mail*'s leader was typical:

> We do not expect the law to protect us against the nosiness of the neighbours. That is one of the hazards of life.
>
> But we do demand protection against these fearsome and inhuman gadgets. And we doubt very much whether even the police should use them.
>
> They may catch a few more crooks that way. But such methods plant dark suspicions in the minds of law-abiding citizens. . . .
>
> For it is the unseen apparatus of microphones, computers and cameras that scares us, not the tingling ears of the couple at the next table.
>
> Instead of puzzling over woolly definitions of privacy, Mr.

Walden's Bill should simply ban the bugs and all the other electronic earwigs.[107]

Brian Walden and those who supported the bill thought it best to let the courts interpret what was in the public interest; the *Daily Telegraph* disagreed. According to that newspaper, to give such power to the courts would place "far too great a burden of discretion on the judges. Indeed, it is to ask them to usurp the functions of journalists."[108]

The national Sunday newspapers were equally adamant. The *News of the World* entitled its comment "Leave the Newspapers Alone." Like some of the daily newspapers, it thought that the computer should be restricted: "The advance of Big Brother computer must be resisted. So must the activities of irresponsible investigators who make secret recordings of conversations at which they are not present." It also suggested: "If any 'bugging' is to be done in Britain, it must be strictly controlled and used only to safeguard national security."[109] In the *Sunday Times* James Evans wrote that the bill was a "gold digger's charter which could lead to a welter of speculative claims." He contended that the defenses provided would be applicable only to articles actually published and not to the investigations that preceded publication.[110]

The press was aligned against the bill; JUSTICE and the NCCL favored it. But those were only some of the groups participating in the debate. One indication of the cumulative effect of years of debate about privacy came from Maurice Trowbridge, who reported in the *Daily Express*: "Exceptional pressure is being put on MPs to support the controversial Privacy Bill. . . . MPs say they have never been subjected to such pressure behind the scenes at Westminster on a private member's Bill apart from the controversial measures of major social reform—such as the death penalty, abortion, divorce, and homosexuality."[111]

The debate in the House of Commons was inevitably something of an anticlimax. The preceding three years had been but prologue to the intense activity of the preceding week, when the issues were widely discussed in newspapers, on television, and on the radio.[112] To add to the artificiality, before the debate began it was known that the government would announce a committee to investigate the subject of privacy. Thus, most speakers addressed their remarks to an evanescent bill.

Brian Walden began the debate by saying: "The right to be left alone may not sound a very exciting freedom, but it is the one about which the British people care most."[113] His catalogue of events that had prompted the proposal illustrate the continuing expansion of the concept of privacy. Walden listed modern technology, private detectives and bugging, newspapers and their intrusion, preemployment checks, civil credit inquiries, and the computer's ability to collate information. With such a miscellany Walden thought that a specific, piecemeal approach to the problems would take too long and would result in inconsistencies. Instead, he thought that a single bill, patterned on the international declarations to which the United Kingdom was a party, was the best solution.[114]

The kind of arguments made by Walden had not changed significantly from those made by Lord Mancroft, or from those made by Warren and Brandeis. The remedies had altered slightly to encompass the technologies that had been developed, but little else differed. The technology of the computer and the electronic listening devices were as new to Lyon and Walden as the photographic technology of the late nineteenth century had been to Warren and Brandeis.

Speakers after Walden adopted positions that had been held in every privacy debate. Sir Lionel Heald, Jasper More, Arthur Davidson, Sir John Foster, and Renee Short all agreed that some greater protection for the press was needed before the bill could be acceptable. Sir Lionel Heald and Angus Maude thought that to enact a new right by a private member's bill was wrong in principle.

After reminding the House of "1984," Alexander Lyon explained that what he feared most was the all-pervasive government that denied an individual any place for seclusion from the state.[115] According to Lyon, the principle of privacy was in need of protection: the principle, rather than the methods by which privacy was invaded, was the "essence of this problem." Therefore, he concluded, the appropriate remedy was comprehensive, not specific, legislation.[116]

The home secretary, James Callaghan, agreed that there was a need for a right to privacy but thought that the bill was not the proper way to proceed. Because Parliament needed to devote further study to the subject before legislating to guide the courts, Callaghan announced the government's intention to appoint a committee, under the chairmanship of Kenneth Younger

> to consider whether legislation is needed to give further pro-

> tection to the individual citizen and to commercial and industrial interests against intrusions into privacy by private persons or organisations, or by companies, and to make recommendations.[117]

The terms of reference were criticized for excluding invasions of privacy by the government, but both Callaghan and his successor refused to change the scope of the inquiry.

Thus the Younger Committee marked the culmination of three years of discussion of privacy. Throughout those years there were repeated examples of the capacity of the concept of privacy to expand to shelter each new concern that arose. Sometimes hidden by the unchanging terminology, however, were the shifting causes of the public's concerns. It was ironic, then, that just as the government again was emerging as the greatest perceived threat to privacy, the committee was prevented from investigating those threats.

9

The Younger Committee and After

i

The full membership of the Younger Committee was not announced until 13 May 1970. Between then and the publication of its report on 12 July 1972, the committee held nearly forty meetings and considered written evidence from over 130 organizations. That evidence was supplemented by an opinion survey and 181 letters that were thought to be relevant. In addition, the committee was no doubt influenced by new episodes that continued to arouse public debate about privacy. Computers were a pivotal factor in many of those episodes—for example, the 1971 census, a workshop on "The Data Bank Society," and, to a lesser extent, student protests about secret files.

A new topic was added to the committee's agenda even before its full membership was appointed. Students at Warwick University accused the university's administrators of spying and of maintaining secret files on the students. Even earlier, at the conference of the National Union of Students (NUS) in October 1969, there had been a debate about the proposed computerization of information held by the Department of Education and Science. But the protests at Warwick were the first widely publicized student reactions against collections of information. Even so, the quickly spreading protests were less evidence of concern with secret files than manifestations of students' mistrust of university officials.

Lord Radcliffe was asked to investigate the Warwick allegations. He reported in April 1970 that there were no political files and suggested that it would be improper for a university to maintain such records. He recommended that each student should be allowed to see his own file, with the exception of the admissions form.[1] In the autumn a joint NUS-NCCL report, "Academic Freedom and the Law," made related but more detailed suggestions.[2]

A similar dispute arose at Cambridge University over a plan to link by computer a graduate's academic and personal record with his first job. Opponents of the plan feared that the computer might allow information about a student to be recalled and used either by an employer or a future government. In contrast to Lord Ritchie-Calder's remarks on Lord Wade's 1969 motion, one proposal made by the opponents was to provide a number for each file rather than the student's name.[3]

Although these student protests had characteristics of an argument about privacy, they were not conducted in terms of a "right to be let alone." No one argued that collection of information should be prohibited. Nor were the debates strictly about the right of an individual to control *all* information about himself. Rather, the students objected because they were not aware of the files, and they feared that the information might be used to their detriment. The students' protests were practical examples of the arguments voiced by Kenneth Baker and Lord Windlesham in their bills to control personal information.[4]

Another topic that again raised privacy questions was the use of technology against criminal activities. At the end of January 1970, Dr. Francis Camps, professor of forensic medicine at London University, renewed the proposal that everyone's fingerprints should be stored on a computer. He thought that "there was a point when attitudes toward defence of privacy could become an accessory to the increase of crime."[5] The *News of the World* responded with a leader that suggested that after the national fingerprint registry would come truth drugs and then a loss of legal advice. The national registry "would place Britain on the way to a police state" and was a "disgraceful intrusion on privacy. It would increase the power of government to an intolerable level."[6]

Jeremy Wallington, executive producer of current affairs for Granada Television, was also concerned about the balance between privacy and the need to investigate certain activities. In a special article for the *Times,* Wallington told of his seven years' experience with "investigative journalism" in both the press and broadcasting.[7] During that time he had "encouraged the use of journalistic methods of investigation which I know most liberal Britons would abhor as gross invasions of privacy. We have taped telephone calls, posed as people we are not, hidden cameras and bugged conversations with concealed microphones." Because he was "convinced that all these actions were totally justified," he was concerned that the Younger Committee would make no distinction between the privacy of individuals and that of commercial activities. Wallington argued that private individuals, a group in which he included journalists, should not have their privacy invaded so long as they lived "within the prevailing legal, social and ethical boundaries." Without suggesting who would determine the prevailing boundaries, Wallington wrote that when individuals were working they were more likely to break those boundaries and thereby make themselves eligible targets for investigating journalists.

In response to a letter challenging his views, Wallington explained that the techniques he used only recorded what the human senses saw or heard; he thought that the use of interception devices should be prevented by criminal penalties.[8] In his opinion the press and the broadcasting media should be allowed to use the recording methods because of an imbalance in society's traditional checks and balances. This imbalance had resulted from "the dangers of depressed newspapers and television economics on one side and, as an example, the formation of international conglomerates on the other."

During 1970, in addition to Jeremy Wallington's article, there were other mentions of electronic eavesdropping devices. In February the Society for Individual Freedom alleged that the telephones of foreign embassies were tapped and that trade details were passed to the Board of Trade.[9] In July, after the general election, the prime minister said that he would not review the immunity of M.P.'s from telephone tapping.[10] And in August seven people were arrested on "bugging" charges.[11]

Computers in particular were used in ways other than to commit or to combat crime, many of which had been forecast in the early 1960s. In March 1970 the Statute Law Society proposed that computers "collate statutes and provide a comprehensive index of the law on any subject."[12] A suggestion was again made that computers could be used to ask routine questions of patients and save valuable time for doctors.[13] Lloyds Bank advertised that every one of its accounts was serviced by a computer.[14] As in the past, there was some discontent; rather than silently awaiting the Younger Committee's findings, various organizations expressed their anxieties. At its annual meeting the Institute of Professional Civil Servants discussed the "increasing watchfulness of Government over the individual" and, in particular, the role of computers.[15] The last motion adopted by the Trades Union Congress (TUC) conference called for a general right to privacy.[16] There were special discussions of the implications of the growing use of computers—for example, their impact on society was considered at the National Physical Laboratory under the title "Man-Computer Interaction."[17] The Council of Europe sponsored a conference in October 1970 and proposed that a model privacy law should be drafted by the end of the year.[18]

The widest publicity, however, was given to a workshop—"The Data Bank Society"—cosponsored by the NCCL and Allen and Unwin, who published a book, *The Data Bank Society*, to coincide with the meeting.[19] The thesis of the book, as well as the dominant thought of the workshop, was that the computer was going to make a greater impact—and make it faster—than any technological innovation in history. Foreseeing potential incompatibility between information storage and freedom, the workshop concluded that there should be an immediate start toward legislation to control computers.[20]

On a broader scale, privacy continued to be a factor in suggestions for a Bill of Rights. Lord Shawcross advocated such a measure in a speech to the Institute of Directors in May 1970.[21] In later remarks to the Commonwealth Press Union, however, he made it clear that he did not favor a right to privacy: "The disadvantage of legislation against press intrusion into privacy would outweigh any mischief caused by such intrusion."[22]

In October of the same year, the earl of Arran introduced a Bill of Rights in the House of Lords.[23] One of only three speakers against Lord Mancroft's measure in 1961, he explained that he had omitted reference to privacy from his bill because the Younger Committee was still sitting.[24] The essence of his proposal was that there should be a parliamentary commissioner who could examine every bill for inconsistencies with the Bill of Rights and who would report to both Houses of Parliament. After the proposal received unenthusiastic comments, it was withdrawn, but the earl of Arran declared that he would continue with his inquiry into the protection of rights.[25]

An alternative suggestion—that the courts be given increased powers to check legislation—was attacked by Lord Lloyd of Hampstead. He argued that the courts should not be so introduced into the political process. An opposing view was expressed in a Haldane

Memorial Lecture by Lord Justice Salmon, who said: "Judges were the last bulwark of individual liberty, and a Bill of Rights might be needed to give them power to declare certain repressive measures to be illegal."[26]

It became apparent early in 1971 that there was to be no scarcity of events involving potential questions about privacy. The Littlewoods pools organization was reported to be computerizing the electoral roll to provide maximum coverage for direct mail promotions.[27] More ominously, in the United States the Senate Subcommittee on Constitutional Rights was told that the average American was the subject of ten to twenty dossiers. In Britain, a Mr. T. F. Durkin responded with the question that probably occurred to many: "Is there any reason to suspect that the authorities do not amass a similar amount of information on the average Briton?"[28]

In the first quarter of 1971 there were three Parliamentary proposals of especial relevance to the privacy debate. Like most private members' bills, the first two were not debated. Nevertheless, their appearance illustrates the continuing variety of privacy concerns. Sally Oppenheim was denied leave to introduce a measure that would have granted discretion to doctors in deciding whether to inform parents of minors of any treatment prescribed.[29] Her bill followed discussion of charges of serious professional misconduct brought against a doctor for telling the parents of a sixteen-year-old girl that she had been given birth control pills by the Brooke Advisory Centre.[30] In the same week that Oppenheim was not allowed to introduce her proposal, Leslie Huckfield's Control of Personal Information Bill was lost when the House adjourned for lack of a quorum before his bill was reached.

The one successful measure was the Unsolicited Goods and Services Bill, introduced by Philip Goodhart.[31] Similar to Arthur Davidson's Inertia Selling Bill[32] of the previous session it was introduced to counter two problems: inertia selling (sending unsolicited goods and then demanding payment) and bogus business directories, which collected money without publishing the advertised directory. Neither of these problems was portrayed as an invasion of privacy although a number of M.P.'s spoke of the bill as adding protection for the privacy of the individual.[33] A complaint not dealt with in the original drafting concerned the sending of unsolicited matter of a sexual nature through the post. Since early 1965 there had been questions in Parliament about similar practices, but they became more numerous as the result of an advertising campaign by Julien Press.[34] The House of Commons had been told that the issue fell under the terms of the Younger Committee.[35] Despite that advice, when the bill was returned from standing committee, David Steel proposed a new clause to ban the unsolicited sending of books and other matter dealing with sexual techniques.[36] The amendment was accepted by a vote of 39 to 7, and the clause remained in the final act passed by Parliament. (The House of Lords did add the word *human* before "sexual techniques" to allow farmers to receive literature about breeding animals.)

Those three Parliamentary proposals and the other events that occurred between the debate on Walden's bill and April 1971 were but minor demonstrations of the topicality of privacy compared with the furor that arose over the 1971 census. Before Parliament adjourned for Easter the House of Lords had approved the draft Census Order in forty-seven minutes.[37] In the House of Commons the order had been approved after seventy-five minutes, during which two junior ministers and only three other M.P.'s had spoken.[38] In both Houses the comments had primarily concerned the need to publicize the reasons for the census and the guarantees of its confidentiality. Closer to the date of the enumeration, Leslie Huckfield had asked two questions about the possible identification of individuals from data sold by the registrar general.[39] In the second question he asked if the secretary for Social Services would "agree that people who wish to preserve the confidentiality and privacy of their personal information would be well advised to risk the £50 fine and not fill out the form?"[40]

Distribution of information for the census had begun during the first week of April, but until Parliament adjourned there was no evidence that privacy was more than the concern of specialists like Huckfield. A meeting of the Young Liberals proved otherwise. Although another Liberal, John Pardoe, first advised the Young Liberals to break the census law, it was Jeremy Thorpe's speech that—in the words of the *Daily Telegraph*—"had them on their feet."[41] Promising to go to prison rather than answer some of the census questions, Thorpe spoke of his objection to the use of computers: "Before the computer had crept into people's lives privacy was assured." He explained that "the computer made the circulation and accumulation of information so much easier that the threat to civil liberties was greater now than in the past."[42]

After Thorpe's statement, protests against the census acquired an impetus that no one could control. For fourteen days in the spring "silly season," the census was the dominant story in the newspapers. Yet, when the day for the enumeration arrived, nearly everyone completed the forms, including Jeremy Thorpe. The *Daily Mail*'s leader on the Saturday before Census Sunday best explained the collapse of the protest:

> Other nations put up barricades; the British grumble. . . .
>
> The last days have echoed with the finest outburst of British grumbling since the days of identity cards, queues, ration coupons, demob suits and snoek. . . .
>
> The census has everything that you need for a first-class grumbling subject. . . .
>
> No wonder it has brought out the ancient British pastime of grumbling in full flower.
>
> It's nice to know we can still do it.[43]

The characteristics of a "first-class grumbling subject" included that it be inflicted "by THEM on US," that it involve computers and the filling out of forms, and that it require answers to personal questions from "faceless strangers for inscrutable purposes." It was made even worse when "THEY" pretended to be friendly by sending brochures to explain the census.

There were other explanations for the furious fortnight. Although all national newspapers supported the census, they gave the Liberal protest daily coverage. The controversy filled an otherwise slack time for the newspapers, as the census had done in 1951. (In 1961 the Cuban invasion had crowded it off the front pages.) The protests of 1971 provided headlines to accompany the journalists' decennial search for census trivia.

But there was some significance to the objections. Anxieties about the use of computers to store information had increased sharply since 1967. They had been used experimentally in the 1961 census and for the sample census of 1966; yet both censuses had been conducted without public protest.[44] Vague fears were heightened by the knowledge that data from the 1966 census had been sold to the BBC, public and private corporations, banks, direct mail organizations, and local governments; the revenue from those sales was three hundred thousand pounds. (Estimates for sales of the 1971 data were five hundred thousand pounds.)[45] In the *Daily Telegraph* a direct mail firm, Market Force, explained how the census data assisted its search for customers.[46] From such sales of data emerged a complaint that was phrased by Peason Philips of the *Daily Mail*: "Why should we be compelled by the majesty of Parliament on penalty of fine to cough up personal details about our families in order that a stranger can flog us a bedroom suite?"[47] Likewise, Anthony Shrimsley, the *Sun*'s political editor, asked why he "should be threatened with a fine to get information which indirectly will make me more likely to be pestered by salesmen on my own doorstep."[48]

Closely related to such anxieties were the suspicions of the use that the government would make of the information. The NCCL did not object to the census or to the sale of data. But its general secretary, Tony Smythe, thought that there was reason for concern because "the massive accumulation of personal information by government is bound to lead to political manipulation and the destruction of liberal democracy."[49]

When Parliament reassembled on 19 April, the lord president of the council and leader of the House, William Whitelaw, responded to Jeremy Thorpe's private-notice question. Whitelaw emphasized that no data on individuals or families would be released and that no names or addresses would be fed into the computer. He also announced that the government had accepted the offer from the British Computer Society to inspect the safeguards for the information.[50] Public anxieties were somewhat allayed by those announcements and by the earlier statements from two people, one a computer expert and the other a member of the Society for Individual Freedom, who had visited Somerset House and declared their satisfaction with the security procedures.[51]

The decline in the volume of protest also resulted because other events, unrelated to the census, provided distraction for the newspapers. Lord Longford visited a Soho strip club in preparation for his motion in the House of Lords on pornography. In the same week there were allegations of a leak of information about the collapse of the Vehicle and General Insurance Company and suggestions that the Department of Trade and Industry had known in November of the leak before the collapse in March.

The 1971 census had provided the most dramatic example of the growth of privacy concerns. Still, no one attempted a rigorous definition of the concept. Yet in that fact probably lay its residual strength, which provided fertile soil for other concerns to grow apace. The concerns were nourished by developments that individually aroused little anxiety. Each new use for a computer seemed beneficial—for example, to organize the American Bar Association's meeting in London.[52] The Parliamentary activities of M.P.'s were to be placed on a computer for analysis by Political Reference Publications.[53] Electoral roles were still sold to debt firms and pools organizations.[54] The *Police Review* described the capabilities of the Home Office central computer, scheduled to be operational in 1974, as "a programme which is to be far more comprehensive than any other computerised intelligence service in the world."[55] But a danger was foreseen that "once a person is in the system he may remain there—there is no means of opting out until the Police consider the subject has reached the age of criminal ineffectiveness."

Along with the new uses occurred new proposals to regulate the computers. In July 1971 Leslie Huckfield initiated a consolidated fund debate on the control of personal information stored in computers. In a short speech he said that his greatest fear arose from the possible integration of data from the various computers operated by the government—integration that would be much easier than in the United States because the United Kingdom began with nationally integrated systems.[56] Seven months later Huckfield was given leave to introduce his Control of Personal Information Bill, which had first been introduced in 1971.[57] The bill had been drafted by Joseph Jacob, an NCCL executive member, following the November 1970 workshop on data banks. According to Huckfield: "Basically, what the Bill does is to set up a data bank tribunal, and to establish a comprehensive legal framework to govern and regulate the supply of private and confidential personal information."[58] He explained that he wanted to avoid the entanglements of the philosophical argument about privacy. Nevertheless, he did voice this general concern:

> We all ought to have the right to be let alone. We all ought to have the right to personal anonymity if we want to drop out of things for a time, just fade out for a time—go unrecognised for a time, which is certainly blissful sometimes in our present occupation. That is a fundamental right which despite the fact that we live in a fairly crowded island we should enjoy.
>
> . . . we all have some right to control the quality and quantity of information about ourselves.[59]

Discussion of the bill ended when the House automatically adjourned at four o'clock during the second reading debate. The minister of state for the home department, Mark Carlisle, probably correctly assessed the feelings of the members when he suggested that legislation should await the report of the Younger Committee.

Other events provoked unsettling questions about the control of information, especially that collected and held by government departments. The *Guardian* demonstrated the ease with which someone could telephone a government office, or a bank, and gather details about an individual.[60] There was an allegation that the Department of Health and Social Security was helping the police trace illegal immigrants.[61] A slightly different issue was raised by Leslie Huckfield when he asked the home secretary about reports that the police were passing information about individuals to professional bodies.[62] Methods of collecting information were the subject of criticism in questions asked about the Social Security investigators who were charged with determining whether a woman was ineligible for supplementary benefits because she was cohabiting with a man.[63]

ii

Some of these issues were discussed by the Younger Committee in its report published on 12 July 1972; others were not, because of the committee's limited terms of reference. The significance of that limitation was emphasized by the results of the public-opinion survey sponsored by the committee. According to the survey, most people valued privacy as the antithesis of totalitarian government.[64] Even so, the committee could investigate neither the National Health Service nor the Department of Health and Social Security. And, most important, it was prevented from considering the computers operated by the government. The report did, however, summarize the public's reaction against computers:

> Almost all the more credible of these apprehensions, however, relate to the use or possible use of computers by central or local governments, in particular to those in the hands of the police, the Inland Revenue and the health and social services, all of which are outside our terms of reference.[65]

Further confirmation of the public's primary concern came from the most intense negative reaction in the survey, which hypothesized a computer that would make available to anyone who asked for it details about an individual's life "such as family circumstances, financial situation, political views and so on." Respondents were asked whether this central computer was an invasion of privacy, whether they would be annoyed by it, and whether it should be prohibited by law. Seventy percent said that they would regard it as an invasion of privacy, that they would be very annoyed, and that it should be prohibited by law. The next-highest percentage giving all three of the extreme responses was 55 percent for an example of a newspaper's reporting the details of a will.[66] The results might have been somewhat distorted because the survey was taken during the discussion of the 1971 census. But it was clear that the committee was not able to examine the issue that most concerned the public.

Besides that inability, a second major theme in the report was the inability to define satisfactorily what was meant by *privacy*. The majority of the committee concluded that the concept had two aspects: "freedom from intrusion upon oneself, one's home, family and relationships"; and "the right to determine for oneself how and to what extent information about oneself is communicated to others."[67] The committee devoted most of its attention to the second aspect because it felt that the first did not need protection of new laws. For instance, after considering complaints about prying by neighbors and landlords, the committee concluded: "We do not think that the practices of neighbours and landlords are so new or offensive or have so changed in character as to justify any change in the law."[68]

This last statement was an example of the third theme of the majority's report. If existing social or legal restraints were sufficient to deter invasions of privacy, the committee saw no need to examine the issues Only if new invasions threatened to overwhelm traditional defenses did the committee investigate. In the words of the majority report, the committee wanted to discover

> whether there is evidence of a substantial body of serious complaint for which the law at present provides no remedy; whether the threat to privacy is growing, either on account of the introduction of new technology or of other new developments in industrial society; and whether any evil which exists or which may develop in the near future seems likely to be checked satisfactorily by other social forces without further assistance from the law.[69]

The result of the combination of these three themes (the exclusion from examining governmental actions, the inability to define *privacy*, and the concentration upon new threats) was the majority's rejection of a general right to privacy and their recommendation of solutions for specific problems. Another important influence upon the content of the report was the majority's view of the proper function of the courts. In their opinion, to allow the courts to interpret a general statute would make the law too uncertain and extend the judicial role "too far into the determination of controversial questions of a social and political character."[70] The most objectionable result of this uncertainty would be its detrimental effect upon the publication of news and opinion.

The committee made recommendations in each of the fourteen areas into which it had divided the privacy issue. Six topics received only brief consideration. Two of the areas, prying neighbors and noise were not considered to involve significant problems. Consideration of issues that fell under the rubric of medicine had been excluded by the terms of reference. The committee thought that the recommendations made after the disturbances at Warwick University would remedy most of the problems in the area of education. Employment considerations were viewed as essentially the concern of unions and management although the committee did make minor suggestions. Banks were advised to be more careful about divulging information over the telephone and to inform the customer of requests for information about him. In a seventh area, broadcasting, minor changes were recommended in the procedure or scope of the existing complaints bodies. In those seven areas the committee repeatedly sought to implement a principle that the individual should be aware of information collected about him and the uses made of it.

A similar guide was also suggested for credit-rating bureaus. The committee felt that the volume of complaints was not serious enough to warrant "serious imposition" on the industry; it did, however, propose that any individual denied credit should be told the reasons for the refusal. To protect the bureaus, the committee recommended that each bureau have qualified privilege for its reports.[71]

Although it based its recommendations concerning credit bureaus in part upon the number of complaints that it received, the committee was not generally swayed by quantity of complaints. Instead, it seemed to rely upon its own subjective evaluation of the quality of the complaints. That reliance was apparent in two other areas, sales-promotion methods and private detectives. Sales-promotion methods included mailings of advertising material, door-to-door salesmen, telephone callers, and market survey polls. The home office and M.P.'s had received an "exceptional number of complaints," and the committee itself had received a large number. Yet the report did not recommend legal sanctions.[72] The committee explained that it thought that no new action was necessary because of the ease with which the annoyance could be ended: postal matter could be discarded, the door could be closed, or a telephone conversation ended. This argument exemplified the committee's tendency not to recommend new laws unless traditional remedies were thought inadequate.

Unlike sales-promotional methods, few complaints were received about private detectives. Even so, it was the committee's opinion that "a small, though in our view significant, number of people had come into contact with the work of private detectives."[73] The committee wrote: "The work of private detectives is of exceptional concern to us because invasion of privacy is the essence of it."[74] Evidence given by the police had revealed that ex-criminals were operating as private detectives and that some private detectives had broken the law in order to obtain information. From that evidence the committee concluded that only "fit and proper" persons should be allowed to be private detectives.[75] The propriety of an invasion of privacy by a private detective, even a "fit and proper" one, was never considered.

Private detectives were also discussed, along with industrial espionage, under the topic of technical surveillance devices. Only one member of the public wrote to complain, and no mention of the subject occurred in the survey definitions. The committee, however, reserved its strongest recommendations for this topic: surrepititious use of surveillance devices should be a criminal offense, and there should be a new tort to allow recovery of damages for unlawful surveillance.[76] These recommendations epitomized the committee's preoccupation with new problems for which there were no apparent traditional defenses. Its aim was "to set at rest the reasonable fear of the public"—summarized as the "widespread if vague fear that they [technical devices] may be used, and a general belief that their use is damaging to innocent individuals and offensive to public feeling."[77] As explained in the report the use of surveillance devices was harmful when a person's expectations of seclusion were violated. The complaint was aggravated because the individual could take no steps to avoid the surveillance.[78] Thus, this explanation was closely related to the problem that arose throughout the report: an individual was wronged when his expectations were violated or when he was not told of information gathered about him.

Like the apprehension surrounding the use of technological devices, the fear of computers was also vague and uncertain. But because the committee was unable to make recommendations about the computers that caused the most anxiety, its major proposals lacked significant content. It suggested that a voluntary code of conduct be formalized for the handling of computerized personal information; it also advised the government to establish a permanent body to investigate and report upon developments in the computer field.[79]

Throughout the report the committee decided in favor of procedures rather than substance: it suggested or approved programs to review consumer credit developments, magistrates to license private detectives, complaints councils for broadcasting, and a permanent overseer for the computer industry. Nowhere was this difference between procedure and substance clearer than when "the press" was discussed. Fearful of the harmful effect a general right to privacy would have upon freedom of the press, the committee thought it best that the Press Council continue to exercise its vigilance over the performance of newspapers. The majority of the committee were convinced that the Press Council had improved the standards of newspapers. But they did believe that the public's respect for the council would be increased if half of the membership were lay (nonjournalist). In addition, to make future decisions more predictable and to guide the newspapers, the council was advised to codify its privacy decisions.[80]

There was no dissent from the specific recommendations that have been briefly summarized. What disagreement there was arose over the importance of the gaps in the report's proposals. Fourteen of the members concluded that the remaining gaps were insignificant and that even if they became significant other specific remedies were possible. They argued that it was better to continue an ad hoc approach than to hamper severely the dissemination of facts by a more general statute.[81]

Both of the dissenting members, Alexander Lyon, M.P., and Donald Ross, Q.C., favored a general right to privacy. Ross emphasized the United Kingdom's acceptance of the various international declarations of rights, which included sections about privacy. Otherwise the two opinions were alike in their rejection of the majority's reasoning. Although there was a failure to argue directly with the majority, Lyon's minority report offers the starkest contrasts. Unconstrained by the terms of reference, he urged that a general right be adopted because it would limit the government.[82] Within the terms of reference he did not perceive the problem of definition as insurmountable. Lyon agreed that the concept of privacy was vague, but he thought that for the purpose of the law "privacy is what the law says it is."[83] The majority's third theme—the bias for new problems without a traditional remedy—was used by Lyon as a reason for a general right. Because no one could foresee all future developments, it would be better to enact a general principle and allow the courts to develop the protection. He did not explain how the courts would develop protection from a law that delimited the meaning of privacy.

The majority had been influenced by their three themes and had favored voluntary procedural protection. Lyon rejected, or adapted, the three themes and wrote of the voluntary bodies: "Like the Highway Code and the Ten Commandments they would be improved by a legal deterrent."[84] He also disagreed with the verdict of the majority about the extent of the problem; he believed that even if the number of people whose privacy was invaded were small "the consequences for the person affected may be catastrophic."[85] Because the effect was so severe, he thought that an individual should have a civil remedy for intrusion upon his privacy. And he considered it an advantage that a jury would be able to express the public's opinion of a particular act.[86]

Probably the most important difference between the two positions was in their view of the function of the law. The majority had excluded the courts from deciding social and political questions and had implicitly argued that the law should intervene only if traditional protections were not likely to be adequate. In disagreeing, Lyon thought that the courts were uniquely capable of balancing "conflicting freedoms."[87] And he explained his concept of the proper function of the law when he said that he preferred "a society where a zeal for the truth is matched by compassion and where even the weakest of our fellow citizens knows that he can call upon the law in his unequal fight with those powerful interests, including the government, who abuse his freedom."[88]

iii

Nearly twelve months passed before the report was debated in Parliament. Events in the interim only highlighted the issues involved in the earlier discussions of privacy. Among those events, the most widely publicized was the attempted "bugging" of the Democratic party headquarters in the Watergate complex in Washington, D.C. As more information became known, it was inevitable that comparisons were drawn between the United States and the United Kingdom. Prominent among the comparisons were discussions of the British press and restrictions imposed by the Official Secrets Act, libel laws, and contempt of court rules. The comparison showed the British press to be more restricted than its American counterpart.

Any inclination to eliminate those restrictions was lessened by the conduct of the British press. On two occasions publicity about Princess Anne recalled similar controversies that had surrounded Princess Margaret nearly twenty years earlier. In December 1972 a faction of the Royal Society for the Prevention of Cruelty to Animals (RSPCA) announced that it had spies to inform on Princess Anne's participation in blood sports. The *Times*, in a second leader entitled "Princess Anne's Right to Privacy," contended that since fox hunting was neither illegal nor a substantial nuisance, the RSPCA should not interfere with her participation in the sport.[89] In the spring of 1973 newspaper reporters' attempts to learn if Princess Anne were to be engaged were thwarted and did not reach the offensive scale of the speculations about Princess Margaret. When Princess Anne's engagement was announced, it occurred during the publicity about the most acute privacy episode of the period before the debates on the Younger Committee.

On 22 May 1973 Lord Lambton, Parliamentary under secretary of state for defense for the Royal Air Force (RAF), resigned and declared that he would not stand again for Parliament. This resignation came at a time when allegations of corruption concerning an architect, John Poulson, were spreading through local government and threatening to reach into the Cabinet itself, at a time of suggestions of presidential involvement in criminal activities in the United States, and, at a time when the financial arrangements of companies such as Lonrho were bringing into disrepute the institutions of government and business.[90] Thus the knowledge that Lord Lambton had resigned because of his association with prostitutes and because he had taken drugs added to the existing malaise. Lord Jellicce, Lord Privy Seal, also resigned after rumors were published that other members of the government were involved with call girls.[91]

Edward Heath, the prime minister, immediately announced a security commission, headed by Lord Diplock, to investigate the implications of the two resignations. While Parliament was in recess for Whitsun, the issues were complicated by the disclosure that the *News of the World* had secreted cameras and a tape recorder in a room to record Lord Lambton in bed with a prostitute. In its defense the *News of the World* said that it had acted to collect material for legal evidence and not for publication.[92] Thus, like the resignation of John Profumo a decade earlier, matters of national security again prompted questions about the relevance of the private lives of public men and questions about the propriety of newspaper activities.

For a short period there was much discussion about Lord Lambton and the *News of the World*. The Press Council decided to investigate the matter before a formal complaint was made, though their report was not published until March 1974.[93] Opinion polls showed that the public was uncertain of its reaction to the resignations.[94] This uncertainty tended to resolve into the belief that private conduct of Ministers was immaterial so long as they did not get caught.[95]

The House of Lords debated the report of the Younger Committee before Lord Diplock completed his investigation. The debate was little more than a summary of the report without any extension of the conclusions of the privacy committee.[96]

Before the House of Commons debated the privacy recommendations, additional facts were revealed that underlined the problems discussed in the Younger Report. In June 1973 the *Times* headlined an article entitled "Turnover of Bugging Industry in Britain 'Above £1m a Year.' "[97] Less than a month later, one of the men mentioned in the article was fined under the Wireless Telegraphy Act 1967 for illegally manufacturing miniature radio microphones.[98] Also in June, two draft laws to protect privacy were placed before the Council of Europe.[99] A new complaint found a home under the privacy rubric when Harry Ewing complained to the home secretary about firms requiring persons paying by check to be photographed.[100]

There were also a number of actions taken in response to the Younger Report. The Press Council refused to reconstitute itself with half its total membership coming from nonjournalists. It did agree, however, that half the membership of its complaints committee would be lay persons, and it proposed to codify its privacy decisions.[101] The British Computer Society published a Code of

Good Practice.[102] A working party that had begun concurrently with the Younger Committee and the 1971 Census discussed the privacy issues raised by surveys and data collection.[103] Their report, *Survey Research and Privacy*, recommended that the standing review committee suggested by the Younger Committee extend its scope to include data collection and survey research. An action that did not evolve from the Younger Report but that was relevant both because it responded to the allegations of corruption and because it involved privacy issues was the prime minister's proposal to establish a voluntary public register of M.P.'s' financial interests.[104]

When the House of Commons began its series of three debates on the Official Secrets Act, the Diplock Commission, and the Younger Committee Report, it was faced with an intricate set of difficulties. Privacy was only of tangential importance in the Franks Report on the Official Secrets Act.[105] A poorly attended House of Commons heard the home secretary say that the government was considering a revision of the controversial Section 2 of the act, but that a criminal sanction was needed to protect information held by the government about a private individual.[106] Questions of privacy were also not of central concern to the security commission's report on Lord Lambton and Lord Jellicoe. The primary risk, according to the commission, had arisen from Lord Lambton's use of drugs and not from his association with prostitutes.[107] The prime minister made a statement in the House of Commons and announced the government's acceptance of the security recommendations.[108] Questions about a minister's private life were not discussed.

The House of Commons considered the Younger Report in an adjournment debate initiated by the home secretary, Robert Carr.[109] Carr first said that the government accepted the recommendation against a general right. Then, after stating that the government was going to consider legal curbs on harassment and pestering by newspapers and broadcasting, he explained the government's observations on the remainder of the report. For the Opposition, Shirley Williams concentrated upon the increased concern for privacy that resulted from the "widespread technological revolution."[110] Another twelve speakers commented upon various aspects of the report. The issue of press intrusion, and particularly the use of bugging devices by reporters, was raised by five M.P.'s, two of whom were journalists. The only new suggestion was Dr. David Owen's proposal that the newspapers establish a fund from which sums could be paid to individuals whose complaints about intrusion were upheld by the Press Council.[111]

Concluding the debate for the Opposition, Alexander Lyon argued for a general right to privacy that would allow opposing arguments to be balanced by the courts rather than by the intruder:

> There must be some mechanism to correct the imbalance that exists in the fact that the intruder himself decides the issue. He may have a commercial reason for deciding in his own favour, and that may overcome any humanitarian instincts of sympathy for the victim.[112]

iv

The debate neither resulted in legislative action nor concluded discussion of the questions raised by claims of a right to privacy. In September 1973 four private detectives were fined for pretending to be government officials in order to gather information about applicants for credit or hire purchase.[113] At Nottingham Crown Court a judge and jury were shown a videotape of the defendant driving—in order to support charges of dangerous driving.[114] Another technological innovation, the "infinity bug," was discussed at a conference of British executives who were concerned about the rapid increase in industrial espionage.[115]

Certain of the Younger Committee's recommendations would have been enacted had the Consumer Credit Bill become law,[116] but the bill was lost when Parliament was dissolved for the 1974 general election. The bill would have established a consumer credit commission, individuals would have been given new remedies against credit bureaus, and canvassing by telephone would have become illegal unless initiated by the prospective debtor.[117]

Another measure that was lost was Kenneth Marks's Rehabilitation of Offenders Bill, which would have allowed persons to keep secret their previous criminal convictions if after a specified number of years they had no further convictions.[118] In 1972 Lord Gardiner had introduced a similar bill, which was passed by the House of Lords but not debated in the House of Commons.[119] Lord Gardiner explained that the bill resulted from a committee set up in December 1970 representing a number of organizations concerned with the difficulties imposed upon persons who early in life served a prison sentence of less than two years. The storage of data in computers had increased those concerns.[120] The concept of privacy was not a factor in the debate. When speaking during the debate, on the

Younger Report, however, Lord Gardiner contended that his bill had been drafted with the intention of protecting privacy.[121] No one else so perceived the bill. Instead, the proponents argued in favor of removing the extra penalties, which amounted to a life sentence, paid by people who had lived exemplary lives after serving their prison terms. Opposition came from those who claimed that the bill authorized lies and would complicate newspaper reporting and the writing of biographies.

The general election of 1974 interrupted the discussions on these subjects. Only the Conservative party included proposals to protect privacy in its manifesto; neither the Labour nor the Liberal party mentioned the subject. Shortly after the election, however, privacy issues briefly returned to prominence with the report of the Press Council on the Lambton affair. There were tangential issues, but of the "bugging" and secret photography the council said:

> Nobody can justify bugging or secret photography for a dishonest purpose or for the purpose of making a profit serving merely private ends and the Council would never condone them when so used. The difficulty is when they are used to frustrate dishonesty or to prevent serious public ill.[122]

The council accepted that the *News of the World* had "kept in touch with the police" during its inquiries into organized crime and prostitution in London. But it offered no opinion about the propriety of the secret photography. The council did say that anyone who used such methods "employs them at the risk of his own reputation and nothing but success is an acceptable excuse." The council proposed no criteria for defining success and no limitation to the use of bugging devices or secret photography.[123] At the end of the report was a statement of the purpose of the press:

> It is a function of the Press to inform the public and it is necessary to bear in mind that it discharges this function on a commercial basis and it cannot on any other terms survive as a free and independent medium. Certainly the Press shares with members of the public the responsibility of reporting to the proper authorities when it has substantial evidence of crime. But the Press is not an arm of the executive. And circumstances may arise when it can reasonably see it as a part of its duty to call public attention to matters about which it suspects the executive is not functioning satisfactorily. Where the subject is ripe for legitimate public debate the

> Press must be free to investigate and report so that debate may take place.[124]

A not-so-veiled hint of legislative action came from a Conservative M.P., John Gorst, who termed the report "pathetic and cynical." He said that it revealed "the gross inadequacy of the Press Council machinery as a watchdog in the interests of both press and public."[125] The NCCL said that the report emphasized the need for a statutory right to privacy. The *News of the World* said that it was unable to defend itself because there was no privilege for procedures before the Press Council. The final word came from Lord Lampton, who said that his privacy had not been invaded.[126]

10

Epilogue

After publication of the Younger Report, private organizations followed certain of the committee's recommendations. But there has been no corresponding legislative response to the issues discussed in the report. What has occurred has been a ready and regular inclusion of new problems under the privacy rubric. Old problems also retain their vitality and make periodic appearance at the forefront of public concern. But since the Younger Report, discussion of privacy has perhaps become less audible. Economic crises may have ended the intellectual leisure that seems required for extended consideration of concepts such as privacy. But there is no indication that the concept of privacy has outlived its appeal.

It is difficult to explain the paradox of continuing popular concern for privacy without any new legal protection. One reason may lie in the malleable nature of the concept of privacy. The concept's appeal comes from the ease with which diverse concerns can be described in terms of the concept. Yet that same ease has made many people reluctant to give the courts an opportunity to manipulate the concept.

At first privacy appeared as a perquisite of the aristocracy. Samuel Warren, for example, thought that the public had no proper interest in his wedding. Likewise, for St. John Ervine, club life became intolerable because of gossip published in newspapers. The years after the Second World War revealed a significantly broader appeal for the concept. The aristocratic element still existed—one need only recall Captain Robert Cecil's wedding and the uninvited photographer. By then, however, the notion of privacy had come to embrace more than the belief that certain journalists intruded too much into people's private lives. Government had become a force that affected individuals without regard to status. Objectors to that force adopted the vocabulary of rights from the rhetoric of post-war discussions. The same objectors relied upon the concept of privacy to provide a pedigree for their arguments. Furthermore, out of the Second World War also came technological devices that later were the source of fear that privacy was threatened.

Each development that provoked claims of a right to privacy also brought an exhibition of the concept's elasticity. Such was the ease of expanding the notion of privacy that it came to embrace opposites: those who objected to the activities of the press complained about the use of true information; those who considered threats from computers complained about the use of false information. Yet both groups easily phrased their arguments in the rhetoric of the privacy debate.

A concept flexible enough to comprise opposite ideas is not a likely subject for legislation. This is an especially valid conclusion in a political system such as that of the United Kingdom where the constitution depends upon Parliamentary action (a legislative-executive combination). In the United States, however, protection of rights is primarily the function of the judiciary. Statutes in the United Kingdom require greater specificity to allow for the more limited judicial role. A statute that creates a right to privacy would be an anomaly in the British system of government. Insofar as this is true, the increasing calls for legislation may foreshadow a fundamental shift of power between the courts and Parliament—a shift instituted primarily by members of Parliament.

But privacy has been more than an anomalous candidate for legislative protection. It has been a source of confusion. Because respect for privacy is an integral part of the British character, it has proved to be an unassailable concept: to assert the right is to conclude the argument. But the use of the concept of privacy without further analysis creates an overly simple image of the issues involved. Behind the façade constructed by those who have claimed a right to privacy lie a number of different issues that involve applications of such fundamental concepts as *justice* or *fairness*, *liberty* or *autonomy*. Rarely is the distinction between *public* and *private* only. In part, the erection of that façade represents recognition that, because concepts such as liberty no longer belong only to a select group, they must be expressed in terms that do not evoke connotations of an elite status. But in popularizing the concept it has all too often been made trivial.

Table of Cases

List of Abbreviations in Notes

Birkett Committee	Report of the Committee of Privy Councillors appointed to inquire into the interception of communications (1957; Cmnd. 283)
Civil Liberty	Annual report of the National Council for Civil Liberties
NCCL Bulletin	The bulletin of the National Council for Civil Liberties, published approximately seven times each year
Porter Committee	Report of the Committee on the Law of Defamation (1948; Cmd. 7536)
Press and the People	Annual reports of the Press Council (and, earlier, the General Council of the Press)
Ross Committee	Report of the Royal Commission on the Press 1947–1949 (1949; Cmd. 7700)
Shawcross Committee	Report of the Royal Commission on the Press 1961–1962 (1962; Cmnd. 1811)
Warren and Brandeis	Samuel Warren and Louis Brandeis, "The Right to Privacy," *Harvard Law Review* 4 (December 1890): 193–220
Wolfenden Committee	Report of the Committee on Homosexual Offences and Prostitution (1957; Cmnd. 247)
Younger Committee	Report of the Committee on Privacy (1972; Cmnd. 5012)

Notes

Introduction

1. Younger Committee, p. 1.

2. Ralph Waldo Emerson, *English Traits*, ed. Howard Mumford Jones (Cambridge, Mass.: Harvard University Press, 1966), p. 70.

3. Erwin Schrödinger, "Equality and Relativity of Freedom," *Listener* 13 (5 June 1935): 953.

4. George Orwell, "The Lion and the Unicorn," *The Collected Essays, Journalism and Letters of George Orwell*, vol. 2, *My Country Right or Left 1940–1943*, ed. Sonia Orwell and Ian Angus (Harmondsworth: Penguin Books, 1970), p. 77.

5. Warren and Brandeis.

Chapter 1: The Warren and Brandeis Argument

1. Warren and Brandeis, p. 196.

2. Ibid., p. 195.

3. Ibid., p. 193.

4. Ibid., p. 193.

5. Ibid., p. 198.

6. Thomas M. Cooley, *A Treatise on the Law of Torts*, 2d. ed. (Chicago: Callaghan & Company, 1888), p. 29. Warren and Brandeis, p. 195. Judge Cooley also wrote *A Treatise on Constitutional Limitations*, a work described as most responsible for the shift in emphasis of the Supreme Court of the United States from procedural to substantive due process and the accompanying acceptance of laissez-faire economic theory. Sidney Fine, *Laissez Faire and the General-Welfare State* (Ann Arbor: University of Michigan Press, Ann Arbor Paperbacks, 1964), p. 162, and Clyde E. Jacobs, *Law Writers and the Courts* (Berkeley: University of California Press, 1954), p. 27.

7. Cooley, *Treatise on Torts*, p. 24.

8. It is worth mentioning that on pages 67 and 69 of Cooley's *Treatise on*

Torts, intrusion upon the privacy of the home is mentioned as an actionable wrong even though no pecuniary loss was suffered.

9. Cf. Warren and Brandeis, pp. 198, 205.
10. Ibid., p. 197.
11. Ibid., p. 194 n. 5.
12. (1613) 9 Co. Rep. 111b; 77 E.R. 895.
13. 77 E.R. 895 at 899.
14. *Russell* v. *Corne* (1704) 2 Ld. Raym. 1031; 92 E.R. 185 at 186.
15. *Satterthwaite* v. *Dewhurst* (1785) 4 Dougl. 315; 99 E.R. 899. Cf. *Grinnell* v. *Wells* (1844) 7 Man. & G. 1033; 135 E.R. 419 at 423 per Tindal C. J., who refused damages because the fourteen-year-old girl supported herself.
16. *Irwin* v. *Dearman* (1809) 11 East. 23; 103 E.R. 912.
17. *Dodd* v. *Norris* (1814) 3 Camp. 519; 170 E.R. 1467.
18. *Thompson* v. *Ross* (1858) 5 H. & N. 16; 157 E.R. 1082 at 1083.
19. *Flemington* v. *Smithers* (1826) 2 Car. & P. 292; 172 E.R. 131.
20. *Hedges* v. *Tagg* (1872) L.R. 7 Ex. 283 at 285.
21. Warren and Brandeis, p. 198.
22. Ibid., p. 198.
23. Ibid., p. 205.
24. Ibid.
25. (1848) 2 De G. & Sm. 652; 64 E.R. 293 (V. Ch.): (1849) 1 Mac. & G. 25; 41 E.R. 1171 (Ch.).
26. 64 E.R. 293 at 300.
27. Ibid., at 301.
28. Ibid.
29. Warren and Brandeis, p. 199.
30. Ibid., p. 200.
31. Ibid., pp. 204–5.
32. Ibid., p. 205.
33. Ibid.
34. Ibid., p. 207.
35. 64 E.R. 293 at 308.
36. (1774) 4 Burr. 2408; 98 E.R. 257.
37. 64 E.R. 293 at 310.
38. Ibid., at 311.
39. Ibid.
40. Ibid., at 312.
41. Ibid.
42. Ibid.
43. Ibid., at 313.
44. Warren and Brandeis, p. 199 n. 5; 64 E.R. 293 at 311–12.
45. Warren and Brandeis, p. 199.
46. Ibid., p. 199 n. 6; 64 E.R. 293 at 311.

47. 64 E.R. 293 at 311.

48. 64 E.R. 293 at 312. *Southey* v. *Sherwood* (1817) 2 Mer. 435; 35 E.R. 1006 at 1007.

49. Warren and Brandeis, p. 200 n. 3. *Gee* v. *Pritchard* (1818) 2 Swanst. 402; 36 E.R. 670.

50. 36 E.R. 670 at 678.

51. Warren and Brandeis, p. 200.

52. Ibid., p. 199.

53. Another of Warren and Brandeis's sources accepted this argument rather than Warren and Brandeis's. New York Superior Court Justice Duerr wrote that the sole foundation of the right was "the right which every man has to the exclusive possession and control of the products of his own labor." *Woolsey* v. *Judd* (1855) 4 Duer. 379 at 386. Cited by Warren and Brandeis, p. 200 n. 3.

54. Warren and Brandeis, p. 201.

55. Ibid., pp. 201–2.

56. *Times* (London), 7 November 1848, p. 7; *Sun* (London), 5 November 1848, p. 3.

57. 41 E.R. 1171 at 1178.

58. Warren and Brandeis, p. 204.

59. Ibid., p. 202; 64 E.R. 293 at 311.

60. Warren and Brandeis, pp. 204–5.

61. (1769) 4 Burr. 2303; 98 E.R. 201.

62. 98 E.R. 201 at 221.

63. Warren and Brandeis, p. 213.

64. Ibid., p. 213 n. 1.

65. (1825) 3 L.J. (o.s.) Ch. 209; Warren and Brandeis, p. 207. In 1835 Parliament passed the Lectures Publication Bill to prevent the publication of lectures without consent; a short debate was reported, 30 Hansard, 3d series, H.C. col. 953–54 (24 August 1835).

66. Warren and Brandeis, pp. 207–8.

67. 3 L.J. (o.s.) Ch. 209; Warren and Brandeis, p. 207.

68. 3 L.J. (o.s.) Ch. 209 at 219.

69. Ibid.

70. (1849) 1 McN. & G. 25; 41 E.R. 1171. Warren and Brandeis, p. 208.

71. 41 E.R. 1171 at 1177.

72. Ibid., at 1178.

73. Ibid.

74. Warren and Brandeis, pp. 204–5.

75. Ibid., p. 205.

76. (1843) 2 Hare 383; 67 E.R. 157.

77. 41 E.R. 1171 at 1179.

78. Ibid.

79. (1887) 19 Q.B.D. 629; Warren and Brandeis, p. 208.

80. (1888) 40 Ch.D. 345; Warren and Brandeis, p. 208.
81. Warren and Brandeis, p. 211.
82. (1854) 4 H.L.C. 815; 10 E.R. 681. Warren and Brandeis, p. 194 n. 6.
83. 10 E.R. 681 at 745.
84. *Caird* v. *Sime* (1887) 12 A.C. 326 at 343 H.L. (Sc.).
85. 2 Swanst. 402; 36 E.R. 670.
86. Warren and Brandeis, p. 212.
87. 36 E.R. 670 at 678.
88. E. J. MacGillivray, *Copyright in Letters* (London: Publisher's Association, 1907), p. 7.
89. Ibid., p. 14.
90. Warren and Brandeis, pp. 214–18.
91. Ibid., pp. 214–15.
92. Ibid., p. 215.
93. Ibid., p. 195 n. 7.

Chapter 2: Judicial Precedent in Britain

1. (1820) 1 J. & W. 394; 37 E.R. 425. Warren and Brandeis, p. 212.
2. (1851) 9 Hare 241; 68 E.R. 492. Warren and Brandeis, p. 212 n. 2.
3. 68 E.R. 492 at 498.
4. 68 E.R. 492 at 500.
5. (1843) 2 Hare 383; 67 E.R. 157.
6. 67 E.R. 157 at 161.
7. (1857) L.J. (n.s.) 26 Ch. 113 at 114.
8. (1857) L.J. (n.s.) 26 Ch. 113 at 116. This is consistent with principles of cases cited by Warren and Brandeis: *Southey* v. *Sherwood* (1817) 2 Mer. 435; 35 E.R. 1006 and *Hopkinson* v. *Lord Burghley* (1867) L.R. 2 Ch. 447.
9. (1577) Cary 62; 21 E.R. 33.
10. *Lord Say and Seal's Case* (1712) 10 Mod. 40; 88 E.R. 617.
11. *R.* v. *Thomas Baillie* (1778) 21 How. St. Tr. 1, 358–61.
12. *Doe ex dim. Jupp* v. *Andrews* (1778) 2 Cowp. 845; 98 E.R. 1393, per Lord Mansfield; *Du Barré* v. *Livette* (1791) Peake 108; 170 E.R. 96; *Duffin* v. *Smith* (1792) Peake 146; 170 E.R. 110, per Lord Kenyon; and *Sandford* v. *Remington* (1793) 2 Ves. Jun. 189; 30 E.R. 587, per Lord Chancellor Loughborough.
13. (1833) 1 My. & K. 98; 39 E.R. 618.
14. 39 E.R. 618 at 621.
15. 39 E.R. 618 at 621. See also *Annesley* v. *Earl of Anglesea* (1743) 17 How. St. Tr. 1139 at 1241, 1242.
16. *Lawrence* v. *Campbell* (1859) 4 Drewry 485; 62 E.R. 186 at 188.

17. *Wheeler* v. *Le Marchant* (1881) 17 Ch. D. 675 at 683 (C.A.).

18. *R.* v. *Cox and Railton* (1884) 14 Q.B.D. 153, per Stephen J.

19. *Bursill* v. *Tanner* (1885) 16 Q.B.D. 1, per Lord Esher M.R. See also *Lowden* v. *Blakey* (1889) 23 Q.B.D. 332.

20. *Cullier* v. *Cullier* (1590) Cro. Eliz. 201; 78 E.R. 457.

21. (1696) 13 How. St. Tr. 1.

22. Ibid., at 17.

23. Ibid.

24. *Harrison* v. *Southcote* (1751) 1 Atk. 528; 26 E.R. 333 at 340. See also *Paxton* v. *Douglas* (1812) 19 Ves. Jun. 225; 34 E.R. 502 at 503, per Lord Chancellor Eldon; and *Thorpe* v. *Macauley* (1820) 5 Madd. 218; 56 E.R. 877 at 882, per Vice-Chancellor Sir John Leach.

25. *Lamb* v. *Munster* (1882) 10 Q.B.D. 110 at 113.

26. *Adams* v. *Lloyd* (1858) 3 H. & N. 351; 157 E.R. 506 at 510, per Pollock C.B.; *R.* v. *Boyes* (1861) 1 B. & S. 311; 121 E.R. 730 at 738, per Cockburn C.J.; *Ex parte Reynolds* (1882) 20 Ch.D. 294 at 297, per Bacon C.J.

27. For a discussion of the origins of the right see Leonard W. Levy, *Origins of the Fifth Amendment* (New York: Oxford University Press, 1968).

28. *Pearse* v. *Pearse* (1846) 1 De G. & Sm. 12; 63 E.R. 950 at 957.

29. *Barker* v. *Dixie* (1736) Cas. t. Hard. 264; 95 E.R. 171.

30. *R.* v. *Cliviger* (1788) 2 T.R. 263; 100 E.R. 143 at 146.

31. *Monroe* v. *Twisleton* (1802) Peake Add. Cas. 219; 170 E.R. 250 at 251.

32. 14 & 15 Vict. c. 99.

33. *Stapleton* v. *Crofts* (1852) 18 Q.B. 367; 118 E.R. 137 at 138.

34. 118 E.R. 137 at 138.

35. (1826) 2 Car. & P. 325; 172 E.R. 147.

36. 172 E.R. 147 at 148.

37. *Foster* v. *The Bank of London* (1862) 3 F. & F. 214; 176 E.R. 96 at 98 (N.P.).

38. 176 E.R. 96 at 98.

39. *Hardy* v. *Veasey* (1868) L. Rep. 3 Exc. 107.

40. *Du Barré* v. *Livette* (1791) Peake 108; 170 E.R. 96 at 97.

41. *Greenlaw* v. *King* (1838) 1 Beav. 137; 48 E.R. 891 at 894.

42. *R.* v. *Hay* (1860) 2 F. & F. 4; 175 E.R. 933.

43. *Wheeler* v. *LeMarchant* (1881) 17 Ch. D. 675 at 681.

44. *R.* v. *Duchess of Kingston* (1776) 20 How. St. Tr. 355, 373.

45. *R.* v. *Gibbons* (1823) 1 Car. & P. 97; 171 E.R. 1117. And see *Broad* v. *Pitt* (1828) 3 Car. & P. 518; 172 E.R. 528 at 529 per Best C.J.

46. (1851) 14 Dunl. (Ct. of Sess.) 177.

47. Ibid., at 180.

48. (1900) 64 J. P. 241, 242.

49. *Cossey* v. *London, Brighton, and South Coast Railway Company* (1870) L.R. 5 C.P. 146; *Friend* v. *The London, Chatham, and Dover Railway Co.* (1877) L.R. 2 Ex 437 (C.A.).

50. *Lafone* v. *The Falkland Island Company* (No. 1) (1857) 4 K. & J. 34; 70 E.R. 14 at 15–16.

51. *Baker* v. *London and Southwestern Railway Company* (1867) L.R. 3 Q.B. 91 at 93. And for the same rule applied to an attorney who overheard negotiations between two parties, see *Griffith* v. *Davies* (1833) 5 B. & Ad. 502; 110 E.R. 876 (K.B.).

52. See, e.g., Warren and Brandeis, p. 213.

53. *Pearse* v. *Pearse* (1846) 1 De G. & Sm. 12; 63 E.R. 950 at 957.

54. Ibid., p. 196.

55. *Walter* v. *Selfe* (1851) 4 De G. & Sm. 315; 64 E.R. 849 at 852.

56. (1865) 11 H.L.C. 642; 11 E.R. 1483.

57. 11 E.R. at 1486.

58. Ibid., at 1488.

59. (1888) 40 Ch. D. 80 (C.A.).

60. Ibid., at 93–94.

61. Ibid., at 98.

62. Warren and Brandeis, p. 197.

63. *Edwards* v. *Wooton* (1607) 12 Co. Rep. 35; 77 E.R. 1316 at 1317.

64. *R.* v. *Burdett* (1820) 4 B. & Ald. 95; 106 E.R. 873 at 885.

65. 106 E.R. at 887.

66. *Parmiter* v. *Coupland* (1840) 6 M. & W. 105; 151 E.R. 340 at 342.

67. *Gathercole* v. *Miall* (1846) 15 M. & W. 319; 153 E.R. 872 at 880.

68. *Seymour* v. *Butterworth* (1862) 3 F. & F. 372; 176 E.R. 166 at 169. For other opinions by Cockburn C.J. see *Cox* v. *Feeney* (1863) 4 F. & F. 13; 176 E.R. 445 at 446; *Campbell* v. *Spottiswode* (1863) 3 B. & S. 769; 122 E.R. 288; and *Hedley* v. *Barlow* (1865) 4 F. & F. 224; 176 E.R. 541 at 543.

69. *Henwood* v. *Harrison* (1872) L.R. 7 C.P. 606 at 622; and *cf. Odger* v. *Mortimer* (1873) 28 L.T. 472 (C.P.).

70. *Merivale* v. *Carson* (1887) 20 Q.B.D. 275 (C.A.).

71. Ibid., at 280.

72. (1860) 5 H. & N. 536; 157 E.R. 1292 (Ex.).

73. 157 E.R. at 1293–94.

74. (1861) 9 H.L.C. 577; 11 E.R. 854.

75. Ibid., at 863.

76. (1884) 54 L.J. (n.s.) Q.B. 113 (C.A.).

77. Ibid., at 116.

78. James Fitzjames Stephen, *Liberty, Equality, Fraternity* (1874; reprint ed., Cambridge: Cambridge University Press, 1967).

79. Ibid., p. 151.

80. Ibid., pp. 161, 162.

81. *Taylor* v. *Blacklow* (1836) 3 Bing. N.C. 235; 132 E.R. 401 at 406.

82. *R* v. *Delaval* (1763) 3 Burr. 1434; 97 E.R. 913 at 915. The courts ex-

tended the common law to protect public morals and public decency as they felt necessary: *R.* v. *Mears and Chalk* (1851) 4 Cox C.C. 423 (C.C.A.); *Dugdale* v. *R.* (1853) 1 El. & Bl. 435; 118 E.R. 499.

83. *R.* v. *Bunyan and Morgan* (1844) 3 L.T. (o.s.) 453 (Cent. Crim. Ct.). The men were alone in the parlor of a public house; they had been seen by the barmaid through a window of another room separated from the parlor by a passage.

84. Ibid.

85. (1847) 2 Cox C.C. 376 (C.C.R.).

86. Ibid., at 377.

87. *R.* v. *Webb* (1848) 3 Cox C.C. 183 (C.C.R.).

88. 34 Ed. III c.1.

89. 4 Bl. Com. 168. In *Raffaelli* v. *Heatly* (1949) S.C. (J.) 101, the judges decided that an indictment for being a peeping Tom did exist in common law.

90. (1604) 5 Co. Rep. 91a; 77 E.R. 194.

91. 77 E.R. 194.

92. Ibid.

93. *In re Agar-Ellis*; *Agar-Ellis* v. *Lascelles* (1883) 24 Ch. D. 317 at 335.

94. (1765) 2 Wils. 275; 19 St. Tr. 1030; 95 E.R. 807; [1558–1774] All E.R. 41.

95. (1763) 19 St. Tr. 1153; 98 E.R. 489.

96. [1558–1774] All E.R. 41 at 45.

97. *Pringle* v. *Bremner and Sterling* (1867) 5 Macph (H.L.) 50.

98. Ibid., at 55.

99. (1670) 1 Mod. Rep. 55; 86 E.R. 727.

100. *Merest* v. *Harvey* (1814) 5 Taunt. 442; 128 E.R. 761.

101. 128 E.R. at 761.

102. (1867) L.R. 5 Eq. 25.

103. Ibid., at 33.

104. (1801) 4 Esp. 69; 170 E.R. 644.

105. (1811) 3 Camp. 80; 170 E.R. 1312.

106. Ibid., at 1313. Comparable cases with arguments for privacy without mention in the decision are *Renshaw* v. *Bean* (1852) 18 Q.B. 112; 118 E.R. 42; and *Hutchinson* v. *Copestake* (1861) 31 L.J. (n.s.) C.B. 19.

107. (1861) 30 L.J. (n.s.) Ch. 801.

108. Ibid., at 803.

109. *Johnson* v. *Wyatt* (1863) 2 De G. J. & S. 18; 46 E.R. 281 at 284 (C.A.).

110. (1862) 31 L.J. (n.s.) C.P. 110; (1862) 31 L.J. (n.s.) C.P. 342 (Exch. Ch.); (1865) 11 H.L.C. 290; 11 E.R. 1344 *sub nom Tapling* v. *Jones*.

111. 31 L.J. (n.s.) C.P. 110 at 115.

112. 31 L.J. (n.s.) C.P. 342 at 347.

113. Ibid., at 353.

114. 11 E.R. 1344 at 1350.

Chapter 3: Legislative Precedents before the First World War

1. 3 Parliamentary History, H.C. col. 131–32 (11 June 1643).

2. 34 Parliamentary History, H.C. col. 1006–14 (1799).

3. 41 Hansard, 1st series, H.C. col. 575–78 (1 December 1819).

4. 41 Hansard, 1st series, H.C. col. 1348 (20 December 1819).

5. Ibid., col. 1364–65.

6. See, e.g., motion by Sir Edward Bulwer Lytton, 23 Hansard, 3d series, H.C. col. 1193–1223 (22 May 1834).

7. 137 Hansard, 3d series, H.C. col. 774–814 (19 March 1855).

8. Ibid., col. 784.

9. 137 Hansard, 3d series, H.C. col. 1120 (26 March 1855).

10. Ibid., col. 1147, 1148.

11. 233 Hansard, 3d series, H.C. col. 935–36 (11 April 1877).

12. 155 Hansard, 3d series, H.C. col. 1368–75 (11 August 1859). A similar clause was also rejected two years earlier during the debate on the Divorce and Matrimonial Causes Bill, 147 Hansard, 3d series, H.C. col. 1758–59 (17 August 1857).

13. 155 Hansard, 3d series, H.C. col. 1373 (11 August 1859).

14. See, e.g., 199 Hansard, 3d series, H.C. col. 994 (1 March 1870); 242 Hansard, 3d series, H.C. col. 1638 (9 August 1878); 298 Hansard, 3d series, H.C. col. 1827–28 (7 July 1885); 310 Hansard, 3d series, H.C. col. 553 (3 February 1887); 313 Hansard, 3d series, H.C. col. 1660–73 (22 April 1887).

15. Report of the Royal Commission on Divorce and Matrimonial Causes (1912; Cd. 6478), p. 153 par. 494.

16. Ibid., p. 158 par. 518.

17. Ibid., pp. 156–57 par. 508, 511, 514.

18. *Scott* v. *Scott* [1913] A.C. 417.

19. Ibid., at 438.

20. Ibid., at 439.

21. "The Taste for Privacy and Publicity," *Spectator* 61 (9 June 1888): 782. A different view was expressed by Aline Gorren. "The Ethics of Modern Journalism," *Scribner's Magazine* 19 (April 1896): 507–13.

22. 22 Hansard, 3d series, H.C. col. 414–15 (18 March 1834). Cf. "The Libel Law," *Blackwood's Edinburgh Magazine* 51 (February 1842) 141–43.

23. 38 Hansard, 3d series, H.C. col. 489 (3 May 1837).

24. 66 Hansard, 3d series, H.L. col. 404 (13 February 1843).

25. Ibid.

26. Report from the Select Committee of the House of Lords appointed to Consider the Law of Defamation and Libel, *Parliamentary Papers 1843* 5 (513): 259–66.

27. 71 Hansard, 3d series, H.C. col. 878-90 (16 August 1843).

28. 9 Parliamentary History, H.C. col. 848 (16 April 1735).

29. 75 Hansard, 3d series, H.C. col 895, 897–98 (14 June 1844).

30. Report from the Secret Committee of the House of Lords Relative to the Post Office, *Parliamentary Papers 1844* 14 (601): 501.

31. Ibid.

32. Report of the Secret Committee on the Post Office, *Parliamentary Papers 1844* 14 (582): 505–602.

33. 77 Hansard, 3d series, H.C. col. 668 (18 February 1845).

34. Ibid., col. 672. Cf. Lord Howick's remarks at col. 894. See also the Earl of Radnor, 75 Hansard, 3d series, H.L. col. 974 (17 June 1844).

35. 77 Hansard, 3d series, H.C. col. 842–43 (20 February 1845). Similar questions were raised about the telegraph service when it was transferred to the government. The postmaster general, William Monsell, assured the House that messages were to be regarded as "strictly confidential communications." 206 Hansard, 3d series, H.C. col. 154 (4 May 1871).

36. 68 Hansard, 5th series, H.C. col. 222 (16 November 1914).

37. 69 Hansard, 5th series, H.C. col. 270 (8 February 1915). 258 Hansard, 3d series, H.C. col. 766 (14 February 1881).

38. 85 Hansard, 5th series, H.C. col. 587 (3 August 1916), col. 851–53 (8 August 1916).

39. 18 Hansard, 5th series, H.L. col. 705 (11 March 1915).

40. 98 Hansard, 5th series, H.C. col. 1270–71 (29 October 1917).

41. Ibid., col. 1271–73.

42. Ibid., col. 1283.

43. 14 Parliamentary History, H.C. col. 1317–65 (1753).

44. Ibid., col. 1318.

45. Ibid., col. 1320, 1323.

46. Ibid., col. 1320.

47. Ibid., col. 1330–31.

48. 35 Parliamentary History, H.C. col. 598–601 (19 November 1800).

49. Report from Select Committee on a General Register of all Deeds and Instruments affecting Real Property in England and Wales, *Parliamentary Papers 1831–1832* 18 (609): 372.

50. Report from the Select Committee on Parochial Registration, *Parliamentary Papers 1833* 14 (669): 505–15.

51. *Times* (London), 22 November 1841, p. 5. Questions were asked about the accuracy of the 1851 religious question: 114 Hansard, 3d series, H.C. col. 1316–17 (14 March 1851); 115 Hansard, 3d series, H.C. col. 112–14 (18 March 1851) and H.L. col. 629–33 (27 March 1851).

52. 159 Hansard, 3d series, H.C. col. 1696 (11 July 1860). Cf. resolution of Nonconformist ministers, *Times* (London), 7 June 1860, p. 12.

53. Ibid., col. 1702–15.

54. 347 Hansard, 3d series, H.C. col. 400 (21 July 1890).

55. *Times* (London), 13 February 1911, p. 13.

56. Ibid., 30 March 1911, p. 14.

57. Ibid., 4 April 1911, p. 10. The president of the local government board said that the number who evaded the census was negligible and that he would show mercy to those who did elude the count. 23 Hansard, 5th series, H.C. col. 2194 (5 April 1911).

Chapter 4: Early Complaints about Privacy

1. 40 Hansard, 5th series, H.L. col. 576 (10 June 1920).
2. Census Bill (1920) H.C. Bill 171.
3. 132 Hansard, 5th series, H.C. col. 2586 (4 August 1920).
4. 79 Hansard, 5th series, H.L. col. 420–21 (3 December 1930) and col. 467–68 (9 December 1930).
5. 245 Hansard, 5th series, H.C. col. 1455–59 (26 November 1930); 251 Hansard, 5th series, H.C. col. 801–2 (21 April 1931).
6. 252 Hansard, 5th series, H.C. col. 1601 (18 May 1931).
7. 329 Hansard, 5th series, H.C. col. 1720–21 (29 November 1937).
8. 328 Hansard, 5th series, H.C. col. 259 (28 October 1937) H.C. Bill 7.
9. 329 Hansard, 5th series, H.C. col. 1731–32 (29 November 1937).
10. Ibid., col. 1740.
11. Ibid., col. 1796. Cf. 331 Hansard, 5th series, H.C. col. 120 (1 February 1938) where he sought to point out the dangers to "personal privacy" in the original bill.
12. 329 Hansard, 5th series, H.C. col. 1820 (29 November 1937).
13. 331 Hansard, 5th series, H.C. col. 105–41 (1 February 1938).
14. Francis Williams, *The Right to Know* (London: Longmans, 1969), p. 104. Soon after the war, Labour MPs began to criticize the concentration of ownership and to request an investigation; see, e.g., 133 Hansard, 5th series, H.C. col. 1966 (28 October 1920), and remarks by Ramsay Macdonald, *Times* (London), 9 December 1922, p. 13.
15. Kennedy Jones, "Journalism, a Branch of Commerce," *Fortnightly Review* 107 (June 1920): 827. (Jones was a joint founder of the *Daily Mail* and *Daily Mirror*.) Jones's views were criticized by Arthur Bauman, "The Functions and Future of the Press," *Fortnightly Review* 107 (April 1920): 620–27.
16. *Report on the British Press* (London: PEP, 1938), p. 156.
17. Ibid.
18. Williams, *The Right to Know*, p. 117.
19. Stephen Leacock, "The British and the American Press," *Harper's Magazine* 145 (June 1922): 1.
20. *Times* (London), 20 February 1922, p. 5.
21. *Russell* v. *Russell, Times* (London), 8 July 1922, p. 4; 12 July 1922,

p. 5; 14 July 1922, p. 4; 15 July 1922, p. 4; 19 July 1922, p. 5; 20 July 1922, p. 5; 21 July 1922, p. 5; 22 July 1922, p. 5; 25 July 1922, p. 5.

22. 156 Hansard, 5th series, H.C. col. 2081 (19 July 1922).

23. *Times* (London), 21 February 1923, p. 5.

24. Ibid., 27 February 1923, p. 12.

25. Ibid., 12 March 1923, p. 7; 3 April 1923, p. 15.

26. H.C. Bill 136. 164 Hansard, 5th series, H.C. col. 248–52 (15 May 1923).

27. Hansard, 5th series, H.C. col. 746 (16 April 1926). The Institute of Journadists also remarked that competition had prevented a voluntary agreement against the publication of evidence. *Times* (London), 11 July 1923, p. 9.

28. Ibid., col. 733–816.

29. 194 Hansard, 5th series, H.C. col. 797 (16 April 1926).

30. 62 Hansard, 5th series, H.L. col. 141 (16 July 1925).

31. 53 Hansard, 5th series, H.L. col. 853 (24 April 1923).

32. 292 Hansard, 5th series, H.C. col. 2453 (31 July 1934); 308 Hansard, 5th series, H.C. col. 1949 (20 February 1936).

33. *Times* (London), 8 September 1923, p. 6. In 1924 Major Kindersley asked the home secretary if he would take action concerning the "ghoulish pictures" taken by newspaper photographers at the scene of a murder. 173 Hansard, 5th series, H.C. col. 911–12 (12 May 1924) and col. 1529 (15 May 1924).

34. *Times* (London), 25 November 1929, p. 15.

35. Ibid., 4 December 1929, p. 15.

36. "The Taste for Privacy and Publicity," *Spectator* 61 (9 June 1888): 782; see chap. 3, p. 63.

37. St. John Ervine, "The Invasion of Privacy," *Spectator* 138 (28 May 1927): 937–38.

38. *Dockrell* v. *Dougall* (1899) 80 L.T. 556. Three similar cases are *Monson* v. *Tussauds Limited* [1894] 1 Q.B. 671, in which the complaint involved a wax representation; *Corelli* v. *Wall* (1906) 22 T.L.R. 532, in which a not very good portrait was sold as a post card; and *Palmer* v. *The National Sporting Club, Ltd.* (1906) *MacGillivray's Copyright Cases* 55 (Ch. D.), in which a defeated boxer complained about the publication of his photograph.

39. *Sports and General Press Agency Limited* v. *"Our Dogs" Publishing Company, Ltd.* [1916] 2 K.B. 880 at 884.

40. Percy H. Winfield, "Privacy," *Law Quarterly Review* 47 (January 1931): 23.

41. *Tolley* v. *J.S. Fry & Sons, Ltd.* [1930] 1 K.B. 467.

42. Ibid., at 478 (citations omitted).

43. *Tolley* v. *J.S. Fry & Sons, Ltd.,* [1931] A. C. 333.

44. Winfield, "Privacy," pp. 23, 24.

45. Ibid., p. 30.

46. During the debate on Lord Mancroft's Right of Privacy Bill, Lord Conesford explained that counsel for Tolley were in his chambers at the time of the case and that all thought that success would depend upon a libel remedy; it had not occurred to anyone that they might succeed on a common law right to privacy. 229 Hansard, 5th series, H. L. col. 654 (13 March 1961).

47. 230 Hansard, 5th series, H.C. col. 608 (18 July 1929).

48. Williams, *The Right to Know*, pp. 107–19.

49. *Times* (London), 22 June 1933, p. 10.

50. Ibid., 23 June 1933, p. 10.

51. Ibid., 25 July 1933, p. 15.

52. Ibid., 23 October 1933, p. 15; 18 October 1933, p. 11.

53. Ibid., 27 January 1934, p. 7.

54. See J. H. Aitken's presidential address to the NUJ, Ibid., 31 March 1934, p. 7.

55. Letter from J. M. Denvir, ibid., 1 February 1934, p. 10.

56. 302 Hansard, 5th series, H.C. col. 1705–6 (4 June 1935).

57. H.C. Bill 110.

58. St. John Ervine, "Privacy and the Lindberghs," *Fortnightly Review* 139 (February 1936): 180–86.

59. Ibid., p. 180.

60. Ibid., p. 186.

61. 318 Hansard, 5th series, H.C. col. 2607–8 (17 December 1936).

62. *Times* (London), 20 January 1937, p. 4.

63. 319 Hansard, 5th series, H.C. col. 1052–53 (28 January 1937).

64. The earlier response was given three days before. 319 Hansard, 5th series, H.C. col. 574–75 (25 January 1937). Similar criticism was voiced after other coroners commented about press intrusions, 319 Hansard, 5th series, H.C. col. 1752–53 (4 February 1937).

65. The resolutions of the Newspaper Society, the Press Association, Limited, and Reuters were printed in 320 Hansard, 5th series, H.C. col. 558–60 (11 February 1937).

66. *Times* (London), 15 February 1937, p. 9.

67. Ibid., 2 March 1937, p. 18.

68. Ibid., 29 March 1937, p. 6.

69. *Times* (London), 4 January 1938, p. 13. Similarly, J. P. Collins wrote that if a principle for compensation could be fixed, then the legislators should act to limit the press intrusions on private grief and other aspects of private life. "The Cult of the Hyena," *Nineteenth Century* 123 (May 1938): 535–49.

70. *Report on the British Press*, pp. 36–37.

71. Ibid., p. 283.

72. (1938) H.C. Bill 18.

73. 343 Hansard, 5th series, H.C. col. 576 (3 February 1939).

74. Ibid., col. 603. See also the discussion "The Freedom of Our Press," *Listener* 20 (22 December 1938): 1337–38, 1370–71. And compare Kenneth Adam, "Press and Public," ibid., 17 (7 April 1937): 641–43.

75. Porter Committee, p. 5, par. 1.

76. H.C. Bill 250. 351 Hansard, 5th series, H.C. col. 288 (3 September 1939), col. 375–401 (4 September 1939), col. 474–91, 501 (5 September 1939). 114 Hansard, 5th series, H.L. col. 998–1002 (5 September 1939).

77. 123 Hansard, 5th series, H.L. col. 1–68 (2 June 1942), col. 115–78 (4 June 1942).

78. 124 Hansard, 5th series, H.L. col. 195–236 (5 August 1942).

79. 128 Hansard, 5th series, H.L. col. 59–98 (23 June 1943).

80. 134 Hansard, 5th series, H.L. col. 373 (19 December 1944).

81. Ibid., col. 385.

82. Ibid., col. 380.

Chapter 5: Privacy and Individual Rights

1. Compare Eric Fletcher's letter to the *Times* (London), 11 December 1947, p. 5, with his remarks in the House of Commons, 447 Hansard, 5th series, H.C. col. 2264 (26 February 1948).

2. Ian Brownlee, *Basic Documents on Human Rights* (Oxford: Clarendon Press, 1971), p. 106.

3. Ibid., p. 109.

4. Ibid., p. 343.

5. 229 Hansard, 5th series, H.L. col. 628–29 (13 March 1961).

6. *Times* (London), 10 December 1963, p. 13.

7. Ibid., 7 February 1950, p. 8.

8. Preservation of the Rights of the Subject Bill (1947) H.L. Bill 61.

9. 167 Hansard, 5th series, H.L. col. 327–79 (17 May 1950).

10. Liberties of the Subject Bill (1950) H.L. Bill 34.

11. 167 Hansard, 5th series, H.L. col. 1083–84 (27 June 1950).

12. 177 Hansard, 5th series, H.L. col. 1168–1242 (16 June 1952).

13. For similar concerns, but with emphasis upon judicial remedies rather than upon Parliamentary ones, see Sir Henry Slesser's special article "The Common Law—Traditional Rights in a Collective Age," *Times* (London), 9 August 1946, p. 5.

14. *Times* (London), 25 May 1951, p. 2; 26 May, p. 8; 29 May, p. 2. *Grove v. Eastern Gas Board* [1951] 2 K.B. 586 (K.B.); [1952] 1 K.B. 77 (C.A.).

15. *Evening News*, 29 May 1951, p. 2. (Emphasis added).

16. *Daily Express*, 29 May 1951, p. 4.

17. *Daily Mail*, 19 June 1950, p. 1.

18. *Evening News*, 7 April 1951, p. 1.
19. *Daily Telegraph*, 6 April 1951, p. 4.
20. *Daily Express*, 3 April 1951, p. 4.
21. Ibid., 7 April 1951, p. 2.
22. *Observer*, 8 April 1951, p. 2.
23. *Times* (London), 1 January 1946, p. 5; 4 January, p. 6; 16 January, p. 6.
24. Ibid., 13 June 1951, p. 2; 26 June, p. 2; 27 June, p. 4.
25. *Willcock* v. *Muckle* [1951] 2 K.B. 844. Lord Chief Justice Goddard's observations are at page 851.
26. *Daily Mail*, 30 June 1951, p. 1.
27. Ibid., 12 June 1951, p. 12.
28. 172 Hansard, 5th series, H.L. col. 1335–74 (26 July 1951).
29. Ibid., at 1336. A published view different from the Marquess of Reading was S. P. Vivian, "Identity Cards and Liberty," *National Review* 127 (August 1946): 143–48.
30. *Daily Herald*, 20 July 1946, p. 1.
31. 428 Hansard, 5th series, H.C. col. 452–576 (29 October 1946).
32. Ross Committee, p. 4.
33. *Justice of the Peace and Local Government Review* 110 (26 January 1946): 38.
34. H. Montgomery Hyde, *Privacy and the Press* (London: Butterworth & Co., 1947), p. 229. (This book told the story of the action and included the argument before the court and the judgment.)
35. Ross Committee, p. 132 par. 491.
36. Ibid., p. 131 par. 483.
37. Ibid., p. 132 par. 489.
38. Ibid., p. 132 par. 490.
39. Ibid., p. 170 pars. 642, 643.
40. Ibid., p. 174 par. 662.
41. Porter Committee, p. 10 par. 26.
42. Sir Lynn Ungoed-Thomas discussed the relationship between the council and the law of defamation during the debate on the Defamation (Amendment) Bill. 495 Hansard, 5th series, H.C. col. 534–38 (1 February 1952).
43. Defamation (Amendment) Bill (1951) H.C. Bill 21.
44. 495 Hansard, 5th series, H.C. col. 523, 528, 544. See also Porter Committee, pp. 20–21 par. 78.
45. Press Council Bill (1952) H.C. Bill 10.
46. *Daily Express*, 22 November 1952, p. 4. *Evening Standard*, 27 November 1952, p. 4.
47. *Sunday Times* (London), 30 November 1952, p. 6.
48. *Times* (London), 28 November 1952, p. 9.
49. *Daily Telegraph*, 1 December 1952, p. 9.
50. *Daily Express*, 16 July 1952, p. 1.

51. *Times* (London), 21 July 1952, p. 5.
52. *Daily Express*, 25 July 1952, p. 1.
53. *Observer*, 2 November 1952, p. 6.
54. *Times* (London), 1 November 1946, p. 2.
55. Ibid., 23 July 1947, p. 5.
56. Ibid., 29 February 1952, p. 3.

Chapter 6: Privacy and the Press

1. *Daily Mirror*, 3 July 1953, p. 1.
2. Ibid., 4 July 1953, p. 1.
3. See the letters in the *Evening Standard*, 9 July to 13 July 1953.
4. *Daily Mirror*, 13 July 1953, p. 1.
5. *Times* (London), 14 July 1953, p. 3.
6. *Daily Sketch*, 14 July 1953, p. 1.
7. *Daily Mirror*, 14 July 1953, p. 1.
8. Ibid., 17 July 1953, p. 1.
9. *Sunday Graphic*, 19 July 1953, pp. 1–2.
10. *Sunday Times* (London), 19 July 1953, p. 6.
11. *Times* (London), 22 July 1953, p. 8. Press and the People, 1954.
12. *Evening Standard*, 22 July 1953, p. 4.
13. *Daily Express*, 24 July 1953, p. 4.
14. *Daily Mirror*, 23 July 1953, p. 16.
15. *Times* (London), 24 July 1953, p. 9.
16. *Sunday People*, 13 March 1955, p. 6.
17. *Times* (London), 15 October 1955, p. 6.
18. *Daily Telegraph*, 15 October 1955, p. 6.
19. *Daily Mail*, 14 October 1955, p. 1.
20. Hugh Cudlipp later said that he regretted publishing that headline. BBC 1 Television, "Cudlipp and Be Damned," 28 November 1973.
21. *Times* (London), 19 October 1955, p. 4. See also Press and the People, 1956, pp. 9–13.
22. BBC Television, Press Conference, 28 February 1958 (transcript in BBC files).
23. *Times* (London), 10 November 1955, p. 11.
24. Ibid., 26 January 1955, p. 4; 2 May 1956, p. 6.
25. Ibid., 17 January 1957, p. 4. Press and the People, 1957, pp. 31–32.
26. *Times* (London), 26 February 1955, p. 4.
27. Ibid., 1 March 1955, p. 9.
28. Ibid., 3 March 1955, p. 9.
29. Ibid., 9 March 1955, p. 4.
30. Ibid., 28 October 1955, p. 11. Press and the People, 1956, pp. 52–53.
31. *Times* (London), 17 January 1958, p. 11.

32. Ibid., 20 January 1958, p. 9.

33. *Daily Mirror*, 20 January 1958, p. 1.

34. BBC Television, Press Conference, 28 February 1958 (transcript in BBC files).

35. *Times* (London), 11 February 1958, p. 9.

36. Ibid., 12 February 1958, p. 8. His motion to "draw attention to the conflict of interest between the liberty of the subject and the freedom of the Press" was not debated. 588 Hansard, 5th series, H.C. col. 1305 (21 May 1958).

37. *Times* (London), 12 February 1958, p. 9.

38. Ibid., 13 February 1958, p. 9.

39. Ibid.

40. *Daily Mail*, 14 February 1958, p. 1.

41. *News Chronicle*, 13 February 1958, p. 1.

42. *Times* (London), 9 April 1958, p. 4. Press and the People, 1958, pp. 33–35.

43. Press and the People, 1958, p. 35.

44. *Times* (London), 7 May 1958, p. 6.

45. *Observer*, 16 February 1958, p. 11.

46. *Times* (London), 8 May 1958, p. 5.

47. Ibid., 26 January 1960, p. 10.

48. Ibid., 27 January 1960, p. 11.

49. Ibid., 30 September 1960, p. 7. Press and the People, 1961, pp. 39–42.

50. Press and the People, 1958, p. 11.

51. *Times* (London), 26 August 1955, p. 5.

52. Press Authority Bill (1956); 200 Hansard, 5th series, H.L. col. 806 (6 December 1956). *Times* (London), 13 July 1956, p. 4.

53. *Times* (London), 18 July 1956, p. 7.

54. *Daily Mirror*, 17 July 1956, p. 2.

55. *News Chronicle*, 13 July 1956, p. 4.

56. Cf. "The Press of Our Times," *Economist* 180 (21 July 1956): 197–98.

57. *Times* (London), 3 March 1955, p. 9.

58. Wills, etc. (Publication) Bill (1956) H.C. Bill 56.

59. Wills, etc. (Publication) Bill (1958) H.C. Bill 19.

60. 459 Hansard, 5th series, H.C. col. 1651 (2 March 1956).

61. Ibid., col. 1656.

62. Ibid., col. 1669.

63. Ibid., col. 1663, 1665.

64. 596 Hansard, 5th series, H.C. col. 746 (28 November 1958).

65. Ibid., col. 762.

66. "The Birthday of Newspapers," *Times* (London), 2 December 1920, p. 15.

67. Ross Committee, p. 88 par. 313.

68. *Times* (London), 21 April 1955, p. 7. *Daily Express*, 21 April 1955, p. 4.

69. *Times* (London), 21 January 1957, p. 7.
70. *Reynolds News*, 26 May 1957, p. 6.
71. 631 Hansard, 5th series, H.C. col. 719–822 (2 December 1960).
72. *Times* (London), 6 June 1955, p. 7.
73. Ibid., 29 June 1955, p. 11.
74. Ibid., 18 May 1957, p. 7.
75. BBC Television, Press Conference, 28 February 1958 (transcript in BBC files).
76. Ibid., 15 January 1960 (transcript in BBC files).
77. *Daily Sketch*, 26 June 1957, p. 2.
78. Those events included the defection of Dr. Pontecorvo, the disappearance of Burgess and Maclean, and the presumed death of Commander Crabb while diving in the vicinity of a Soviet ship anchored near Portsmouth Harbour during the visit of Bulganin and Khrushchev.
79. 555 Hansard, 5th series, H.C. col. 1305–7 (4 July 1956); 555 Hansard, 5th series, H.C. col. *24* (11 July 1956).
80. *Times* (London), 7 June 1957, p. 4. 571 Hansard, 5th series, H.C. col. 1461–63 (6 June 1957).
81. The nature of the impropriety was not disclosed. It is, however, noteworthy that a barrister would be in breach of bar ethics for talking with his lay client in the absence of the lay client's solicitor or the solicitor's clerk.
82. 571 Hansard, 5th series, H.C. col. 1565–71 (7 June 1957).
83. *News Chronicle*, 7 June 1957, p. 4.
84. *Sunday Times* (London), 9 June 1957, p. 12.
85. *Manchester Guardian*, 24 June 1957, p. 6.
86. *Evening Standard*, 7 June 1957, p. 4.
87. Ibid., 26 June 1957, p. 4.
88. *Times* (London), 8 June 1957, p. 7.
89. *Daily Mail*, 7 June 1957, p. 1.
90. *Daily Telegraph*, 8 June 1957, p. 6.
91. *Manchester Guardian*, 7 June 1957, p. 8; 24 June 1957, p. 6.
92. Birkett Committee, p. 15 par. 51.
93. *Times* (London), 1 November 1957, p. 11; cf. *Reynolds News*, 3 November 1957, p. 6.
94. Birkett Committee, p. 27 par. 121.
95. 614 Hansard, 5th series, H.C. col. 1378–90 (3 December 1959). The lord chancellor, Viscount Kilmuir, also defended the home secretary on the grounds that there was a distinction between Dr. Fox's case and the case investigated by the Birkett Committee. 220 Hansard, 5th series, H.L. col. 529–35 (17 December 1959).
96. 615 Hansard, 5th series, H.C. col. 1521–1600 (16 December 1959).
97. Ibid., col. 1521.
98. Ibid., col. 1528.
99. Ibid., col. 1534–35. Bernard Levin and the Warden of All Souls, John

Sparrow, disputed this point in the *Spectator* 203 (18 December 1959) : 903; (25 December 1959) : 934; 204 (1 January 1960) : 11; (29 January 1960) : 130–32.

100. 615 Hansard, 5th series, H.C. col. 1571 (16 December 1959).

101. Wolfenden Committee.

102. 529 Hansard, 5th series, H.C. col. 2313–14 (8 July 1954).

103. *Times* (London), 27 August 1954, p. 7.

104. Wolfenden Committee, p. 21 par. 52. A similar conclusion about prostitution was expressed at p. 79 par. 224.

105. Ibid., p. 24 par. 61.

106. Ibid., p. 22 par. 54.

107. The debate was published in three Oxford University Press Paperbacks: Patrick Devlin, *The Enforcement of Morals* (Oxford: Oxford University Press, 1968) ; H. L. A. Hart, *Law, Liberty and Morality* (Oxford: Oxford University Press, 1968) ; and Basil Mitchell, *Law, Morality, and Religion* (Oxford: Oxford University Press, 1970).

108. Devlin, *Enforcement of Morals*, pp. 13, 22.

109. Ibid., p. 15.

110. Ibid., pp. 16–20.

111. Ibid., p. 19.

112. Ibid.

113. Hart, *Law, Liberty, and Morality*, p. 47.

114. 206 Hansard, 5th series, H.L. col. 737 (4 December 1957).

115. Ibid., col. 738.

116. Ibid., col. 753.

117. Ibid., col. 796.

118. Ibid., col. 822.

119. 596 Hansard, 5th series, H.C. col. 365–508 (26 November 1958).

120. Ibid., col. 440–45.

121. Ibid., col. 473.

122. Ibid., col. 477–78.

123. Ibid., col. 499.

124. In June 1960 the House of Commons debated a motion calling on the government to take early action on the homosexuality recommendations of the Wolfenden Report. Again, there was no significant argument in terms of a right to privacy. Those who favored a change argued that the law had major defects and that a change would not encourage the spread of homosexuality. Those who opposed the change said that it would imply that the House condoned homosexual conduct and that public opinion was not ready for the change. 625 Hansard, 5th series, H.C. col. 1453–1514 (29 June 1960).

125. *Sunday Graphic*, 9 June 1957, p. 8.

126. Ibid., 30 June 1957, p. 5.

127. *News Chronicle*, 29 June 1957, p. 4.

128. Ibid.

129. *Times* (London), 22 January 1952, p. 2; 2 February 1952, p. 3. 495 Hansard, 5th series, H. C. col. 54 (30 January 1952).

130. *Times* (London), 18 August 1956, p. 4.

131. Ibid., 20 July 1957, p. 4; 20 August 1957, p. 5.

132. Ibid., 20 July 1957, p. 4; 20 August 1957, p. 5.

133. Ibid., 27 July 1956, p. 13; 23 October 1956, p. 6. ERNIE's full name was Electronic Random Number Indicating Equipment.

134. Ibid., 17 May 1957, p. 9.

135. Ibid., 15 January 1959, p. 5; 29 July 1959, p. 5. 603 Hansard, 5th series, H.C. col. *29–30* (8 April 1959).

136. Vance Packard, *The Hidden Persuaders* (London: Longmans, Green & Co., 1957).

137. *Times* (London), 16 September 1957, p. 7; 28 September 1957, p. 3.

138. Ibid., 5 July 1958, p. 5. *Subliminal Communication* (London: Institute of Practitioners in Advertising, 1958), p. 6.

139. *Times* (London), 17 April 1959, p. 15.

140. Ibid., 6 May 1955, p. 7; 8 September 1955, p. 7.

141. Ibid., 16 October 1958, p. 6.

142. Ibid., 28 January 1959, p. 9.

143. *Daily Express*, 4 November 1952, p. 3; *Times* (London), 23 October 1958, p. 5.

144. *Times* (London), 26 October 1954, p. 2.

145. Ibid., 29 November 1960, p. 12; 30 November 1960, p. 6.

146. Ibid., 23 November 1959, p. 8.

Chapter 7: First Attempt at Legislation

1. *Williams* v. *Settle* [1960] 1 W. L. R. 1072 at 1076. See also the *Times* (London), 16 December 1959, p. 13; 18 December, p. 6.

2. *Williams* v. *Settle* [1960] 1. W. L. R. 1072 at 1082.

3. *Times* (London), 11 May 1960, p. 15.

4. Ibid., 6 January 1961, p. 10.

5. 227 Hansard, 5th series, H.L. col. 1193 (25 January 1961).

6. Shawcross Committee, p. 9.

7. Right of Privacy Bill (1961) H.L. Bill 35.

8. Younger Committee, Appendix F, p. 273.

9. Right of Privacy Bill (1961) cl. 1.

10. Ibid., cl. 2(d).

11. Ibid., cl. 3.

12. BBC Radio, Home Service, "Matters of Moment," 27 April 1961 (transcript in BBC files).

13. 229 Hansard, 5th series, H.L. col. 607, 617 (13 March 1961).

14. *Daily Mirror*, 20 January 1958, p. 1. See discussion in chap. 6, p. 110.

15. *Daily Mail*, 16 February 1961, p. 1.

16. *Times* (London), 13 March 1961, p. 15.

17. *Guardian*, 13 March 1961, p. 1.

18. *Observer*, 19 March 1961, p. 10.

19. *Sunday Times* (London), 19 February 1961, p. 10; *Sunday People*, 19 March 1961, p. 12.

20. 229 Hansard, 5th series, H.L. col. 618–21 (13 March 1961).

21. Ibid., col. 621.

22. Ibid., col. 629–30.

23. 232 Hansard, 5th series, H.L. col. 289–99 (15 June 1961).

24. *Daily Telegraph*, 7 February 1970, p. 12.

25. *Times* (London), 22 July 1961, p. 8. *Lewis* v. *Daily Telegraph* [1963] 1 Q.B. 340; [1964] A.C. 234.

26. *Times* (London), 14 December 1962, p. 6.

27. The Census Order was approved by the House of Commons without objection. 622 Hansard, 5th series, H.C. col. 1181–98 (4 May 1960). In the House of Lords there were scattered objections before the order was approved. 224 Hansard, 5th series, H.L. col. 205–16 (1 June 1960).

28. *Daily Express*, 18 April 1961, p. 8.

29. Ibid., 24 April 1961, p. 8.

30. *Times* (London), 22 April 1961, pp. 4, 9, 10.

31. *Daily Mail*, 25 April 1961, p. 11.

32. *Daily Sketch*, 25 April 1961, p. 9.

33. *Sunday Express*, 23 April 1961, p. 5.

34. *Times* (London), 7 April 1961, p. 6.

35. Ibid., 12 April 1971, p. 1 (where the figure was 80); 17 December 1963, p. 4, (where the figure was 89).

36. Shawcross Committee, p. 101 par. 323.

37. *Times* (London), 25 January 1963, pp. 4–5; *Att.-Gen.* v. *Clough* [1963] 1 Q.B. 773; [1963] 2 W.L.R. 343.

38. See discussion in chap. 2, pp. 41–42.

39. *Att.-Gen.* v. *Mulholland*; *Att.-Gen.* v. *Foster* [1963] 2 Q.B. 477 at 491.

40. *Daily Express*, 7 March 1963, p. 10; *Daily Mirror*, 7 March 1963, p. 2.

41. *Daily Mail*, 7 March 1963, pp. 1–2.

42. *Observer*, 10 March 1963, p. 10. See also leading article "Conditions of Freedom," *Spectator* 210 (15 March 1963): 311.

43. *Daily Telegraph*, 7 March 1963, p. 12; *Times* (London), 7 March 1963, p. 13.

44. *Daily Sketch*, 7 March 1963, pp. 1–2.

45. *Daily Sketch*, 18 March 1963, p. 11. Lord Parker made the statement when giving guidance to Desmond Clough during his testimony at the trial. *Times* (London), 25 January 1963, p. 4.

46. *Daily Telegraph*, 11 March 1963, p. 12; *Times* (London), 18 March 1963, p. 11.

47. *Daily Express*, 15 March 1963, p. 1.

48. For discussions of the newspapers' behavior, see the *Daily Mail*, 7 June 1963, p. 1; *News of the World*, 9 June 1963, p. 10; *Sunday Express*, 16 June 1963, p. 16.

49. *Times* (London), 11 June 1963, p. 13.

50. *Daily Sketch*, 12 June 1963, p. 20.

51. Ibid., 19 June 1963, p. 20.

52. *Daily Telegraph*, 6 June 1963, p. 14.

53. Ibid., 27 September 1963, p. 16.

54. Ibid.

55. *News of the World*, 23 June 1963, p. 10.

56. Ibid., 6 October 1963, p. 1.

57. *Observer*, 9 June 1963, p. 10. Cf. Press and the People, 1964, pp. 17–20.

58. *Observer*, 29 September 1963, p. 10. The phrase "trafficking in scandal for reward" was used by Lord Denning at the conclusion of his report (1963; Cmnd. 2152), p. 112 par. 342.

59. In a widely-publicized case, the duke of Argyll used his wife's diary as evidence against her to obtain a divorce. *Times* (London), 9 May 1963, p. 9. Later the duchess of Argyll successfully applied for an injunction to restrain the duke from publishing excerpts from the diary in the *Sunday People*. Ungoed-Thomas J. awarded the injunction on the grounds of breach of marital confidence. *Argyll* (*Duchess*) v. *Argyll* (*Duke*) [1967] Ch. 302; [1965] 1 All E.R. 611.

60. *The Law and the Press*, the report of a joint working party of JUSTICE and the British Committee of the International Press Institute (Stevens: London, 1965), p. 1.

61. Ibid., p. 32 par. 105.

62. Ibid., p. 33 par. 107.

63. Ibid.

64. *Times* (London), 11 January 1961, p. 7.

65. Questionnaire on privacy and the computer, a technical project of the Privacy and Public Welfare Committee of the British Computer Society, 1973, p. 32.

66. *Times* (London), 25 January 1961, p. 6.

67. Ibid., 10 November 1961, p. 17.

68. Ibid., 7 February 1963, p. 6.

69. Ibid., 9 January 1963, p. 13.

70. Ibid., 10 January 1963, p. 11; 12 January, p. 13; 13 January, p. 13; 14 January, p. 7; 16 January, p. 11; 17 January, p. 11; 18 January, p. 11. The advertisement was published 20 January, p. 14.

71. *Daily Sketch*, 19 November 1963, p. 2; cf. the *Times* (London), 19 November 1963, p. 8.

72. *Times* (London), 30 October 1965, p. 9.

73. Ibid., 13 July 1965, p. 6; 7 January 1966, p. 10.

74. Ibid., 3 May 1966, p. 17.

75. Ibid., 24 November 1966, p. 12.

76. Ibid., 21 May 1966, p. 11.

77. Ibid., 14 July 1966, p. 14; 23 December 1966, p. 8.

78. Ibid., 3 January 1966, p. 6.

79. Ibid., 11 January 1966, p. 8.

80. Ibid., 7 December 1965, p. 9. *General Report, Census 1961* (London: Her Majesty's Stationery Office, 1968), p. 12.

81. *Times* (London), 11 March 1964, p. 12; 20 May 1964, p. 12; 2 September 1965, p. 12.

82. *Daily Express*, 17 January 1958, p. 6.

83. *News of the World*, 14 April 1963, p. 9.

84. *Times* (London), 27 January 1964, p. 6. Press and the People, 1964, p. 52.

85. *Times* (London), 26 August 1959, p. 5.

86. Ibid., 30 November 1965, p. 5.

87. 721 Hansard, 5th seriees, H.C. col. 1422 (1 December 1965).

88. Ibid., col. 1423.

89. *Times* (London), 4 December 1965, p. 6.

90. Ibid., 21 April 1966, p. 6.

91. Ibid., 20 August 1965, p. 5; 24 August 1965, p. 5; 2 September 1965, p. 9; 3 September 1965, p. 5. There is no record of his asking a question about the allegations.

92. Ibid., 14 November 1966, pp. 10, 11; 17 November 1966, p. 1; 736 Hansard, 5th series, H.C. col. 634–41 (17 November 1966).

93. *Times* (London), 19 November 1966, p. 9.

94. Ibid., 23 November 1966, p. 6. 278 Hansard, 5th series, H.L. col. 122–23 (22 November 1966).

95. *Times* (London), 13 December 1966, p. 11.

96. Tests to determine the alcohol content of the blood were first proposed in Graham Page's Road Safety Bill (1959) H.C. Bill 24.

97. *Times* (London), 23 March 1961, p. 7.

98. Road Safety Bill (1965) H.C. Bill 44. 714 Hansard, 5th series, H.C. col. 1080–1140 (18 June 1965).

99. Road Safety Legislation 1965–1966 (1965; Cmnd. 2859).

100. *Times* (London), 22 December 1965, p. 5.

101. Ibid., 23 December 1965, p. 9.

102. Road Safety Bill (1966) H.C. Bill 58 cl. 2.

103. Road Safety Bill (1966) H.C. Bill 109. See, e.g., 735 Hansard, 5th series, H.C. col. 981–1048 (7 November 1966) (second reading debate).

104. The first tests of the addition of fluorides to a water supply, announced in 1952, were to take place in Kilmarnock. Some years later there was a single objection to the "unwarrantable invasion of the liberties of

the private subject," 600 Hansard, 5th series, H.C. col. 18 (16 February 1959).

105. *Times* (London), 29 March 1963, p. 6.

106. Ibid., 12 July 1965, p. 11.

Chapter 8: The Lyon and Walden Bills

1. Right of Privacy Bill (1967) H.C. Bill 181; 794 Hansard, 5th series, H.C. col. 881 (23 January 1970).

2. Right of Privacy Bill (1969) H.C. Bill 25. *Times* (London), 18 January 1970, p. 2.

3. 740 Hansard, 5th series, H.C. col. 1565 (8 February 1967).

4. Ibid., col. 1568.

5. Right of Privacy Bill (1967) cl. 1.

6. BBC Radio, Home Service, "The Week at Westminster," 11 February 1967 (transcript in BBC files).

7. 740 Hansard, 5th series, H.C. col. 1567 (8 February 1967). The divorce case was *Trehearne* v. *Trehearne*, *Times* (London), 18 October 1966, p. 9.

8. H.C. Bill 190.

9. 741 Hansard, 5th series, H.C. col. 1054–55 (20 February 1967).

10. NCCL Bulletin, July/August 1965.

11. Letter to the author dated 30 May 1973; cf. Sargant's letter to the *Times* (London), 21 January 1970, p. 9.

12. Alan F. Westin, *Privacy and Freedom* (New York: Atheneum, 1970). Professor Westin's book contains copious notes and bibliographical references for the discussion of privacy in the United States prior to 1967.

13. *Times* (London), 16 June 1967, p. 2. The working paper for the conference was published: Stig Strömholm, *Right of Privacy and Rights of the Personality* (Stockholm: P. A. Norstedt & Söners förlag, 1967). The conclusions of the conference were reprinted in Appendix B, *Privacy and the Law*, a report by JUSTICE (London: Stevens & Sons, 1970).

14. *Times* (London), 16 June 1967, p. 11.

15. Post Office (Data Processing Service) Bill (1967) H.C. Bill 228.

16. 745 Hansard, 5th series, H.C. col 507 (19 April 1967).

17. 4 Standing Committee B, col. 82 (15 June 1967).

18. Professor Westin discusses many of the events in the United States in chap. 12 of his book *Privacy and Freedom*.

19. 4 Standing Committee B, col. 91–92 (15 June 1967).

20. 749 Hansard, 5th series, H.C. col. 1668–1723 (4 July 1967). 284 Hansard, 5th series, H.L. col. 1373–98.

21. *Times* (London), 12 January 1967, p. 9.

22. Ibid., 18 February 1967, p. 2. The public's reaction to fingerprinting

was unpredictable. As part of a number of criminal investigations, the police were able to conduct mass fingerprinting without significant objection. Ibid., 24 May 1948, p. 4 (Blackburn police to fingerprint all men in city); ibid, 1 April 1957, p. 10 (seven hundred workers fingerprinted after theft); ibid., 4 June 1957, p. 6 (sixteen thousand to be fingerprinted during murder investigation). Yet the identification of fingerprints with criminals and police states had prevented their use on identity cards during the Second World War. In 1966 the NCCL labeled proposals to fingerprint the entire nation as "the first step in the creation of a police state." NCCL Bulletin, May 1966. But even then there was no explicit privacy argument.

23. *Times* (London), 30 November 1967, p. 2. Similar remarks were made by Lord Stonham, minister of state, home office, 287 Hansard, 5th series, H.L. col. 141–42 (29 November 967). Smaller police authorities were also making use of computers: the Cheshire County Police, for example, told of their plans to use a computer to establish crime trends and to identify the areas with the greatest likelihood of crime. *Times* (London), 7 January 1967, p. 7.

24. *Times* (London), 20 May 1968, p. 1

25. Wireless Telegraphy Bill (1967) H.C. Bill 205, cl. 2. 745 Hansard, 5th series, H.C. col. 308–68 (18 April 1967).

26. *Times* (London), 10 March 1967, p. 13.

27. Ibid., 12 September 1967, p. 1.

28. Ibid., 15 July 1968, p. 2. A similar use that aroused some speculative remarks was the proposal that checks on vehicle and drivers' licenses be computerized. Vehicle and Driving Licenses Bill (1968) H.C. Bill 11. When the bill was in committee, Robert Cooke expressed the fear of "1984" effects from this use of computers. 1 Standing Committee A, col. 24–26 (10 December 1968).

29. BBC Radio, Third Program, "The Computer and Personal Freedom," 18 April 1968. In 1969 the Post Office announced plans to extend the use of postal codes to the entire country. *Times* (London), 13 June 1969, p. 11.

30. *Times* (London), 26 September 1967, p. 14.

31. *Computers and Freedom* (Old Queen Street Paper: 8) (London: Conservative Research Department, 1968). *Times* (London), 2 December 1968, p. 10.

32. Data Surveillance Bill (1969) H.C. Bill 150. Lord Windlesham's Personal Records (Computers) Bill introduced in the House of Lords had much the same intent.

33. 783 Hansard, 5th series, H.C. col. 288 (6 May 1969).

34. *Times* (London), 28 March 1968, p. 2.

35. Ibid., 24 May 1968, p. 2.

36. Ibid., 21 September 1968, p. 9.

37. Ibid., 31 October 1968, p. 11. The commission reported in 1973; Royal Commission on the Constitution 1969–1973 (1973; Cmnd. 5460). The majority report ruled out a Bill of Rights for the regions because it would

involve judges in political disputes, among other reasons. Pp. 228–31 pars. 746–55.

38. *Times* (London), 2 July 1968, p. 3. Lord Shawcross made similar suggestions in his presidential speech to the British Hotels and Restaurants Association. Ibid., 17 July 1969, p. 3.

39. Ibid., 24 September 1968, p. 3.

40. Ibid., 12 October 1968, p. 10. Cf. his article "A New Bill of Rights," *Listener* 81 (24 April 1969): 549–51.

41. *Times* (London), 21 November 1968, p. 3.

42. See, e.g., Louis Heren, "The Case for a Second Bill of Rights," ibid., 21 December 1968, p. 7.

43. 750 Hansard, 5th series, H.C. col. 1542–1605 (17 July 1967).

44. Ibid., col. 1582–83.

45. 755 Hansard, 5th series, H.C. col. 808–909 (1 December 1967).

46. Ibid., col. 862.

47. Bill of Rights (1969). The same bill was introduced by Lord Arran in October 1970, H.L. Bill 19.

48. 782 Hansard, 5th series, H.C. col. 475 (23 April 1969).

49. Ibid., col. 477.

50. Bill of Rights (No. 2) (1969) H.C. Bill 205, cl. 10.

51. 787 Hansard, 5th series, H.C. col. 1519 (22 July 1969).

52. Ibid., col. 1519–20. Cl. 11 of his bill provided for control of personal information.

53. 302 Hansard, 5th series, H.L. col 1026 (18 June 1969).

54. Ibid., col. 1027–28.

55. Ibid., col. 1031.

56. Ibid.

57. Ibid., col. 1048–49. In 1963 he had been coeditor of a Society of Labour Lawyers' publication in which Aubrey Diamond said that Lord Mancroft's bill should become law and establish a tort of invasion of privacy. Gerald Gardiner and Andrew Martin, eds., *Law Reform Now* (London: Victor Gollancz, 1963), p. 78.

58. 302 Hansard, 5th series, H.L. col. 1059–62 (18 June 1969).

59. Ibid., col. 1071. Cf. his article "On Snooping," *New Statesman* 53 (22 June 1957): 800–801, where he uses similar analogies to oppose wire-tapping.

60. Peter Hamilton, *Espionage and Subversion in an Industrial Society* (London: Hutchinson, 1967). Other instances of industrial espionage are mentioned in Ronald Payne, *Private Spies* (London: Arthur Barker, 1967).

61. Philip Hickson, *Industrial Counter-Espionage* (London: Institute of Directors, 1968).

62. Ibid., p. 61. This was discussed by the Younger Committee, pp. 93–98.

63 *Times* (London), 11 March 1967, p. 1.

64. Ibid., 11 August 1967, p. 3.

65. Industrial Information Bill (1968) H.C. Bill 31

66. 775 Hansard, 5th series, H.C. col. 805 (13 December 1968).
67. Ibid., col. 803.
68. Ibid., col. 826.
69. Ibid., col. 827.
70. Ibid., col. 819.
71. *Times* (London), 1 August 1967, p. 1.
72. Ibid., 1 September 1967, p. 3.
73. *R.* v. *Senat* (1968) 52 Cr. App. R. 282 at 286–87.
74. *Gabbitas* v. *Gabbitas* (1967), *Times* (London), 30 November, p. 2.
75. 744 Hansard, 5th series, H.C. col. 433–34 (6 April 1967).
76. *Times* (London), 8 April 1967, p. 2.
77. Ibid., 10 April 1967, p. 11.
78. Ibid., 29 November 1969, p. 1. Shaw J. agreed, after argument, that the tapes could be admitted in evidence; *R.* v. *Robson*; *R.* v. *Harris* [1972] 1 W.L.R. 651.
79. *Times* (London), 4 October 1968, p. 7.
80. Ibid., 10 October 1968, p. 9.
81. Ibid., 1 February 1968, p. 9. Cf. letter from Professor R. B. Welbourn, director, Department of Surgery, Hammersmith Hospital, ibid., 8 February 1968, p. 9
82. *Times* (London), 4 May 1968, p. 1.
83. Ibid., 2 October 1968, p. 3. Press and the People, 1969, p. 70.
84. *Times* (London), 22 October 1968, p. 2. A member of the heart-transplant team later said that the publicity had eliminated donors. Ibid., 4 December 1968, p. 1. Professor Calne echoed those sentiments and accused the intrusions of causing deaths because of the effects on donors' relatives. Ibid., 28 April 1969, p. 2.
85. *Daily Telegraph*, 20 May 1969, p. 18; 22 May 1969, p. 18; 26 May 1969, p. 6; 28 May 1969, p. 16; 29 May 1969, p. 1; 30 May 1969, pp. 1, 18.
86. *Times* (London), 7 November 1969, p. 4. Press and the People, 1970, p. 50.
87. *Times* (London), 1 October 1969, p. 2.
88. Ibid., 2 October 1969, p. 1.
89. Ibid., 25 September 1969, p. 11; 27 September 1969, p. 7; 30 September 1969, p. 11.
90. Ibid., 8 October 1969, p. 11.
91. Ibid., 17 October 1969, p. 1. Press and the People, 1970, pp. 70–73.
92. *Times* (London), 19 February 1969, p. 8.
93. NCCL Bulletin, February 1969.
94. Civil Liberty, 1970, p. 6. *Times* (London), 5 March 1969, p. 2.
95. NCCL Bulletin, October 1969.
96. *Times* (London), 8 November 1969, p. 2.
97. Ibid., 13 November 1969, p. 3.
98. All events were reported in ibid.: 29 November 1969, pp. 1, 6 (in-

vestigation of police); 4 December 1969, p. 6 (Lord Windlesham); 5 December 1969, p. 4 (Law Commission); 20 December 1969, p. 3 (royal commission); 22 December 1969, p. 7 (leader); 31 December 1969, p. 7 (JUSTICE).

99. 306 Hansard, 5th series, H.L. col. 103 (3 December 1969).

100. Ibid., col. 107.

101. Ibid., col. 110.

102. Ibid., col. 127.

103. Right of Privacy Bill (1969) H.C. Bill 25.

104. *Privacy and the Law*, pp. 2–3, par. 10. The report was criticized in a letter from the general secretary of the Institute of Journalists. The *Times* (London), 23 January 1970, p. 11.

105. *Privacy and the Law*, p. 5 par. 18.

106. *Times* (London), 16 January 1970, pp. 1, 5.

107. *Daily Mail*, 19 January 1970, p. 1.

108 *Daily Telegraph*, 15 January 1970, p. 18. Other opposition to the bill was expressed by the *Times* (London), 16 January 1970, p. 8, and the *Guardian*, 16 January 1970, p. 10.

109. *News of the World*, 18 January 1970, p. 12. Other Sunday newspapers with leaders opposed to the bill included the *Sunday Mirror*, 18 January 1970, p. 2, and *Sunday People*, 18 January 1970, p. 2.

110. *Sunday Times* (London), 18 January 1970, p. 11.

111. *Daily Express*, 21 January 1970, p. 1.

112. Examples of the BBC television reports include "Law of Privacy" on "Daytime," 29 October 1969, and an interview with Brian Walden on "Midlands Today," 23 January 1970. Radio 4 devoted parts of numerous programs to the NCCL campaign; e.g., Kenneth Baker was interviewed alone on 2 December 1968 and with Tony Smythe on 18 February 1969 on "The World at One": the Third Program "Talks" series devoted two programs to "Computer and Society—the Potent Machine," 26 and 29 May 1969.

113. 794 Hansard, 5th series, H.C. col. 862 (23 January 1970).

114. Ibid., col. 863–76.

115. Ibid., col. 881–82.

116. Ibid., col. 882, 888–89.

117. Ibid., col. 941.

Chapter 9: The Younger Committee and After

1. *Times* (London), 15 April 1970, p. 2.

2. Ibid., 20 October 1970, p. 5. The recommendations were reprinted in Appendix G/2, Younger Committee, p. 285.

3. *Times* (London), 21 December 1970, p. 2; 20 January 1971, p. 4.

4. Kenneth Baker's Data Surveillance Bill (1969); Lord Windlesham's Personal Records (Computers) Bill (1969). The Police Federation also complained that secret files about its members hindered their professional opportunities. Ibid., 20 May 1971, p. 4.

5. *Times* (London), 29 January 1970, p. 2.

6. *News of the World*, 1 February 1970, p. 12.

7. "A Journalist's Case for the Use of Bugging Devices," *Times* (London), 31 January 1970, p. 7.

8. The challenging letter was published in the *Times* (London), 6 February 1970, p. 11; the response, 24 February 1970, p. 9.

9. Ibid., 4 February 1970, p. 1.

10. Ibid., 17 July 1970, p. 7.

11. Ibid., 12 August 1970, p. 3. Later cases included those reported in ibid., 17 June 1971, p. 1, and 6 January 1972, p. 3.

12. Ibid., 26 March 1970, p. 2. Cf. ibid., 6 August 1968, p. 1.

13. Ibid., 5 August 1970, p. 8.

14. Ibid., 28 October 1970, p. 3.

15. Ibid., 13 May 1970, p. 2; 6 May 1970, p. 4.

16. Ibid., 12 September 1970, pp. 1, 3.

17. Ibid., 5 August 1970, p. 8.

18. Ibid., 2 October 1970, p. 10; see also "Special Reports on Computers," 10 October 1970.

19. Malcolm Warner and Michael Stone, *The Data Bank Society* (London: George Allen & Unwin, 1970). The proceedings of the workshop were later published. B. C. Rowe, ed., *Privacy, Computers and You* (Manchester: National Computing Centre, 1972).

20. *Times* (London), 18 November 1970, p. 12; 19 November 1970, p. 2; 20 November 1970, p. 28. *Daily Telegraph*, 18 November 1970, p. 16; 20 November 1970, p. 2. *Guardian*, 19 November 1970, p. 5; 20 November 1970, p. 12.

21. *Times* (London), 14 May 1970, p. 2.

22. Ibid., 7 October 1970, p. 2. Cf his remarks in the 1970 Annual Report of JUSTICE, ibid., 25 June 1970, p. 3.

23. Bill of Rights (1970) H.L. Bill 19. 312 Hansard, 5th series, H.L. col. 17 (27 October 1970). Lord Lambton had been refused leave to introduce the same bill in the House of Commons 782 Hansard, 5th series, H.C. col. 474–82 (23 April 1969).

24. 313 Hansard, 5th series, H.L. col. 245 (26 November 1970).

25. Letter to the *Times* (London), 2 December 1970, p. 11.

26. Ibid., 4 December 1970, p. 3.

27. Ibid., 26 January 1971, p. 2.

28. Ibid., 3 March 1971, p. 13.

29. 814 Hansard, 5th series, H.C. col. 1515–24 (31 March 1971).

30. *Times* (London), 8 March 1971, p. 3. A similar case was reported in ibid., 11 March 1971, p. 4. The doctor was acquitted by the General Medical Council. At its annual meeting the British Medical Association decided, after a one-hour debate, that a doctor should respect the confidences of the patient. Ibid., 22 July 1971, p. 2.

31. Unsolicited Goods and Services Bill (1970) H.C. Bill 37.

32. Inertia Selling Bill (1969) H.C. Bill 26.

33. 807 Hansard, 5th series, H.C. col. 1655, 1706, 1707–8, 1710. (4 December 1970).

34. See, e.g., 705 Hansard, 5th series, H.C. col. *156* (26 January 1965); 708 Hansard, 5th series, H.C. col. 1042–44, *233–34* (16 March 1965). For the Julien Press see, e.g., 787 Hansard, 5th series, H.C. col. *266* (21 July 1969) and 803 Hansard, 5th series, H.C. col. *210* (15 July 1970).

35. 798 Hansard, 5th series, H.C. col. *45* (16 March 1970); 800 Hansard, 5th series, H.C. col. 618–20 (23 April 1970).

36. 813 Hansard, 5th series, H.C. col. 1876–95 (19 March 1971).

37. 308 Hansard, 5th series, H.L. col. 21–37 (24 February 1970).

38. 796 Hansard, 5th series, H.C. col. 329–58 (17 February 1970).

39. 812 Hansard, 5th series, H.C. col. 303–4 (23 February 1971).

40. 815 Hansard, 5th series, H.C. col. 227–28 (6 April 1971).

41. Pardoe's remarks were reported in the *Guardian*, 10 April 1971, p. 1; *Daily Telegraph*, 13 April 1971, p. 10.

42. *Daily Telegraph*, 13 April 1971, p. 1.

43. *Daily Mail*, 24 April 1971, p. 1.

44. *Times* (London), 5 April 1966, p. 7; 25 April 1966, p. 5.

45. *Daily Mirror*, 14 April 1971, p. 8; *Daily Telegraph*, 15 April 1971, p. 1.

46. *Daily Telegraph*, 17 April 1971, p. 13.

47. *Daily Mail*, 14 April 1971, p. 6.

48. *Sun* (London), 15 April 1971, p. 6.

49. *Daily Telegraph Magazine*, 19 February 1971, p. 5

50. 815 Hansard, 5th series, H.C. col. 814–21 (19 April 1971).

51. *Times* (London), 22 April 1971, p. 2.

52. Ibid., 12 July 1971, p. 3.

53. Ibid., 8 November 1971, p. 12.

54. Ibid., 6 January 1972, p. 3.

55. *Police Review* 80 (5 May 1972): p. 556. *Times* (London), 8 May 1972, p. 4.

56. 822 Hansard, 5th series, H.C. col. 487–97 (27 July 1971).

57. Control of Personal Information Bill (1972) H.C. Bill 80. 830 Hansard, 5th series, H.C. col. 1139–42 (8 February 1972).

58. 835 Hansard, 5th series, H.C. col. 967–68 (21 April 1972).

59. Ibid., col. 969.

60. *Guardian*, 11 May 1971, p. 1; 12 May 1971, p. 2. *Times* (London), 21 June 1972, p. 8.

61. *Times* (London), 17 January 1972, p. 1.

62. 839 Hansard, 5th series, H.C. col. 1640–42 (29 June 1972). A report of the police activity was published in the *Sunday Times* (London), 11 June 1972, p. 15.

63. *Times* (London), 18 December 1971, p. 2; 9 May 1972, p. 3; 10 May 1972, pp. 2, 12; 27 May 1972, p. 3; 8 June 1972, p. 6.

64. Younger Committee, p. 32 par. 100.

65. Ibid., p. 180 par. 582.

66. Ibid., Appendix E, questions 140–42. See also table 76, p. 84, of the full report "Privacy: Report on Survey of Public Attitudes" (London: Office of Population Censuses and Surveys, 1972).

67. Younger Committee, p. 10 par. 38; also compare pp. 58–59 pars. 17–18.

68. Ibid., p. 119 par. 398.

69. Ibid., p. 8 par. 26.

70. Ibid., p. 203 par. 653.

71. Ibid., p. 78 par. 267; p. 82 par. 275; p. 88 par. 298.

72. Ibid., pp. 121–22 pars. 403–5.

73. Ibid., p. 128 par. 427.

74. Ibid., p. 133 par. 445.

75. Ibid., p. 135 pars. 452, 453.

76. Ibid., pp. 172–74 pars. 560–65.

77. Ibid., p. 166 par. 538.

78. See, e.g., p. 172 pars. 558, 560.

79. Ibid., p. 191 pars. 620, 621.

80. Ibid., p. 55 pars. 190–93.

81. In his speech during the debate on the Younger Report, Alexander Lyon said that the actual division was more nearly 10 to 6 on the question of a general right but that some members did not want to dissent. 859 Hansard, 5th series, H.C. col. 2042 (13 July 1973).

82. Younger Report, p. 209 par. 8; p. 211 par. 23.

83. Ibid., p. 209 par. 2.

84. Ibid., p. 208 par. 2.

85. Ibid., p. 208 par. 4.

86. Ibid., p. 211 par. 21.

87. Ibid., p. 211 par. 18.

88. Ibid., p. 212 par. 27.

89. *Times* (London), 14 December 1972, p. 17; the letters published concerning this leader dealt not with the concept of privacy but with the nature of the sport, 16 December, p. 13; 19 December, p. 17; 20 December, p. 13.

90. See, e.g., leaders in the *Times* (London), 24 May 1973, p. 19;

23 June 1973, p. 13.

91. Ibid., 22 May 1973, p. 1; 23 May, p. 1; 24 May, p. 1; 25 May, p. 1.

92. See issues of the *Times* (London), of early June 1973 and the leader of 4 June 1973, p. 15.

93. *Press Conduct in the Lambton Affair,* Press Council Booklet No. 5.

94. *Daily Mail,* 1 June 1973, p. 9 (National Opinion Poll). *Times* (London), 8 June 1973, pp. 1–2 (Opinion Research Centre).

95. See Lord Devlin's article "Gauging Public Sentiment Towards a Probing Press," *Times* (London), 11 June 1973, p. 14.

96. 343 Hansard, 5th series, H.L. col. 104–78 (6 June 1973).

97. *Times* (London), 8 June 1973, p. 4.

98. Ibid., 6 July 1973, p. 2.

99. Ibid., 12 June 1973, p. 4.

100. 858 Hansard, 5th series, H.C. col. 1123–24 (25 June 1973).

101. *Times* (London), 29 November 1972, p. 6; 19 March 1973, p. 3. See also Lord Pearce's remarks as chairman of the Press Council, 343 Hansard, 5th series, H.L. col. 126–29 (6 June 1973). In March 1974 the Press Council said that its codification would be published in the summer of 1974.

102. *Times* (London), 1 February 1973, p. 3.

103. *Survey Research and Privacy* (London: Social & Community Planning Research, 1973).

104. *Times* (London), 29 June 1973, pp. 1–2.

105. Departmental Committee on Section 2 of the Official Secrets Act 1911 (1972; Cmnd. 5104).

106. 858 Hansard, 5th series, H.C. col. 1885–1973 (29 June 1973). *Times* (London), 30 June 1973, p. 1.

107. *Times* (London), 13 July 1973, pp. 1, 4.

108. 859 Hansard, 5th series, H.C. col 1782–90 (12 July 1973)

109. 859 Hansard, 5th series, H.C. col. 1955–2058 (13 July 1973).

110. Ibid., col. 1974.

111. Ibid., col. 2033.

112. Ibid., col. 2047.

113. *Daily Mail,* 6 September 1973, p. 15.

114. *Times* (London), 13 November 1973, p. 2.

115. Ibid., 25 January 1974, p. 6. The "infinity bug" was first reported in ibid., 9 July 1973, p. 2, and was described as enabling any phone to be used as a microphone that could be activated by dialing from any other phone in the world.

116. Consumer Credit Bill (1973) H.C. Bill 8.

117. 864 Hansard, 5th series, H.C. col. 509–98 (14 November 1973).

118. Rehabilitation of Offenders Bill (1973) H.C. Bill 28. 867 Hansard, 5th series, H.C. col. 2110–40 (25 January 1974). *Times* (London), 25 January 1974, p. 5; 26 January 1974, p. 13.

119. Rehabilitation of Offenders Bill (1972).

120. 338 Hansard, 5th series, H.L. col. 708–25 (1 February 1973). *Living it Down*, report of a committee set up by JUSTICE, The Howard League for Penal Reform, The National Association for the Care and Resettlement of Offenders (London: Stevens & Sons, 1972). Lord Gardiner was chairman of the committee.

121. 343 Hansard, 5th series, H. L. col. 115 (6 June 1973).

122. *Press Conduct in the Lambton Affair*, p. 21 par. 75.

123. Ibid., p. 22 par. 78.

124. Ibid., pp. 36–37 par. 141.

125. *Times* (London), 11 March 1974, p. 1.

126. *News of the World*, 10 March 1974, p. 4.

Selected Bibliography

PARLIAMENTARY PAPERS: Reports of Committees

Committee of Privy Councillors appointed to inquire into the interception of communications (1957; Cmnd. 283).

Committee on Homosexual Offences and Prostitution (1957; Cmnd. 247).

Committee on the Law of Defamation (1948; Cmd. 7536).

Committee on Privacy (1972; Cmnd. 5012).

Royal Commission on the Press 1947–1949 (1949; Cmd. 7700).

Royal Commission on the Press 1961–1962 (1962; Cmnd. 1811).

Secret Committee of the House of Lords Relative to the Post Office. *Parliamentary Papers 1844* 14 (601) : 501.

Secret Committee on the Post Office. *Parliamentary Papers 1844* 14 (582) : 505.

Select Committee of the House of Lords Appointed to Consider the Law of Defamation and Libel. *Parliamentary Papers 1843* 5 (513) : 259.

Select Committee on a General Register of all Deeds and Instruments Affecting Real Property in England and Wales. *Parliamentary Papers 1831–1832* 18 (609) : 365.

Select Committee on Parochial Registration. *Parliamentary Papers 1833* 14 (669) : 505.

PARLIAMENTARY PAPERS: Debates, House of Commons

Bill for Registering the Number of the People, 10 Parliamentary History col. 1317–65 (1753).

Population Bill (1800), 35 Parliamentary History col. 598–601 (19 November 1800).

Newspaper Stamp Duties Bill (1819), 41 Hansard, 1st series, col. 575–78, 705–6, 1175–78, 1299–1300, 1319–74, 1409–14, 1459–1515, 1582–89, 1589–91 (December 1819).

Stamps on Newspapers, 23 Hansard, 3d series, col. 1193–1223 (22 May 1834).

Newspaper Stamp Duties, 30 Hansard, 3d series, col. 835–62 (21 August 1835).

Opening Letters at Post Office, 75 Hansard, 3d series, col. 892–906 (14 June 1844); col. 1264–1308 (24 June 1844); 76 Hansard, 3d series, col. 212–59 (2 July 1844).

Opening Letters at Post Office, 77 Hansard, 3d series, col 668–745 (18 February 1845); col. 834–923 (20 February 1845); col. 932–1025 (21 February 1845).

Newspaper Stamp Duties Bill, 137 Hansard, 3d series, col. 1109–67 (26 March 1855).

Census (England) Bill, 158 Hansard, 3d series, col. 1762–66 (25 May 1860); 159 Hansard, 3d series, col. 1695–1741 (11 July 1860).

Judicial Proceedings (Regulation of Reports) Bill, 194 Hansard, 5th series, col. 733–816 (16 April 1926); 200 Hansard, 5th series, col. 2437–2527 (10 December 1926).

Population (Statistics) Bill, 329 Hansard, 5th series, col. 1717–1838 (29 November 1937); 331 Hansard, 5th series, col. 105–41 (1 February 1938).

Press (Control and Ownership), 428 Hansard, 5th series, col. 452–578 (29 October 1946).

Royal Commission on the Press (Report), 467 Hansard, 5th series, col. 2683–2794 (28 July 1949).

Defamation (Amendment) Bill, 495 Hansard, 5th series, col. 507–94 (1 February 1952).

Press Council Bill, 508 Hansard, 5th series, col. 962–1062 (28 November 1952); 515 Hansard, 5th series, col. 748–806 (8 May 1953).

State of the Press, 570 Hansard, 5th series, col. 725–819 (17 May 1957).

Homosexual Offences and Prostitution (Report), 596 Hansard, 5th series, col. 365–508 (26 November 1958).

Telephone Tapping, 615 Hansard, 5th series, col. 1521–1600 (16 December 1959).

Closure of Newspapers, 631 Hansard, 5th series, col. 719–822 (2 December 1960).

Journalists (Imprisonment), 674 Hansard, 5th series, col 682–771 (21 March 1963).

Postal Giro Service, 716 Hansard, 5th series, col. 1589–1643 (21 July 1965).

Sexual Offences (No. 2) Bill, 738 Hansard, 5th series, col. 1068–1148 (19 December 1966).

The Press, 740 Hansard, 5th series, col. 1663–1785 (8 February 1967).

Right of Privacy Bill, 740 Hansard, 5th series, col. 1565–68 (8 February 1967).

Unauthorised Telephone Monitoring Bill, 741 Hansard, 5th series, col. 1051–55 (20 February 1967).

Post Office (Data Processing Service) Bill, 744 Hansard, 5th series, col. 465–71 (6 April 1967) ; 745 Hansard, 5th series, col. 502–42 (19 April 1967), col. 1088–1113 (24 April 1967).

Rights and Liberties of the Individual, 750 Hansard, 5th series, col. 1542–1605 (17 July 1967).

Liberties of the Subject, 755 Hansard, 5th series, col. 808–909 (1 December 1967).

The Press, 787 Hansard, 5th series, col. 2021–32 (23 July 1969).

Right of Privacy Bill, 794 Hansard, 5th series, col. 861–960 (23 January 1970).

Computers (Control of Personal Information), 822 Hansard, 5th series, col. 487–502 (27 July 1971).

Control of Personal Information Bill, 835 Hansard, 5th series, col. 967–1011 (21 April 1972).

Privacy (Younger Report), 859 Hansard, 5th series, col. 1955–2058 (13 July 1973).

PARLIAMENTARY PAPERS: Debates, House of Lords

Law of Libel, 66 Hansard, 3d series, col. 395–409 (13 February 1843.

Newspaper Stamp Duties Bill, 138 Hansard, 3d series, col. 952–70 (24 May 1855).

Census (Great Britain) Bill, 6 Hansard, 5th series, col. 66–96 (12 July 1910), col. 286–303 (19 July 1910).

Judicial Proceedings (Regulation of Reports) Bill, 62 Hansard, 5th series, col. 130–59 (16 July 1925).

Newspaper Reports of Law Cases, 53 Hansard, 5th series, col. 847–66 (24 April 1923).

Controls and Regulations, 135 Hansard, 5th series, col. 325–41 (6 March 1945), 417–44 (8 March 1945).

Preservation of the Rights of the Subject Bill, 147 Hansard, 5th series, col. 762–810 (15 May 1947).

Liberties of the Subject Bill, 167 Hansard, 5th series, col. 1041–1110 (27 June 1950).

Identity Cards, 172 Hansard, 5th series, col. 1335–74 (26 July 1951).

Liberties of the Subject, 177 Hansard, 5th series, col. 1168–1242 (16 July 1952).

Homosexual Crime, 187 Hansard, 5th series, col. 737–67 (19 May 1954).

Homosexual Offences and Prostitution, 206 Hansard, 5th series, col. 733–50, 753–832 (4 December 1957).

Right of Privacy Bill, 229 Hansard, 5th series, col. 607–62 (13 March 1961).

The Press and the Law, 274 Hansard, 5th series, col. 1371–84, 1386–1447 (25 May 1966).

Human Rights: The State and the Individual, 302 Hansard, 5th series, col. 1026–96 (18 June 1969).

Computers and Personal Records, 306 Hansard, 5th series, col. 103–75 (3 December 1969).

Bill of Rights, 313 Hansard, 5th series, col. 243–319 (26 November 1970).

Younger Committee Report, 343 Hansard, 5th series, col. 104–178 (6 June 1973).

GENERAL PRINTED SOURCES: Books

Cudlipp, Hugh. *At Your Peril.* London: Weidenfeld and Nicholson, 1962.

Devlin, Patrick. *The Enforcement of Morals* (Oxford University Press Paperbacks number 137) Oxford: Oxford University Press, 1968.

Hamilton, Peter. *Espionage and Subversion in an Industrial Society.* London: Hutchinson, 1967.

Hickson, Philip. *Industrial Counter-Espionage.* London: Institute of Directors, 1968.

Hart, H. L. A. *Law, Liberty, and Morality* (Oxford University Press Paperbacks number 140) Oxford: Oxford University Press, 1968.

Hyde, H. Montgomery. *Privacy and the Press.* London: Butterworth & Co., 1947.

Levy, H. Phillip. *The Press Council: History, Procedure and Cases.* London: Macmillan & Co., 1967.

Madgwick, Donald. *Privacy under Attack.* London: National Council for Civil Liberties, 1968.

Martin, James, and Norman, Adrian R. D. *The Computerized Society.* Harmondsworth: Penguin Books, 1973.

Miller, Arthur R. *The Assault on Privacy.* Ann Arbor: University of Michigan Press, 1971.

Mitchell, Basil. *Law, Morality, and Religion in a Secular Society.* (Oxford University Press Paperbacks number 198) Oxford: Oxford University Press, 1970.

Packard, Vance. *The Naked Society.* London: Longmans, Green & Co., 1964.

Payne, Ronald. *Private Spies.* London: Arthur Barker, 1967.

Pennock, J. Roland, and Chapman, John W., eds. *Privacy* (Nomos 13) New York: Atherton Press, 1971.

Robertson, A. H., ed. *Privacy and Human Rights.* Manchester: Manchester University Press, 1973.

Rowe, B. C., ed. *Privacy, Computers and You.* Manchester: National Computing Centre, 1972.

Rule, James B. *Private Lives and Public Surveillance.* London: Allen Lane, 1973.

Seymour-Ure, Colin. *The Press, Politics and the Public.* London: Methuen & Co., 1968.

Street, Harry. *Freedom, the Individual and the Law.* 3d ed. Harmondsworth: Penguin Books, 1972.

Strömholm, Stig. *Right of Privacy and Rights of the Personality.*

Working paper prepared for the Nordic Conference on privacy organized by the International Commission of Jurists, Stockholm, May 1967. Stockholm: P. A. Norstedt & Söners förlag, 1967.

Tapper, Colin. *Computers and the Law*. London: Weidenfeld and Nicholson, 1973.

Westin, Alan F. *Privacy and Freedom*. New York: Atheneum, 1967.

Westin, Alan F., and Baker, Michael A. *Databanks in a Free Society*. New York: Quadrangle Books, 1972.

Williams, David. *Not in the Public Interest*. London: Hutchinson, 1965.

Williams, Edward Francis. *Dangerous Estate*. London: Longmans, Green and Co., 1957.

———. *The Right to Know*. London: Longmans, 1969.

Wintour, Charles. *Pressures on the Press*. London: Andre Deutsch, 1972.

GENERAL PRINTED SOURCES: Articles

Adam, Kenneth. "Freemen of the Press?" *Fortnightly* 144 (July 1938): 34–41.

———. "Press and Public." *Listener* 17 (7 April 1937): 641–43.

Andrews, W. Linton, "The Conscience of the Press." *Fortnightly* 174 (September 1950): 178–84.

———. Letter to *Spectator* 189 (26 December 1952): 875.

"Are Interviewers a Blessing or a Curse?" *Idler* 6 (January 1896): 583–94.

Arndt, H. W. "The Cult of Privacy." *Australian Quarterly* 21 (September 1949): 68–71.

Baistow, Tom. "Privacy versus Freedom." *New Statesman* 79 (23 January 1970): 108

Bartlett, James. "The New Journalism." *Fortnightly* 166 (September 1946): 202–7.

Baumann, Arthur A. "The Functions and Future of the Press." *Fortnightly* 107 (April 1920): 620–27.

Belloc, Hilaire. "A Few Kind Words on the Press." *Nineteenth Century* 120 (October 1936): 438–51.

Beloff, Michael. "The Inquisitive Society." *Encounter* 35 (December 1970): 49–57.

"Breeze Down Fleet Street." *The British Printer* 73 (December 1960): 66–75.

"The British Press—its Growth, Liberty, and Power." *North British Review* 30 (May 1859): 367–402.

Calder, Nigel. "Averting Technological Tyranny." *New Statesman* 79 (6 February 1970): 177–78.

Calder, Ritchie. "On Snooping." *New Statesman* 53 (22 June 1957): 800–801.

Carson, John. "Defining and Protecting Civil Liberties." *Political Quarterly* 41 (July–September 1970): 316–27.

"The Census." *Cornhill Magazine* 23 (April 1871): 415–24.

"Census Hazards." *New Statesman* 41 (31 March 1951): 362–63.

"The Census of 1871." *Chamber's Journal* 48 (19 August 1871): 518–22.

"Census of Great Britain, 1851." *Christian Observer* (January 1855): 18–35.

Christianson, Arthur. "The Right to Privacy." *New Statesman* 61 (24 February 1961): 288.

Churchill, Randolph S. "The Privacy of the Individual." *Spectator* 200 (23 May 1958): 649–50.

Cline, R. A. "The Argyll Decision." *Spectator* 213 (18 December 1964): 837–38.

———. "Invasion of Privacy." *Spectator* 204 (10 June 1960): 830–31.

———. "Not All That's News is Fit to Print." *Spectator* 224 (10 January 1970): 39–40.

Clogger, T. J. "Fingerprints." *Quarterly Review* 303 (October 1965): 444–49.

Collins, J. P. "The Cult of the Hyena." *Nineteenth Century* 123 (May 1938): 535–49.

Collins, Guy J. M. "Fluoridation in Question." *Month*, n.s. 30 (September 1963): 167–71.

"The Contemporary British Press." *Economist* 107 (3 November 1928): 786–87; 107 (10 November 1928): 833–35; 107 (17 November 1928): 878–79; 107 (24 November 1928): 930–31; 107 (1 December 1928): 987–88.

"Control of the Press." *Economist* 151 (20 July 1946): 85–86.

A Correspondent. "Homosexuality: A Medical Viewpoint." *Spectator* 193 (17 December 1954): 778.

"Counting People by Machinery." *Conquest* 2 (May 1921): 293–96.

Curran, Charles. "All the News That's Fit to Print." *Spectator* 215 (17 December 1965): 800.

"The D-Notice Rumpus." *New Statesman* 73 (16 June 1967): 817.

"The Defence of Privacy." *Spectator* 66 (7 February 1891): 200–201.

Dodd, J. H. B. "Privacy and the Occupational Psychologist." *Occupational Psychology* 44 (1970): 137–40.

Dworkin, Gerald. "The Common Law Protection of Privacy." *University of Tasmania Law Review* 2 (1967): 418–45.

———. "The Right to Be Let Alone." *Listener* 67 (22 March 1962): 503–4.

———. "The Younger Committee Report on Privacy." *Modern Law Review* 36 (July 1973): 399–406.

"Economics of the Press." *Economist* 200 (9 September 1961): 949–60.

Ervine, St. John. "The Future of the Press." *Spectator* 146 (22 November 1930): 773–74; 146 (29 November 1930): 836–37.

———. "The Invasion of Privacy." *Spectator* 138 (28 May 1927): 937–38.

———. "Privacy and the Lindberghs." *Fortnightly*, n.s. 139 (February 1936): 180–86.

"Ethics and Circulation." *New Statesman* 44 (23 August 1952): 199–200.

Fitzgerald, Anthony. "How Human a Year?" *New Society* 12 (5 December 1968): 841.

Foot, Dingle. "Our Civil Liberties." *Contemporary Review* 147 (January 1935): 31–37.

"The Freedom of Our Press" (discussion on BBC National Program). *Listener* 20 (22 December 1938): 1337–38; 20 (29 December 1938): 1370–71.

"From Essay to Stunt." *Nation and the Athenaeum*, 31 (19 August 1922): 678–80.

Fyfe, Hamilton. "Pestering by the Press." *Fortnightly*, n.s. 141 (March 1937): 304–11.

Galton, Francis. "Identification by Finger-tips." *Nineteenth Century*

30 (August 1891): 303–11.

Gerstein, Robert S. "Privacy and Self-Incrimination." *Ethics* 80 (1970): 87–101.

Gillie, Oliver. "Rogue Detectives." *New Society* 15 (16 April 1970): 629–30.

Golsong, N. "The European Convention on Human Rights before Domestic Courts." *British Yearbook of International Law* 38 (1962): 445–56.

Gorren, Aline. "The Ethics of Modern Journalism." *Scribner's Magazine* 19 (April 1896): 507–13.

Hall, Peter. "Computer Privacy." *New Society* 14 (31 July 1969): 163–64.

———. "What the Census Really Means." *New Society* 17 (22 April 1971): 665–67.

Hanbury, J. C. "Fluoridation: An Answer." *Month*, n.s. 217 (April 1964): 218–23.

Hogg, Quinton. "A New Bill of Rights." *Listener* 81 (24 April 1969): 549–51.

Hollerith, Herman. "The Electrical Tabulating Machine." *Journal of the Royal Statistical Society* 57 (December 1894): 678–82.

"Influence of the Newspapers." *Fraser's Magazine* 4 (September 1831): 127–42; (October 1831): 310–21.

"The Influence of the Press." *Blackwood's Edinburgh Magazine* 36 (September 1834): 373–91.

Inglis, Brian. "Press Postcript." *Spectator* 210 (3 May 1963): 558–59.

———. "Press and Profumo." *Spectator* 210 (21 June 1963): 799–800.

Jacob, Joseph. "Seven Dangers of Computers." *New Society* 14 (11 December 1969): 940–41.

Johnson, Timothy. "Fingerprints—and how they're recognised." *Illustrated London News* 248 (4 June 1966): 14–15.

Jones, Kennedy. "Journalism, a Branch of Commerce." *Fortnightly Review* 107 (June 1920): 826–33.

Jourard, Sidney. "Privacy: the Psychological Need." *New Society* 9 (25 May 1967): 757–58.

King, Cecil. "The Morality of the Popular Press." *20th Century* 172 (Spring 1963): 98–102.

"Letter-opening at the General Post Office," *Chamber's Journal* 19

(20 June 1863) : 395–97.

M. "Public Life and Private Morals." *Fortnightly Review*, n.s 49 (February 1891) : 211–28.

Mann, Arthur. "The Press in Our Time." *National Review* 114 (March 1940) : 309–16.

Martin, Kingsley. "The Press." *Listener* 7 (27 January 1932) : 116–18; (3 February 1932) : 156–58; (10 February 1932) : 210–11; (17 February 1932) : 249–50.

McCloskey, H. J. "The Political Ideal of Privacy." *Philosophical Quarterly* 21 (October 1971) : 303–14.

Middleton, K. W. B. "A Right to Privacy?" *Juridical Review* 8 (August 1963) : 178–89.

"Mortgaging the Fourth Estate." *New Statesman* 79 (30 January 1970) : 133–34.

Nathan, Lord. "Eavesdropping." *Law Times* 225 (7 March 1958) : 119–20; (14 March 1958) : 135–36; (21 March 1958) : 149–50.

Neill, Brian. "The Protection of Privacy." *Modern Law Review* 25 (July 1962) : 393–405.

Nokes, G. D. "Professional Privilege." *Law Quarterly Review* 66 (January 1950) : 88–103.

"Opening Letters at the Post Office." *Law Magazine*, n.s. 2 (May 1845) : 248–57.

Owen, David. "Electronic Crime." *Observer Magazine* (12 March 1972) : 9ff.

Paterson, David. "Ordeal by Computer." *Listener* 82 (10 July 1969) : 38–39.

Paton, G. W. "Broadcasting and the Tort of Privacy." *Law Quarterly Review* 54 (July 1938) : 319–21.

Perkin, H. J. "The Origins of the Popular Press." *History Today* 7 (July 1957) : 425–35.

Phillips, Evelyn March. "The New Journalism." *New Review*, n.s. 13 (August 1895) : 182–89.

Poole, J. B. "Information Services for the Commons: A Computer Experiment." *Parliamentary Affairs* 22 (Spring 1969) : 161–68.

"The Press and the People." *Economist* 206 (9 March 1963) : 877–78.

"The Press under Pressure." *Economist* 183 (25 May 1957) : 709–12.

Priestly, J. B. "Thoughts on the Popular Press." *New Statesman* 52 (25 August 1956) : 208.

"Princess Margaret." *Spectator* 195 (21 October 1955) : 513.

"Princess Margaret." *Economist* 177 (29 October 1955) : 369.

"Private Lives and their Public Enemies." *20th Century* 170 (Spring 1962) : 4–122.

"Privacy and the Law." *Law Times* 228 (20 November 1959) : 233–34.

"The Protection of Privacy" (the legal protection of privacy: a comparative survey by the International Commission of Jurists). *International Social Science Journal* 24 (1972) : 417–583.

R. S. R. "The Press." *Cambridge Journal* 3 (March 1950) : 323–44.

Ratcliffe, S. K. "The Revolution in Fleet Street." *Nineteenth Century* 107 (July 1930) : 15–24.

Rolph, C. H. "The Englishman's Front Door." *New Statesman* 36 (20 November 1948) : 435–36.

———. "Fingerprints for All?" *New Statesman* 71 (20 May 1966) : 721.

———. "Privacy." *New Statesman* 61 (12 May 1961) : 746, 748.

———. "The Right to Be Let Alone." *New Statesman* 77 (21 February 1969) : 252–53.

Samuel, Sir Herbert. "Liberty." *Contemporary Review* 131 (May 1927) : 566–75.

———. "The War and Liberty." *New Statesman* 9 (26 May 1917) : 174–76; (2 June 1917) : 200–202; (9 June 1917) : 223–25; (16 June 1917) : 246–48; (23 June 1917) : 272–74; (30 June 1917) : 297.

"Setting the Pace for Privacy." *Economist* 239 (12 June 1971) : 68–69.

Slade, C. J. "Privacy and the Press." *Spectator* 189 (12 December 1952) : 804–5.

Speed, J. A. "Privilege of Communications Between a Solicitor and his Client." *Modern Law Review* 28 (January 1965) : 18–26.

"A Statute of Liberty?" *Economist* 152 (3 May 1947) : 658–60.

Stone, M. G., and Warner, Malcolm. "Politics, Privacy, and Computers." *Political Quarterly* 40 (July-September 1969) : 256–67.

Street, Harry. "Privacy and the Law." *Queen's Quarterly* 77 (Autumn 1970) : 318–32.

———. "What the Law Can Do." *New Society* 9 (25 May 1967) : 758–60.

"The Tappers Return." *Spectator* 203 (4 December 1959) : 811–12.

"The Taste for Privacy and Publicity." *Spectator* 61 (9 June 1888) : 782–83.

Taylor, G. D. S. "Privacy and the Public." *Modern Law Review* 34 (May 1971) : 288–304.

"They Come Not Single Spies." *Economist* 207 (27 April 1963) : 303–4.

Vetch, Edward. "Interests in Personality." *Northern Ireland Legal Quarterly* 23 (Winter 1972) : 423–59.

Vivian, S. P. "Identity Cards and Liberty." *National Review* 127 (August 1946) : 143–48.

Warren, Samuel D., and Brandeis, Louis D. "The Right to Privacy." *Harvard Law Review* 9 (December 1890) : 193–220.

Williams, Francis. "Curbing Press Freedom." *New Statesman* 65 (15 March 1963) : 366, 368.

———. "I Was All Right, Jack." *New Statesman* 65 (14 June 1963) : 889.

———. "Radcliffe and the Press." *New Statesman* 65 (26 April 1963) : 622.

———. "Should We Tell?" *New Statesman* 56 (9 August 1958) : 160.

Willis, Margaret. "Designing for Privacy." *Architects' Journal* 137 (29 May 1963) : 1137–41; (5 June 1963) : 1181–87; (12 June 1963) : 1231–36.

Winfield, Percy H. "The Law of Libel and the Press." *Fortnightly* 170 (December 1948) : 374–77.

———. "Privacy." *Law Quarterly Review* 47 (January 1931) : 23–42.

Zellick, Graham. "Offensive Advertisements in the Mail." *Criminal Law Review* (1972) : 724–43.

GENERAL PRINTED SOURCES: Reports and Miscellaneous

British Computer Society. *Privacy and the Computer—Steps to Practicality*. London: British Computer Society, 1972.

Council of Europe. *Stock-taking on the European Convention on Human Rights*. Strasbourg: Council of Europe, 1971.

———. *Problems Arising from the Co-existence of the United Nations Covenants on Human Rights and the European Convention on Human Rights*. Strasbourg: Council of Europe, 1970.

Institute of Practitioners in Advertising. *Subliminal Communication*. London: Institute of Practitioners in Advertising, 1958.

JUSTICE. *The Law and the Press*. London: Stevens and Sons, 1965.

———. *Privacy and the Law*. London: Stevens and Sons, 1970.

National Council for Civil Liberties. *Civil Liberty* (Annual Report of the NCCL) 1962–73.

Political and Economic Planning. *Report on the British Press*. London: Political and Economic Planning, 1938.

Press Council. *The Press and the People* (Annual Report of the Press Council) 1954–72.

Social and Community Planning Research. *Survey Research and Privacy*. London: Social and Community Planning Research, 1973.

Times (London), 1 January 1946—30 March 1974.

Index